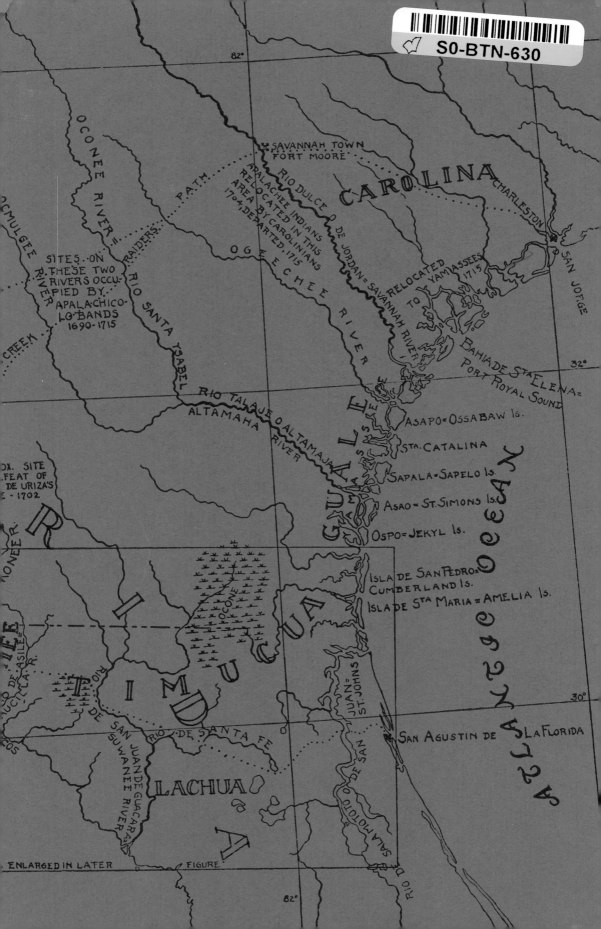

Here They Once Stood

Idealized Reconstruction of a Typical Florida Chapel

Here They Once Stood

The Tragic End of the Apalachee Missions

by

MARK F. BOYD, HALE G. SMITH,
and
JOHN W. GRIFFIN

Gainesville
UNIVERSITY OF FLORIDA PRESS
1951

975.9
BL92h

643956

Printed in the United States of America by
The Record Press, Incorporated, of St. Augustine, Florida

DEDICATION

To the late James Alexander Robertson, scholar and historian, and Secretary of the Florida State Historical Society, in appreciation and acknowledgment of his stimulating encouragement to explore the lacunae of Florida's colonial history.

Authors' Preface

ALTHOUGH HISTORY AND ARCHAEOLOGY are often considered as distinct and unrelated disciplines, they are, in fact, but different techniques of approaching historical problems. The present volume presents a joint historical-archaeological attack on some of the problems of the Spanish mission era in the Apalachee region of Florida, and the authors feel that this joint effort has illuminated the picture of the times to a degree that would have been impossible if only one of the disciplines had been employed. It is to be hoped that similar studies will be conducted, to the end that the documentary sources may be enriched by the data recovered by excavation and the archaeological objects may be enlivened by the insight provided by contemporary documents.

The majority of our acknowledgments have been made at appropriate places in the following pages, but we should like to express our appreciation to the Florida Park Service, under whose auspices the studies were made, and particularly to Mr. Lewis G. Scoggin, Director, and Mr. M. B. Greene, Assistant Director, of that Service. We should also like to thank Mr. James Messer, owner of the site of San Luis, for his interest in our work and for permitting us to examine the site.

November, 1950

M. F. B.
H. G. S.
J. W. G.

Foreword

WHEN ONE REFLECTS that the "Mission Era" of Florida's history lasted for nearly two hundred years, 1567 - 1763, the importance of a book that deals with the climactic moments of that period can be readily appreciated. *Here They Once Stood* focuses our attention upon the most crucial years of that era. The historical section comprises documents of the years 1693 to 1708 which include an eye-witness account of the destruction of the missions of West Florida by Colonel James Moore of South Carolina in 1704. The archaeological sections are studies of two of these very mission sites, San Luis and San Francisco de Oconee. We have, therefore, for the first time in print a detailed picture of the Franciscan Missions of Florida at the very moment of their greatest historical interest.

When James Moore and his army of 1500 Creek Indians and 80 Carolina ruffians marched back to Charleston in 1704, they left the Florida missions almost completely destroyed. The few that were left standing were ravaged by other raiding parties in the succeeding years. In effect the mission era had come to an end, for even though there was a later revival of the *doctrinas,* they could not again attain to their former grandeur. Those Indians who had escaped Moore's armies fled in terror to the woods (some of them are reported to have gone as far west as Mobile), thus leaving the mission provinces almost completely depopulated. It may never be known exactly how many captives Moore took with him, but by his own estimate he took several thousands whom he settled in villages among the Yamassee or sold into slavery. The Franciscan missionaries were disheartened. With their villages ravaged and several of their number killed in the fighting, they were forced to abandon West Florida for a time.

These tragic events wrote *finis* to an illustrious work that had its beginning in 1567, when Menéndez introduced the first Jesuit missionaries into Florida. The sons of St. Ignatius Loyola labored five years in Florida, Georgia, South Carolina, and Virginia until their numbers were decimated by treacherous uprisings. They were succeeded in the work by the Franciscans, the first band of whom arrived in St. Augustine in 1573. By the time that the Franciscan endeavor had reached its zenith in 1675, there were thirty-four missions scattered along the coastline from St. Augustine up to St. Catherine's Island, Georgia, and extending in a second line westward from St. Augustine to Tallahassee. Some seventy friars carried on the spiritual labors in the crude chapels and *doctrinas*. For the most part they were devoted and zealous men who took on willingly a life of hardship and loneliness with the hope of converting the Timucuan, Apalachee, and Guale Indians of Florida to Christian ways and European culture. When Colonel Moore launched his attack against Ayubale Mission on the morning of January 25, 1704, the "Golden Age" of the Florida missions had long since passed. The settlements along the coastline of Georgia had been abandoned because of repeated incursions from South Carolina. Moore himself had descended upon St. Augustine in 1702 to besiege the town, leaving all the East Coast missions in ruins as he passed by. Thus it was that the nine flourishing *doctrinas* which remained in Timucua and the fourteen in Apalachee constituted the whole mission field in 1704. Moore was striking at the heart of it. As the Carolinians and their Creek allies marched back to Charleston, the peace of death settled over the Franciscan provinces of Florida. Most of the villages had been put to ashes or depopulated; the few that survived were utterly cowed. Though some of them were revived after the South Carolina Yamassee Revolt of 1715, when a few of the Apalachees whom Moore had captured returned to their former homes, this revival was doomed to failure.

Heretofore, this exciting chapter in Florida's long history has been known only in outline. *Here They Once Stood* now gives it to us in intimate detail. Not only are the historical events themselves told by eye witnesses in the documents, but the very mode of life of the Indians in the mission *doctrinas* is painted in clearly by the archaeological studies of John W. Griffin and Hale G. Smith. Both the San Luis and the San Francisco sites figure prominently in the story described in Dr. Mark F. Boyd's documents. The picture thus drawn is one unique to Florida. It is interesting in its own right, and need not borrow from the mission lore of California or the Southwest. There are no great architectural monuments to be found, no great churches, no massive structures; the story is one of flimsy buildings, crude implements, primitive utensils. It is also a story of poverty, suffering, and bloodshed. As a result of the studies of the San Luis and San Francisco missions, we can picture for the first time accurately the forlornness of the Florida mission compounds and the simple

Foreword

life of their inhabitants. It is to be hoped that these studies only herald more in the near future.

Here They Once Stood is a significant contribution to a little-known period of Florida history. It is a shaft of light, like a searchlight in a dark cave, which has focused upon something of great interest. We look forward to the day when the whole Mission Era will be floodlighted by the publication of other works of this nature.

Gainesville, Florida   Rev. Charles W. Spellman, M.A.
December 4, 1950

Contents

SECTION I.

𝔉ort 𝔖an 𝔏uis: 𝔇ocuments 𝔇escribing the 𝔗ragic 𝔈nd of the 𝔐ission 𝔈ra

BY MARK F. BOYD

Here They Once Stood

Contents

Here They Once Stood

SECTION II.
A Spanish Mission Site in Jefferson County, Florida
BY HALE G. SMITH

SECTION III.
Excavations at the Site of San Luis
BY JOHN W. GRIFFIN

APPENDIX.
Leon-Jefferson Ceramic Types
BY HALE G. SMITH
and
Trait List of Two Spanish Sites of the Mission Period
BY JOHN W. GRIFFIN and HALE G. SMITH

Illustrations

SECTION I.

Fort San Luis:

Documents Describing the Tragic End of the Mission Era

Translated and Annotated, Together with an Introduction

by

MARK F. BOYD

Historian, Florida Park Service

Introduction

HE COLONIAL PERIOD of that portion of Florida lying between the Suwannee *(San Juan de Guacára)* and Apalachicola rivers has received little attention from historians, and as a consequence it has become one of the most conspicuous lacunae in our knowledge of the history of the United States. This region, as the provinces of Apalachee and Timuqua, is vaguely known to have been an important field for the proselyting efforts of the Franciscan fathers, and to have become the seat of numerous villages or *doctrinas* of Christianized Indians, which were finally destroyed by ruthless attacks of pagan Indians who were instigated by the English settlers in Carolina. Garbled tales of those days were told by some of the Indians (probably not descendants of the ancient villagers) to the earliest Anglo-Americans who penetrated this region after the United States had achieved independence, and who viewed with awe the ruins and relics encountered at various sites. The unavailability of factual narratives by residents who passed through the trying times of the mission period has permitted some of their more imaginative successors in this favored territory to present some highly idealized and romantic concepts of this period.

Actually there are considerable data bearing on the traditional identification of the site of San Luis, village and fort, but localization of the other *doctrinas* is either unknown or conjectural. Thus, on the sketch map of the environs of "Apalachy" made in 1767 by George Gauld and Philip Pittman[1] an "Old Spanish Fort" is marked in the appropriate situation. Pittman,[2] speaking of the source of the Wakulla River, says

it is near where a Spanish Fort formerly stood, and which the Indians obliged them to abandon many years ago. One can trace

I

the ditch, and there remain many broken pieces of Ordinance, and an entire bell was taken from thence some little time since by the Indians.

It is indicated as the "ruins of San Luis Fort and Town" on the Purcell-Stuart map of 1778.[3]

Although De Lacy[4] visited the lower Creek towns in 1801, it is uncertain whether his itinerary took him into Apalachee, or whether his description of the site of St. Lucea (San Luis) is solely derived from Indian description. He speaks of St. Lucea as being

situated on the top of a steep hill of the form of a horse shoe and walled in all around with a Citadell, ditch Fosse, Counter Fosse, Ramparts &c, &c. . . . The site of it only Remains together with the Cannon, most of which have lost their arms [*sic*][5] or have been split or otherwise broken by the Indians, lying on the ground, most of them overgrown with grass and weeds, some few of these are, that if cleaned from the Rust might be again serviceable, the Church Bells also lye in the same way as does all the other things of that nature, not touched nor meddled with by the Indians, all of whom still view the place with Horror.

The credibility of this statement suggests an actual visit, but De Lacy's account of the conflicts of the early eighteenth century is highly garbled.

The following three narratives by visitors after the cession of Florida merit attention:

(1) Williams[6] relates under date of October 31, 1823, that

. . . meeting an Indian hunter, we inquired of him the situation of an Old Spanish fort which had been mentioned as being in the neighborhood. The Indian for a quarter of a dollar undertook to guide us to it and we reached it about 8 o'clock. It is situated on a commanding eminence at the north point of a high narrow neck of highlands surrounded by a deep ravine and swamp. . . . About 12 o'clock we returned to our camp. . . . After dinner Dr. Simmons proceeded to old Tallahassee to visit a very old Indian, who was said to recollect the capture and destruction of the old fort we had visited. He informed the doctor that the country was formerly settled thick with Spanish villages; that the Yamasses, or bone tribe, were their allies, but the Muscogees were their enemies and finally conquered them; that he well remembered when they took the old fort, or rather when the Spaniards evacuated it in the night, after laying trains of powder to burst their cannon. . . . The Yamasses were nearly destroyed in that war.

(2) A few days after the visit to the site by Williams and Simmons, it was viewed by Captain Daniel E. Burch, of the United States Army, who was engaged in laying out the road from Pensacola to St. Augustine. Burch's reports to General Jesup[7] do not mention his observations, but the *Pensacola Gazette* of October 9, 1824, copies an interview with Captain Burch published in the *National Intelligencer*, from which the following is condensed:

. . . The first is Fort St. Louis, at least its ruins, situated about 6 miles east of Ockolockony, and N. by W. 25 miles from St. Marks. This place has more the appearance of having been a fortified town than a mere fortification. . . . Fort St. Louis was built on an elevated spot of ground around a hollow, from the bottom of which issue 2 springs that furnish an abundant supply of water, but which after running but a few yards, again sink into the ground. One of these on being opened by Captain Burch, displayed the wooden box or trunk in which it had been enclosed; they were overshadowed by a beautiful live oak tree. . . . Captain Burch met with an old Indian [probably the same individual encountered by Williams and Simmons] near Tallahassee of the Creek nation, who appeared to be of great age, and who informed him that he had been in the war which had destroyed these settlements. . . . The Indians had made repeated attempts on St. Louis, but were repeatedly repulsed, being unable to withstand the cannon. They then mustered their whole force . . . endeavoring to starve them out. . . . The Spaniards prepared everything for evacuating it and retired in the night to the fort on the Ockolockony. The first intimation to the Indians of the retreat was the explosion of the fort. . . . The country having thus fallen to their hands with the Yamassy tribe of Indians, with whom the Spaniards had intermarried. . . . The males were all destroyed and the women taken for wives or slaves. But the country had been so entirely cleared that there was no game, and the domestic animals having been destroyed during the war, the great body of Indians returned to their nation. The old Indian himself went to the Apalachicola, no Indians lived near St. Louis until the forests grew up, when

3

he returned. He represents the Spanish population to have . . . had horses but no wheeled carriages. Their principal highway . . . was not more than 6-8 feet wide, but well made, everything transported on horseback, except hogsheads, which were rolled by men.[8] The Indians had no firearms, being armed with bow and arrows and clubs. In order to protect themselves from the effect of the shot, they suspended thick boards about their necks. . . . The Indians have preserved a superstitious story, which keeps them at a distance from St. Louis. . . . They cannot be prevailed upon to accompany the whites there, even to show the place.

(3) An anonymous contributor in the issue of the *Apalachicola Commercial Advertiser* of June 7, 1843, said of Old Fort St. Louis:

About two miles west of the city of Tallahassee, lie the remains of what tradition says was once the Spanish fort of St. Louis. Our attention has been recently directed to these ruins, from the circumstance that a very intelligent gentleman, formerly of Georgia, now of Alabama, has at this time many laborers engaged in excavating the site of this old fort, on a search after hidden treasure. Whether or no he may succeed in bringing to light any considerable deposit of the precious metals is not for us to say. But he has already thrown up from beneath the soil where they have long been entombed, many articles which will possess great interest with the antiquarian.

In presenting the tale of these dramatic events, it appears most fitting to let the story be told by the participants, which is done in the chronologically arranged documents which follow. The first forty-three here presented are from Spanish sources, and cover the period from 1693 to 1708. They were selected as representative of the period from the construction, to the destruction, of the blockhouse of San Luis, of legendary fame as Fort San Luis. Its destruction clearly marked *finis* to what may be recognized as the first mission era.

Documents numbered 4, 5, 11, 19, 33, and 35 were furnished the writer by the late Dr. James A. Robertson, former secretary of the Florida State Historical Society, from the John B. Stetson, Jr. collection of photostats of documents of Spanish Florida from the Archives of the Indies of Sevilla, Spain. The Stetson collection is now in the Library of Congress. Photostats of the other thirty-seven documents, from the same source in Spain, are in the collections of the North Carolina State Department of Archives and History, and were made available through the courtesy of the director of the archives, Mr. Henry Howard Eddy. The last two documents are letters of James Moore, which are preserved in the Library of Congress.[9]

The documents were transcribed and translated by the writer. Here and there an undecipherable word is represented by square brackets, and an occasional untranslatable word is given in its apparent spelling. The handwriting of the various writers did not on the whole afford any unusual difficulties in transcription, excepting the scrawl in which Document 20 was written. The problem which this document afforded, as well as the necessity for lucid translation of certain involved passages in Documents 6, 7, 10, 13, 16, and 17, moved the writer to solicit the aid of Dr. and Mrs. Duvon C. Corbitt, which was cheerfully afforded, and to whom my sincere thanks are due. I am also under obligation to Reverend Father Maynard Geiger, O. F. M., who reviewed the script and offered helpful suggestions regarding the employment of various religious and ecclesiastical terms, for which I am equally appreciative, as well as for assistance from Dr. Irving A. Leonard.

In most instances the documents are reproduced in their entirety. The cédulas, or letters from the King, being copies, did not bear the customary formal closing phrases or signatures. The principal abridgment is in Document 39, which has been stripped of all unessential paragraphs of legal verbiage. Of particular importance have been the documents assembled in A. I. 58-2-8:B³, by order of Governor Zúñiga at the close of his administration, evidently to serve as his defense before a *residencia;* and those in A. I. 58-2-7/2, assembled by order of the viceroy, the Duke of Albuquerque, to exhibit the concern felt in that quarter over the predicament of Florida, and the efforts made to render assistance.

It would appear that any attempt to summarize these documents or to incorporate their substance in a narrative would be superfluous, as they themselves tell a sufficiently vivid, and on the whole, connected story.

However, a brief sketch of the background against which this drama was played may be of service to the casual reader, and an analysis of the sequence of the destruction of the villages, as well as of the parallel accounts of the important engagements, will afford a clearer picture. These accounts afford so many tantalizing glimpses into the social and economic life of the province that one wishes a satisfying broader view were available.

After the establishment of St. Augustine in 1565, as a consequence of the attempted settlement of the French in a location where a colony might menace the security of the Spanish navigation of the Bahama Channel, no serious threat to Spanish occupation of the southeastern North American mainland arose until 1670. In that year the Lords Proprietors of Carolina established a settlement at the estuary known by the Spaniards as San Jorge (St. George), to which was given the name of Charles Town (Charleston), located only a short distance from San Felipe (Port Royal), the arrivals being welcomed by Indian elements disaffected with the Spaniards. In an openhanded manner the munificent Charles II had previously given in 1663 to the Lords Proprietors a grant of which the southern limit ran to 29° N., an extension sufficient to include the greater part of the territory in Florida actually occupied by the Spaniards. Shortly thereafter in the same year, but probably without the knowledge of either party of the establishment of Charles Town, a treaty was signed between England and Spain, in which the latter recognized the settlements then established by the English. This did not establish a boundary between Carolina and Florida. Despite this convention, the Spanish authorities in Florida continued to regard the English as intruders, and delayed proclamation of the treaty for several years. Imperative economic necessity led the English to develop trade with the Indians, and traders were soon exchanging their wares with their back-country neighbors for prisoners of war, who were enslaved, and for deerskins.

The century following the establishment of St. Augustine was not, for the Spaniards, wholly one of tranquillity, as raids by pirates on various points of the coast were not infrequent. These vexations, however, did not materially retard significant progress into the interior, more particularly along the coast of the present Georgia, then known as Guale, and westward from St. Augustine through Timuqua into Apalachee.[10] The motivation for this penetration was more particularly the security of St. Augustine, to be effected through the conversion and stabilization of the Indians, rather than through settlement or commerce. The patient efforts of the missionaries resulted in the establishment of numerous villages or *doctrinas* of Christianized Indians. These are tentatively located on Figure 1. Proselyting, which had begun in Timuqua in 1608, was extended to Apalachee in 1633. Although the converts for the most part appear to have accepted the restraint of Spanish discipline, spiritual and temporal, with surprisingly good grace, their tranquillity was rather

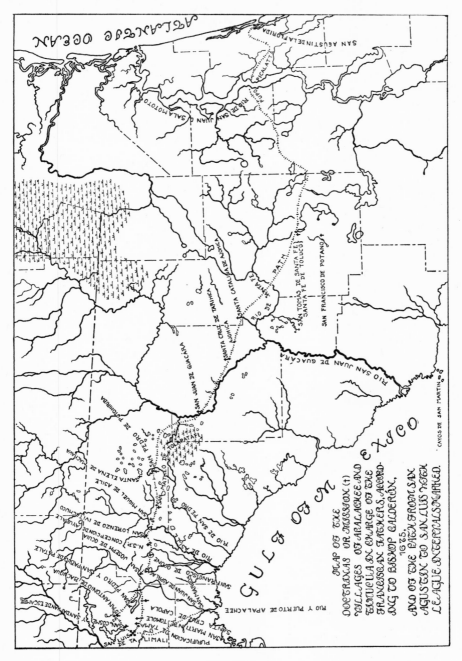

FIGURE I

more apparent than real, as several open revolts to Spanish rule occurred; and as will be shown in the documents presented, smoldering resentment and open rebellion contributed materially to the final outcome. It is probable that the Spanish influence and mission settlements had attained their maximum development in Timuqua and Apalachee at the time of the pastoral visit of Bishop Calderón in 1675.[11]

The first decade after the establishment of Charles Town was one of ominous quiet that terminated in 1680 when the English incited a series of Indian raids into Guale, which soon caused the withdrawal of the mission settlements to the region of the St. Marys River, although many of the Indians removed to the proximity of the English settlements. Meanwhile a settlement of Scots under Lord Cardross had been made at Port Royal in 1683. It was this individual who, in 1685, incited the Yamassee to the raid on Santa Catalina de Afuica (Ahoica of Calderón) in Timuqua. In the following year, however, Port Royal was destroyed in retaliation by a Spanish force. At this time the Indians living on the Chattahoochee River near the falls (Apalachicolos to the Spaniards, later known to the English as the Lower Creeks) became objects of intensified Spanish interest, probably in an effort to forestall the English in that quarter. In 1679 an effort to effect their conversion was rejected, only to be resumed with military aid in 1681, with similar insuccess. It did, however, result in the temporary establishment of the mission of Santa Cruz de Sábacola near the Chattahoochee and Flint rivers. But Dr. Henry Woodward, who played such a large part in the early Indian relations of the Carolina settlements, justified Spanish apprehensions by reaching the Apalachicola River villages in 1685. Learning of Woodward's presence, the deputy governor in Apalachee, Antonio Matheos, led two expeditions to the Apalachicolos in the same year, with the object of apprehending the doctor and driving out the English traders. During the second expedition, he received the submission of eight towns, and burned four which were recalcitrant—Coweta, Kasihta, Tuskegee, and Kolomi—but was eluded by Woodward. Despite three later expeditions in successive years, the Indians could not be dissuaded from their preference for the English traders. Finally, in 1689, the Spaniards built a blockhouse near Coweta, where a garrison was maintained until 1691, when exigencies in St. Augustine required withdrawal of the small force. The fort failed of its purpose, as the presence of the garrison and memories of the burned villages impelled

8

the Indians to leave the Chattahoochee and move nearer to the English on the banks of the upper Ocmulgee River, which from the name of the Indian tribes settling there became known as Ochese Creek by the English—a circumstance which accounts for the English application of the name *Creeks* to these Indians. The attitude of the Apalachicolos was not limited to disavowal of whatever may have been the claims of the Spanish to their allegiance, but developed into an animosity expressed by active raids on the mission settlements of Apalachee and Timuqua, in one of which the mission of San Juan de Guacára was destroyed. When the Spanish efforts to check the excursions of the English traders proved ineffective, they soon began to range as far westward as the Mississippi River.

Meanwhile a further threat to Spanish possession of the Gulf Coast arose from another quarter. The exploration of the Mississippi River by the French was proceeding apace. In 1682 La Salle claimed the valley of this river for the French crown, and in 1684 he set out from France to establish a colony on the lower river. He was shipwrecked on the Texas coast, and his plans otherwise miscarried. In 1687 he lost his life in an attempt to reach Canada. News of his project caused consternation in Spanish circles, and numerous expeditions, some of them based on Apalachee, were sent out over several years to discover his settlement,[12] the ruins of which were finally found in 1689. After some delay arising from this setback, Iberville was sent out from France to make a fresh effort to colonize the lower river. Instead, he occupied Mobile Bay, and to the westward established Biloxi in 1699. In the meantime the Spanish, aroused over the incursion of La Salle, sent out an expedition in 1693, under Admiral Pez and Dr. Sigüenza, to reconnoiter the Gulf Coast from Pensacola Bay *(Santa María de Galve)* to the mouth of the Mississippi River. On their return Pez and Sigüenza recommended the occupation of the former bay. After interminable delay, but finally in a frenzy stimulated by fear of French designs, Andrés de Arriola was sent from Mexico in 1698 to occupy and fortify the bay. However, Captain Juan Jordán, who came directly from Spain, anticipated his arrival by a few days. A settlement and fortification were constructed at the Barranca. The Spanish occupation came none too soon, for the force was barely installed in a meager fashion before the French expedition of Iberville appeared off the port, and being refused admission, proceeded westward to execute the operations already noted.

Despite the hostilities in the Southeast between the English and

Spanish subsequent to the foundation of Charles Town, their home governments in Europe either had been at peace or had participated in the coalitions against Louis XIV (1660-1715) of France in the War of the Grand Alliance, which began in 1689 and terminated with the peace of Ryswick in 1697. Prior to his death, Charles II of Spain (1665-1700) willed his dominions to his grandnephew, the Duke of Anjou, grandson of Louis XIV, who ascended the Spanish throne as Philip V (1700-1746), thus beginning the Bourbon dynasty. This defection of Spain to the side of France initiated the so-called War of the Spanish Succession, which lasted from 1701 to 1714, and in which the French and Spanish were opposed to the English and their allies. In England, Charles II had been succeeded by William II (1689-1702), who was followed by Queen Anne (1702-1714). Among the English peoples this war is commonly known by the queen's name. As a consequence of this realignment, the French and Spanish began active collaboration.

A more extensive description of the events described in these documents may be secured from the brief sketch afforded by Bolton,[13] or the more adequate account given by Crane.[14] Although Geiger's work[15] deals with Franciscan activities in Florida at an earlier period, his introductory chapter provides an admirable orientation on the organization of the order.

Several years ago the writer[16] undertook a critical analysis of the available data relating to the missions of Timuqua and Apalachee, with the hope of tentatively identifying some of the sites in middle Florida where Spanish artifacts have been found. In this effort the Calderón letter of 1675[17] was of especial value, for it is likely that at the time of Calderón's visit, or shortly thereafter, the mission settlements were flourishing to a degree never again attained. Those of Apalachee are stated[18] to have comprised, when most flourishing, fourteen villages with a total population of eight thousand persons. This number coincides with the number in the 1680 list in the Lowery transcripts. It is unlikely that all these were communities of Apalachee Indians, although it may be presumed that this tribe had largely been converted. Some of the villages, judging from their specific names, appear to have been settlements of converts from tribes to the northward. There is no reason to believe that, once established, all villages remained continuously at a particular site. The buildings and dwellings were simply constructed of materials collected in the vicinity, and it is unlikely that their meager intrinsic value would be a deterrent to their abandonment and relocation else-where, if such exigencies as failing fertility of the soil, a devastating epidemic,[19] or security were sufficiently compelling. A deliberate change of site would afford ample opportunity for the removal of all possessions, and the abandoned structures would quickly disappear from the site through rotting. Thus the Calderón letter states that one league (2.5 miles) was traveled from San Damian de Cupahica or Escambé to San Luis (1675); and Torres y Ayala in 1693[20] states that on his departure from San Luis he crossed the Amarillo (Ock-locknee) River before reaching the village of San Cosme and San Damian de Yecanbí, a distance of three leagues. In 1704 Solana[21] speaks of Escambé as being only a cannon shot distant from San Luis. This close proximity to San Luis may have been, of course, a com-pliance with the order to bring the villagers closer to the fort for protection. Both the Spanish and English accounts of Moore's raid specifically mention only Ayubale as a victim, although they admit there were other sufferers. An analysis of the data of the documents, undertaken in an attempt to elucidate the time when the individual settlements were destroyed, is presented herewith:

A. TIMUQUAN MISSIONS	FATE	AUTHORITY FROM DOCUMENTS
San Tomás de Santa Fé	Attacked on May 20, 1702.	14
	Evacuated prior to Novem-ber 30, 1706.	43
San Francisco de Potano	Uncertain whether this or San Francisco de Oconi attacked in 1703, but this place would appear more likely.	25
	Apalachee garrison with-drew to here in 1704.	28
	Evacuated prior to Novem-ber 30, 1706.	43
Santa Cathalina de Ahoica (Afuica, *Bolton*)	Destroyed in term of Gov. Cabrera. Destroyed February 7, 1685.	14 (Bolton, 1925)
Santa Cruz de Tarihica	Fate not mentioned.	
San Juan de Guacára	Destroyed in term of Gov. Quiroga (prior to 1690).	14

A. TIMUQUAN MISSIONS	FATE	AUTHORITY FROM DOCUMENTS
San Pedro de Potohiriba	Attacked in 1702, subsequent to the siege (Pilitiriva).	25
	Raided September 3, 1704.	35
Santa Helena de Machaba	Fate not mentioned.	
San Matheo de Tolapatafi	Raided September 3, 1704.	35
San Miguél de Asyle	Fate not mentioned.	
B. APALACHEE MISSIONS		
San Lorenzo de Ivitachuco	Never attacked.	
	Governor Moore claims it compounded with him.	44, 45
N.S.P. Concepción de Ayubale	Destroyed by Moore January 25, 1704.	25, 44, 45
San Francisco de Oconi	Probably not the San Francisco mentioned as attacked in 1703, subsequent to the siege. Probably a victim of Moore.	25
San Juan de Aspalaga	Destroyed June 23, 1704.	27
San Joseph de Ocuia	Attacked in 1703.	25
San Pedro y San Pablo de Patale	Destroyed June 24, 1704.	27
San Antonio de Bacuqua	Perhaps a victim of Moore.	
San Cosmo y San Damian de Escambé	Attacked June 29, 1704.	27
San Carlos de Chacatos		
San Luis de Talimali	Evacuated and destroyed by the Spaniards in July, 1704.	30
Nuestra Señora de la Candelaria de la Tama		
San Pedro de los Chines		
San Martín de Tomole	Probably a victim of Moore.	
Santa Cruz y San Pedro de Alcántara de Ychuntafun (Capola)	Probably a victim of Moore.	

Note: The dates, being taken from Spanish sources, are to be regarded as New Style.

It is thus seen that of the nine missions in Timuqua, the fate of six is described in the documents, and of the fourteen in Apalachee, the fate of eight is similarly mentioned.

Fort San Luis

In his report of the Ayubale raid, Moore[22] specifically mentions only Ivitachuco and San Luis, and is vague about his operations at other places. According to his statements, he effected the following results:

		ACCORDING TO:	
TOWNS		Doc. 44	Doc. 45
Ayubale destroyed		1	1
Surrendering unconditionally		2	2+2
Accompanied by:			
All people of		3	4
Greater part of		4	4
Destroyed all people of		2	0
Remaining:			
Compounded (Ivitachuco)	1		1
St. Lewis	1		
Population fled but burned village	1	3	
Total		15	14
INHABITANTS			
Removed into exile		300	300
Captured as slaves			
Men			325
Women and children			4,000
Killed			
Men			168+
Women and children			1,000

According to Zúñiga,[23] Moore did not approach closer to San Luis than two leagues, and effected the destruction of five (perhaps including Ayubale) places, and was accompanied by the entire population of two of these, numbering more than six hundred persons. It is seen that one of Moore's totals[24] exceeds the number of known villages, although the other is consistent with the Spanish enumeration of the settlements. Moore acknowledges that Ivitachuco and San Luis survived, leaving twelve to be accounted for. San Joseph de Ocuia was destroyed earlier, in 1703, leaving eleven. From Document 27 we learn that Aspalaga, Patale, and Escambé were destroyed in June, 1704, which leaves eight. According to Zúñiga, Moore did not approach nearer than two leagues to San Luis, which radius would, according to the distances from San Luis given by Calderón,[25] embrace and eliminate Escambé, San Carlos de Chacatos, Nuestra Señora de la Candelaria de la Tama, and San Pedro de los Chines. Since Escambé has already been accounted for, our subtraction leaves five, the number which Zúñiga acknowledges as having been lost. Corroboration for this opinion is afforded by Document 29, dated July 16, 1704, which mentions that the villages had been reduced to four, which probably did not include San Luis. As a result of this elimination, one may infer that San Francisco de Oconi, San Antonio de Bacuqua, San Martín de Tomole, and Santa Cruz y San Pedro de Alcántara de Ychuntafun, as well as Ayubale, were the victims of Moore's raid.

As previously mentioned, there is reason to believe that some of these villages were not peopled by Apalachee Indians. According to Swanton,[26] it would appear that the missions of La Purificación de la Tama (probably the same as Nuestra Señora de la Candelaria de la Tama) and Assumpcion del Puerto were Yamassee settlements, whereas San Carlos de Chacatos and San Pedro de los Chines were Chatot. San Francisco de Oconi was probably a village of Oconee Indians. The others may have been Apalachee settlements. Especial interest attaches to Ivitachuco, lying to the eastward on the confines of Timuqua. A village of this name was encountered by De Soto in this general location.[27] Don Patricio Hinachuba, the cacique of this village at the period considered, appears to have been a man of considerable character and discernment, and unswerving in his attachment to the church, if not to the Spaniards. His letters[28] afford much insight into the prevailing situation in Apalachee, and he forecast the later troubles. His complaints were sympathetically received by the crown,[29] but the local officials largely evaded the royal instructions.[30] One may surmise that Don Patricio must also have been held in respect by the Apalachicolos, as it is difficult to believe that ransom would have sufficed to spare Ivitachuco had the Apalachicolos entertained an inveterate hatred for Don Patricio and his people. At any rate, Ivitachuco was the only village to survive the holocaust, and its Indians the only group to flee eastward to St. Augustine, the others preferring the vicinity of Pensacola and Mobile.

It is to be inferred that the structures which Moore calls forts with strong walls, were, as he in fact states, not fortifications, but mud-plastered walls surrounding the compound attached to the church and convent. The large mud-walled house was probably the council house. However, from Document 28 it would appear that ultimately Ivitachuco and some other places were surrounded by palisades.

Fort San Luis

In view of the importance of the engagements fought at Ayubale and Patale, there is some advantage in synthesizing an account of these affairs from the different narratives.

Colonel James Moore surprised the village of Ayubale on the morning of January 25 (N.S.), 1704, and apparently succeeded in entering it without substantial opposition other than that afforded by Indian archers, and in gaining the council house, which must have been on the central square, adjacent to the church. The opposition delayed his advance sufficiently to permit Father Angel de Miranda to gather many Indians, men, women, and children in the church enclosure, where they stoutly and successfully defended themselves against direct attack, in which very few of Moore's Indians participated. An attempt by Moore's men to breach the church doors with axes was repulsed, with fourteen Englishmen being wounded. Moore finally succeeded in setting fire to the church early in the afternoon, and by another assault effected entry, during which he lost three men. Father Miranda, his munitions exhausted by nine hours' resistance, then surrendered, and in the church and the convent the English captured twenty-six men and fifty-eight women and children, the besieged having lost twenty-four men. Elsewhere in the village the Indian allies captured about as many more.

Word of the surprise attack having reached San Luis, the deputy governor, Captain Juan Ruíz Mexía, set out immediately for Ayubale with about thirty mounted Spaniards and four hundred Indians, and en route spent the night at Patale. On the following morning before resuming march, the force was exhorted to fight by Father Parga, the missionary at Patale, who insisted on accompanying them. The Spanish force found the invaders still occupying Ayubale, which they surrounded, and in impetuous attacks twice drove the English back to the council house. Captain Mexía was wounded, dislodged from his horse, and with six (or eight) other Spanish soldiers, was captured and bound. Father Parga, who continued to exhort the living and minister to the wounded, was captured, and two Spaniards, Marcos Delgado and Juan Solana, were killed in attempting his rescue. Parga's body, mutilated by decapitation, was later found in a canebrake. The munitions of the Spanish force were finally exhausted, whereupon both Spaniards and Indians fled. Moore claimed that his Indian allies killed five or six whites, and at least one hundred sixty-eight, and perhaps up to two hundred, Apalachee Indians. Moore lost one white. The retreating Spaniards were met next day at Capola by Manuel

Solana, Jr. *(hijo)*, who was belatedly bringing up munitions. The Indian allies of Moore proceeded to wreak vengeance on the captives by burning at the stake, within sight of the other prisoners, several Indians, including Antonio Cuipa Feliciano, *enija* of San Luis, and Luis Domingo, as well as two Spanish soldiers. During these events Father Miranda, who was unbound, upbraided Moore for these barbarities, to which Moore replied that his force of whites was greatly outnumbered by his Indian allies, whom he could not restrain. Later, while the Indian raiders were absent searching for cattle, four of the Spanish soldiers escaped, and Captain Mexía and Father Miranda were liberated in the hope that they would subsequently pay ransom to their captors. However, Captain Jacinto Roque, who had been left in charge at the blockhouse of San Luis, refused to furnish the ransom. During the fracas four Gallegan recruits from the Spanish force escaped to Moore, and an Irishman from Moore's party fled to the Spaniards. As soon as Moore's force left Ayubale, Father Juan de Villalva of Ivitachuco came over to search for the body of Father Parga, which was taken to Ivitachuco for burial. With the final departure of Moore from Apalachee, a small party of Spaniards and Indians under Captain Roque went to Ayubale to bury the Christian dead, many of whom gave evidence of having been subjected to torture. The defeat Moore administered to the Spaniards, while not so complete as he claimed, was nevertheless a heavy blow and a severe loss, while the tortures which many prisoners suffered caused further and extensive desertions of Indians to the English and their allies. The morale of the remaining Spaniards and Indians was severely shaken.

Though apprehension must have mounted following the disaster of Ayubale, there does not seem to have been much, if any, distinct effort to consolidate the population of the surviving villages closer to San Luis. Another large raiding party, evidently without English leadership, struck Patale on the night of June 23. Father Manuel de Mendoza was lured to the door of his convent by a friendly hail and shot to death, the convent was burned, and many villagers were made captive. The following day what appears to have been the same band of raiders struck Aspalaga and made the entire population captive. One of these, Estevan, who later escaped, reported at the blockhouse some days later that the departing raiders soon encountered a larger band, under English leadership, which planned to strike Escambé, close to San Luis. Meanwhile Adjutant Manuel Solana, who had succeeded Mexía as deputy, led a small force to reconnoiter Patale. Not finding the priest or his body, Solana and his party supposed him to be a captive and followed the trail of the raiders in the hope of effecting his rescue. In this they were unsuccessful, but they did encounter a mortally wounded woman who told them the father had not been a captive. They returned to Patale, and found his body while digging in the ruins.

Some encouragement being afforded by the sighting of the Pensacola felucca off the coast on June 28, word was sent to its commander, Adjutant Juan de Torres, to repair to San Luis with all his force, the sentinels were recalled from the watchtower at St. Marks, and Don Patricio was summoned with his warriors from Ivitachuco. Learning that a raid on Escambé was in imminent prospect, the population of that village was ordered to take refuge in the blockhouse and, as a consequence, all except a few who were sceptical of the warning escaped, although some of the raiders entered the very environs of San Luis. On the following day most of the expected reinforcements had arrived at the blockhouse, but a party of drovers who came in the felucca were killed, as well as the returning sentinels who disobeyed orders as to the route they should follow. It became evident that the raiders had withdrawn from the immediate vicinity of San Luis, and word was received that they had retired to Patale, which was again in their hands. With the removal of the raiders to the eastward, Don Patricio became apprehensive for the safety of Ivitachuco and returned there with his force. On the way his party captured four rebellious Apalachee Indians, who related that the raiding party was much smaller than supposed. The presence of the Spanish reinforcement afforded encouragement, and when it was reported that the raiding party was small, some degree of enthusiasm for an attack on it developed. The Indians did not share this feeling, as they refused to participate unless the Spaniards would agree to fight on foot, a condition which Solana was obliged to accept. Leaving Captain Roque in the blockhouse with fourteen Spaniards, Solana set out on the night of July 3 with about forty Spaniards, including twelve musketeers, ninety-three Indians armed with guns, and sixty Indian archers, to rendezvous with Don Patricio near Patale. While Solana's party awaited these reinforcements early in the morning, some of the enemy came along the path and were, against orders, ambushed unsuccessfully by some of the Spaniards. Escaping this attack, they made their way to Patale and aroused their comrades, who, to the number of a few English and two hundred pagans, sallied forth and encountered the Spaniards on open ground. About two hours after the fighting began, a rumor became current among the Apalachee Indians that the enemy was encircling them in the woods which surrounded the field, and most of them abandoned the fight. Retreat was now necessary, and as the surviving Spaniards made their way back to the horses as best they could, the retreat became a rout in which eleven of the musketeers were lost. Demoralization of those who attained the blockhouse that night was complete, and most of the Indians who applied for admission were turned away. The accounts of the Spanish losses are somewhat confusing because the loss of the drovers and sentinels are included, but it would appear that at least fifteen failed to return from Patale, including five from the Pensacola contingent. On July 6 the Adjutant Solana, surmising that the enemy had withdrawn, sent a group to reconnoiter the field. The party reported the discovery of two bodies, presumably Christian, on the field, and in the plaza at the village sixteen burned bodies were found about the square, bound to the stations of the cross. An escaped captive who was encountered related that eight Spaniards had been burned, and several carried off captives. All the Spaniards were now convinced that the outlook was hopeless, and most of the settlers and their families implored permission to leave in the felucca for Pensacola. Rumors of a projected overpowering English attack became current, and the remaining Indians flatly refused to participate in further resistance. As a consequence, Solana recommended to Governor Zúñiga the abandonment of Apalachee.

From Document 35 to Document 43 of January, 1708, in our series, excepting Numbers 40 and 41, there is a hiatus of firsthand accounts of these discouraging developments in Florida. Though not seen by the writer, the following documents are mentioned as probably pertinent, in the hope that they may come to the attention of some subsequent student:

(1) 58-2-8:4. Bitachuco (Ivitachuco), May 29, 1705. Cacique Patricio to Governor.

(2) 58-2-8:4. Bitachuco, August 23, 1705. Francisco de Florencia to Andres Garcia.

(3) 58-2-8:4. Bitachuco, August 27, 1705. Francisco de Florencia to Sr. Cabo de Lachua, Juan Francisco.

(4) 58-1-27:87. San Augustín, April 30, 1706. Royal Officials to King. The Indians in revolt continue war on the Apalachinos, killed a chief, carried off a friar.

Fort San Luis

(5) 58-1-27:90. San Augustín, May 3, 1706. Governor Corcoles y Martínez to King. Spanish driven out of La Chua, garrison fell back on San Francisco.

(6) 58-1-27:92. San Augustín, August 13, 1706. Royal Officials to King. In the last three months twenty-six Spaniards have been killed, a general falling back on San Augustín, the only place not abandoned.

Joseph de la Zúñiga y Zerda was succeeded in the governorship by Francisco Corcoles y Martínez probably some time in April of 1706. Zúñiga had distinguished himself by his successful defense of St. Augustine during the siege by Moore in 1702, and considering the meager force and supplies available to him, subsequent events herein described probably could not have taken any different course. But as the future unfolded and in spite of the later reverses, it was evident that in saving St. Augustine, he had saved Florida. For this achievement he was promoted to the governorship of Cartagena, which one may hope he actually attained. Not until after the return of peace in 1714 did Apalachee receive further attention from the Spanish authorities.

One forms the opinion from the perusal of these documents that the depopulation of Apalachee was not wholly due to the vicious attacks of the Lower Creeks, incited and abetted by the English, but that a formidable element of rebellion on the part of the Apalachians was an important factor. While the teachings and deportment of the missionary priests appear to have won the respect and devotion of many influential Indians, this effect was largely nullified by the treatment they received from the administrative officials and settlers, which in many aroused a deep-seated and slumbering resentment that flared into open rebellion under the derision of their pagan kinsmen who had been liberated from all restraint by their contact with the English. The Spanish had been chary about permitting their proselytes to have firearms, which the English introduced extensively among their adherents, against whom the Apalachian bowmen were largely defenseless. Spanish prestige steadily diminished with the regular progression of unfavorable events, until all substantial Indian support was irretrievably lost. Although the outnumbered Spaniards fought bravely at both Ayubale and Patale, as proved by their heavy losses, they were, without substantial relief from outside and from the defection of their Indians, in a hopeless position, faced with the alternatives of withdrawal or extermination. Their choice was natural.

19

Documents

1. Royal Cédula, Madrid, November 4, 1693.[31]

THE KING

Don Laureano de Torres y Ayala, my governor and captain general of the Provinces of San Augustín of Florida, or the person or persons in whose charge is the government:

Don Diego de Quiroga, your predecessor, related in a letter of April 1st of 1688[32] that he, with the royal officials, had visited those provinces, among them Apalachee, whose caciques had offered, if aided with tools, to make at their cost a wooden blockhouse for the infantry which compose the garrison there, as well as a stone watchtower at the port of San Marcos, because it is not sufficiently spacious [there] for a fort. In view of which, and from the endorsement by my fiscal, I have decided to inform you of the former, and of the voluntary offer made by the Indians of the Province of Apalachee, to aid with their personal labor in the construction of the fabric of a blockhouse and watchtower. We are informed that the Governor Pablo de Hita Salazar in his time constructed a wooden fort in the port of San Marcos, as you may know; and if [it is] not built as is supposed, you are to build it, without bothering or obliging the Indians to work upon it, but persuading them with blandishments, under the exact [conditions] which they proposed. Of whatever you will do in this, [you] will give me a detailed account, in order that I may be informed of it.

2. Royal Officials to the King. San Augustín, April 6, 1696.[33]

In a royal cédula of Your Majesty dated December 30, 1693, Your Majesty was pleased to ask us to be observant of what the governor of this province is to execute in the matter of the blockhouse which he is to build in the Province of Apalachee. Upon the receipt of the said royal cédula, we inform Your Majesty whether the Indians of the said province, in fulfilment of what they proposed, have begun to build the house of wood for the shelter and residence of the infantry which compose the garrison of that province, giving their personal labor and handicraft. Because of their poverty, they petition that you aid them at Your Majesty's expense with some sustenance, as they have none, neither tools for its construction, [nor] spikes, for this is not their responsibility, as was arranged by agreement of the governor and ourselves, of which we have given an account to Your Majesty, which we will resume on its completion, [giving] that which has been spent upon it. Our Lord protect the Catholic royal person of Your Majesty many years, as your vassals desire. Florida, April 6, 1696.

> Thomas Menéndez Marqués [rubric]
> Joachin de Florencia [rubric]

3. *Governor Torres y Ayala to the King. San Augustín, April 15, 1696.*[34]

I received a royal cédula from Your Majesty in which you ordered me to execute the construction of the wooden blockhouse in the Province of Apalachee, where is situated the garrison of infantry which Your Majesty has there. After I had gone to that province on taking possession of this government, much cut timber was found already weakened from the time elapsed since it was cut. Recognizing the necessity for the blockhouse, I assembled the caciques and explained to them [that] the reason they should labor was to assure the security of the people. In this they willingly concurred, offering again to cut the timber which was lacking, with the stipulation that they should have aid from Your Majesty [as regards] tools, and some corn for their sustenance, which I offered them, to further the royal service of Your Majesty.

Today it is completed, except for the third part of the roof, and [there are] placed in it two pieces of artillery, and all the infantry [can pass] the night in it with security, as can also all the people on the nights when the alarm is sounded, which happens repeatedly at the present. The Indians have worked without compulsion more than they would have voluntarily, and from the royal treasury [have received] only the assistance of some axes, *vasuras*, and assorted nails, [together with] corn for their sustenance. It receives all my solicitude for its construction, as it is not yet complete, lacking the third part of the roof, as was mentioned to Your Majesty. I have considered the representations which the said caciques made to me, that they are occupied at present with their agricultural labors. Notwithstanding, I have ordered the deputy whom I have in that province to pursue the marauding and rebellious Indians who are accustomed to surprise them, so that as soon as possible the matter may be closed, upon which I will give a report to Your Majesty. For that which relates to the stone watchtower, which Your Majesty touched upon in the royal cédula mentioned, [I may say that] although I arrived at the said port of San Marcos where it should be,[35] I saw no such thing nor had [it] brought to my attention before its mention by Your Majesty in the said royal cédula. The only [tower] they have there is of wood, from where it is possible to see the sea and coast, and where sentinels are continually stationed. Neither did I find the fort built by the Governor Don Pablo de Hita de Salazar, as it was burned and cut down by the enemy, in the government of Don Juan Marqués de Cabrera.[36] I have ordered my said deputy to give a report to the royal comptroller of the cost and amount of the corn, so that in conjunction with whatever may be spent for the tools, it may be furnished to Your Majesty on conclusion. Our Lord protect the Catholic royal person of Your Majesty many years, as Christianity requires and as we your vassals desire. Florida, April 15, 1696.

Don Laureano de Torres y Ayala

4. *Certification by Officials of the Royal Hacienda of the Construction Costs of the* [Block]*house in Apalachee. San Augustín, July 3, 1697.*[37]

The officials of the royal treasury of these Provinces of Florida, the Captains Don Thomas Menéndez Marqués, comptroller [by commission] of Your Majesty, and Joachin de Florencia, who fills the office of treasurer and storekeeper *ad interim* by reason of the absence of the proprietor, and who, by order of Your Majesty, is engaged in the collection of the subsidy of this presidio:

We certify that from the account and vouchers received in the auditor's office, there has been prepared a statement of the expenses incurred in the Province of Apalachee in the construction of a wooden [block]house for the lodgment and defense of the infantry assigned there as garrison. The Indians of the said province furnished the timber and labor as they promised, and as Your Majesty commanded by your royal cédula, [we] assisted and aided them only with food, some tools, and spikes, the expense in construction being entirely at

22

the cost of Your Majesty; and what has been spent and the time consumed are shown in the following manner:

Firstly, it appears from two certificates submitted by Captain Jacinto Roque Pérez, deputy [governor] of the said province, who supervised the said work, that from October 3, 1695, when it was begun, until its conclusion, there was spent on food for the Indians, master workmen, and laborers that worked on said house, 353 measures of corn for their food, which at 2 reals amount to 88 pesos and 2 reals......................... P 88 R 2

For 6 quintals of new iron at 10 pesos per quintal and 2½ quintals of old iron at 20 reals, and 6 pounds of steel, all to be forged and pointed into large and small spikes, with some other necessary tools, which amount in all to 91 pesos............ P 91

For three new axes, two adzes, one crowbar, and three augers which were bought for the said works, at a cost of 29 pesos.... P 29

For two thousand new nails for shingles, which were bought for its roof, and which amount to 25 pesos................. P 25

For 71 pesos which were spent for two blacksmiths who fashioned and dressed the various spikes and iron tools........... P 71
_____

P 304 R 2

In which manner the cost of the said house amounts to P 304 R 2. The said 304 pesos and 2 reals, which were spent in that province, were furnished from the tithes of the years 1695 and '96, as more clearly appears from the said certifications which we transmit, and from which it may be clear to Your Majesty. By order of the governor and captain general we submit the present. In San Augustín of Florida on the 1st of July, 1697.

Thomas Menéndez Marqués
Joachin de Florencia

5. Royal Cédula. Madrid, March, 1698.[38]

THE KING

Don Laureano de Torres y Ayala, Knight of the Order of Santiago, my governor and captain general of Florida, or the person or persons that govern them:

In a letter of July 3, 1697, you reported that the [block]house in the Province of Apalachee for the infantry which there constitute the garrison is completed; that it is sufficiently capacious to shelter all who reside in the place, some Spanish settlers and all the natives of the village; that you have therein placed two pieces of artillery on two *travesos* which project from the house; and that you submitted a certificate given on the 1st of July of the same year '97 by the royal officials of that city. From this it appears that its cost amounted to 304 pesos and 2 reals, in order that I might be pleased to approve it [what follows in quotation marks is scratched out] . . . "to the relief of all the residents of the village of San Luis of Apalachee."

The letter was submitted to my Council of War for the Indies and examined by the fiscal, and in consideration of [scratched out] the moderate [insert illegible] expense, which the construction of the blockhouse entailed, and because there will be no subsequent expense in maintaining it, and it can serve as a reasonable shelter or defense for the natives from the incursions which the neighboring Indians make at the instigation of the English of Saint George (San Jorge), I have decided to give my approval (as by the present I do) for this which you have effected, and give you thanks for the care with which you have attended to its defense and to the security of that province. Herein I acknowledge I have been well served by your anticipation of what you would have to execute, and in the letter [I offer] proposals to the Council in order that it may decide whatever is most advantageous to my service.

6. *Don Patricio, Cacique of Ivitachuco, and Don Andrés, Cacique of San Luis, to the King. February 12, 1699.*[39]

Don Patricio Hinachuba, the principal cacique of the Province of Apalachee, and Don Andrés, cacique of San Luis, in the name of all the province, and for themselves, humbled at the feet of Your Majesty (whom God protect), say that in the time when the Sergeant Major Don Pablo de Hita Salazar was governor of this plaza, he granted permission for some Spanish families to settle in this province at the place of San Luis, where are stationed the infantry of its garrison. One of these families was that of Captain Juan Fernández de Florencia, who was deputy [governor] and superior magistrate, and who has remained until the present, inasmuch as Captain Jacinto Roque [Pérez], the present deputy [governor], got him to establish a ranch of cattle, swine, and horses, from which we receive considerable injury to our fields from his cattle, as well as [from] those of Diego Florencia and Francisco de Florencia, his brothers-in-law, who reside with him. Although we have sought redress from various sources, we have not had it, since they are so powerful, and we are without a person to protect and defend us. Justice is not administered to us in this, nor in other lesser injuries, [such] as committed by Juana Caterina, wife of the said deputy, who gave two slaps in the face to a cacique of [the Indians] of San Luis, because he had not brought her fish on one Friday, and obliged the village to furnish six Indian women for the grinding every day without payment for their work; and although this was [contrary to] an order of the inspector, it is not observed, and notwithstanding, [they] continue doing it. As also that she be given an Indian to go and come every day with a pitcher of milk for the house of the said deputy.

And that they likewise built a house of singular architecture for the infantry, with notable detriment to us and to the natives, since in addition to the donation of their personal labor, they brought their own axes and food, and with the remainder of the timber they made houses for one of his brothers-in-law and other Spanish settlers. And as a consequence, the natives of San Luis are found withdrawn a league into the woods, for their places have been seized for the Spaniards. For this reason, and because they flee from the continued labor of the deputy's house, they do not even go to Mass on feast days. And not only this, but there are many Apalachee Indians withdrawn to the Province of Guale, where many die without confession, because they do not understand the language of the missionaries of that province. All this is because of the great hardships imposed on us by the families which are settled in our village of San Luis; and we are sufficiently annoyed by the said deputy and brothers-in-law, since they compelled the *mico*[40] of la Tama, who is new in the faith, [and] who is skilled in tanning, to prepare skins for them without pay for his work, [because of which] he went to the place of Saint George; from his revolt we are disconsolate, for fear others may follow him.

All, Sir, arises from our lack of a protector who was petitioned [for], to hear our grievances and redress them, for which we ask of Your Majesty, [whom] God protect, the necessary relief of our afflictions, [by your] sending us shortly alleviation through your royal decree, and [by your] appointing for us a person who can defend us, or by giving authority to Don Laureano de Torres y Ayala, governor and captain general, that for the present we name one to his satisfaction and ours. Thus we will be relieved from all these grievances and many more, which we have not expressed in order not to bother Your Majesty, whom God protect and prosper with succession to the crown as Christianity needs. San Luis, February 12, 1699.

> Don Patricio Hinachuba
> Don Andrés, Cacique of San Luis

7. *Don Patricio Hinachuba to Don Antonio Ponce de León. Ivitachuco, April 10, 1699.*[41]

Don Antonio Ponce de León: I wish that the Divine Majesty may give to Your Grace the most perfect health, which I desire in company with all your children. I and all my subjects are at Your Grace's service. Here [we continue] subject to many annoyances and are much aggrieved for many reasons, the principal being what Francisco Florencia did this past winter to the pagan Indians of the Province of Tasquique [Tuskegee]. The said señor having departed on a hunt for buffalo [*civo=cibolo*] with forty Chacato Indians, they unexpectedly encountered twenty-four Indians coming peacefully to trade in this province, to sell their buffalo skins, leather shirts, and madstones [*piedras besales*=kissing stones, bezoars, madstones]; and having amicably conversed with them, he asked them where they would spend the night. They replied they would halt nearby, as they did. And the said Francisco de Florencia said that he would go to another part of the woods, and at midnight he returned with his party and killed sixteen men, the others fleeing. He gathered up the spoils and brought them to his province, and they painted the shirts in Ayubale; and it is very well known in this province that they have sold all the plunder, [and] it is certain that the deed is such that all of us will have to pay for these activities, since this aggravation has aroused misgivings, although to this date the opening of hostilities which we expect has not begun. Furthermore, the cattle of the said Francisco de Florencia and of the deputy [governor], his brother-in-law, are within the villages, with no effort made to remove them to their ranches, and those of the adjutant Salinas in the same manner. Although we have complained to the deputy, since these matters are his responsibility, he has done nothing, nor has he done anything about the murders committed by his brother-in-law; and [he has] even informed the governor that he was attacked by the pagans, when the truth is quite the contrary, since the very Indians who accompanied him are telling the truth, all of which was done without fear of God. He is also permitting the adjutant Salinas and the said Francisco de Florencia to detain on their ranches the youths of the mission, and although our missionary father sent for them, they did not wish to let them go, and they rear them without learning prayers or hearing Mass. They also have women on their ranches, and although on your visit Your Grace ordered that it should not be thus, after you left the deputy said that [this order] signified nothing; that what he desired would prevail as indeed [it] did; and it is for this that we are most unhappy and the natives are fleeing from these [parts] in disorder. Some have fled to the woods, others to Saint George with the English, prompted by the heavy labor exacted by the Florencias for which they are not paid anything; and as we do not have other support than that of Your Grace, I give you an account of this and could give you much more except that it would trouble you; and of all Your Grace will learn from those who go from here. And as you are our father and defender at this time, attempt our aid for the love of God, hinting of all this to the Sergeant Major Don Nicolas Ponce, your father, who has loved and protected us so much, for as he has been governor of that plaza, he can tell to the present governor what he should do to give us the comfort that would be afforded by withdrawing these families to the presidio, as they are depriving us of our manner of living, and our sweat and labor should be for God to whom we would leave it; and we ask that His Divine Majesty protect Your Grace for our protection and aid. Ivitachuco, April 10, 1699.

I kiss the hands of Your Grace, your great servant and friend.

Don Patricio Hinachuba

8. *Don Antonio Ponce de León to the King on Behalf of Don Patricio Hinachuba. Havana, January 29, 1702.*[42]

Don Antonio Ponce de León, chaplain organist in the parish church of San Augustín of Florida, for Your Majesty:

Prostrated at the royal feet of the Most Catholic person of Your Majesty, he says that in the time when Don Laureano de Torres Ayala was governor of these provinces of Florida, in whatever criminal charges [were] made against the natives of these said provinces, he was always designated as their defender, for which reason they seek me whenever an injury is done, entreating by means of my small efforts to provide some relief from their afflictions, as has [been] done [in the present instance]. The cacique Don Patricio Hinachuba, who is the greatest of all of the caciques of the Province of Apalachee, [seeks the attention of Your Majesty] by means of the enclosure, since consideration, although sought, was not received in the said city of San Augustín, and nothing to relieve the natives was achieved. Giving charitable attention to the subject of the letter, [you will see] it is thus that the natives, made obstinate from bad treatment and continued labor, desert their women and children and abandon the law of God and gather at the settlement of Saint George where they live in license, because the families of the Florencias in the said province, with their cattle, cows, swine, and horses, cause great damage to the fields of the wretched natives, and employ them in their service without compensation, together with many other grievances which are not expressed.

It being necessary, at the pleasure of Your Majesty, to institute action before [an] ecclesiastical judge, [in order] that these [conditions] be censured and rectified, for if it is not [done] thus, nothing will be effected, because these people always have cattle by consent of the governors, through whose aid they effect these injuries, and from their being related to most of [the families] of the presidio. The Captain Juan de Ayala Escobar is related to these by marriage.[43] Since I have visited those provinces, I have reliable information that no charges were placed before him, and that he left them in much discontent; and I am very certain that the withdrawal of the said families [would] be their chief relief [as well as] desire. Since Your Royal Majesty (whom God protect) is spending your royal patrimony solely for the purpose of converting souls to the holy faith, there is no reason that for private interests they be lost in the woods or in the settlement of Saint George. They must have the benefit of encouragement for their increase, or you will lose a soul. I affirm to Your Majesty that in the said province I have seen, in the vicinity of San Luis, the houses of the Indians located a league's distance, because their building sites and fields have been taken by the Spanish settlers. The missionary fathers assured me that in the entire year the [Indians] have not heard Mass because of their dispersion and flight, so that they will not be ordered about as the Spaniards are accustomed to do. On a former occasion, letters for His Majesty

Don Carlos II (who rests in glory) were brought to that court by the hand of the Reverend Father Francisco Gutiérrez. These natives have not had justice, and if some help has come, it is concealed, for which reason I beg that Your Majesty will be pleased to harken with all compassion to these wretched Indians, giving them the relief which they request, in order that these provinces be not destroyed and made waste, to which I am prompted only by charity and zeal for the honor of God and the advancement of Your Majesty, whom heaven protect and favor as Christianity requires. Havana, January 29, 1702.

Prostrate at the royal feet of Your Majesty, which in submission I kiss.

Antonio Ponce de León

9. Royal Cédula, Madrid, May 7, 1700.[44]

THE KING

Field Master Don Joseph de Zúñiga y la Zerda, my governor and captain general of the Provinces of San Augustín of Florida, or the person or persons who may be charged with their government:

Don Patricio Hinachuba, the principal cacique of the entire province, and Don Andrés, cacique of the village of San Luis, in their names and for the entire province, have written to me in a letter dated the 12th of February, 1699, of the continuous affronts, vexations, and annoyances which they receive from the families that in the time of Governor Don Pablo de Hita Salazar, and with his permission, went to settle in that province, as well as from its deputy [governor]. [As a consequence of these conditions], they are driven from their home sites for the houses which they have constructed, obliging them to work for them without giving them food or otherwise compensating for their labor, by which they are obliged to withdraw to the woods where they do not hear Mass or go to confession, some even passing to Saint George. He requests me that for the correction of these evils you appoint some person to protect them, [or] that I give authority to the governor of those provinces to select someone to the satisfaction of him and of those Indians, before whom their grievances may be rectified. His letter and representations were presented to my Royal Council for the Indies and viewed by the fiscal, who has approved sending them with this dispatch, [a] copy of which is signed by my undersigned secretary; and I direct you, and I command you (as I do), that, informed of its contents, you assume the office of magistrate and investigate the allegations of these unhappy caciques and Indians of the said Province of Apalachee.

If they are found to be so oppressed and annoyed as they give to understand—and it must be presumed that they are—and upon finding it to be thus, and after having done this, [you should] make effective restitution to them of all that in which they have been injured, and then attend with all the power of the law to the punishment of those who have annoyed them, of which you shall give me an account by *autos* at the first opportunity offered, and apply as many measures as you judge necessary to put a stop to these and similar injuries.

You should always remember and have ever present before you that one of your principal duties is to exercise the greatest care so that the caciques and Indians of the said Province of Apalachee live without annoyance, and to remove whatever is prejudicial, taking note that the council will be always observant of the zeal and diligence which they expect of you in this matter and of other [duties] which are presented by my service, as I desire greatly that these poor caciques and natives should be well treated, and that you help, protect, and defend them, as is your duty and as I have ordered in repeated cédulas to the governors, your predecessors, with which again I charge you, that thus my resolution and the service of God be advanced and my [ending].

10. An Order from the Governor Don Joseph de Zúñiga. San Augustín, November 5, 1700.[45]

Don Joseph de Zúñiga y Zerda, field master of the Spanish Infantry, by the King Our Lord, governor and captain general of this city of San Augustín of Florida and of all its provinces by His Majesty:

Inasmuch as it is desirable and necessary to the service of His Majesty that in the Province of Apalachee there exist that good order which is required for the preservation of the province, as well as for the relief of its inhabitants, Spaniards and Indians, I therefore order and command the Captain Jacinto Roque Pérez, my deputy [governor] of the said Province of Apalachee, to be attentive in the first place to the protection of the Indians, because of his obligation to them, and because of the deteriorated condition in which the province is found; to bring back those who are in a state of servitude in other parts, sending the soldiers and people that may be necessary to effect it; and on every occasion when [a violation] occurs, to make investigation, punishing those who transgress in the form which appears appropriate to the situation *(yende a la mano)*, whether Spaniards, both settlers and soldiers, in order that they do not commit any injury whatsoever against them, neither in their fields nor regarding their stock, [or in] buying them against their wishes or at a low price. They [are to] be allowed to raise their swine and fowl, and these are not to be taken from them; and my said deputy will take particular care not to hinder anyone from coming to this city to sell bacon, lard, swine, as well as hides and skins, which they have raised or acquired; because regarding this there have been given me various complaints, and since [all] this appears to me mischievous, those who obstruct [this order] will be punished severely.

I likewise order and command my said deputy to notify all the proprietors of ranches that they shall not for any reason, or purpose, or need that they may have, sell or kill any calf which has not attained more than two to three years, under penalty of ten pesos for the first time; for the second, thirty; and for the third, chastisement and punishment (for non-observance) at my discretion. And in order to encourage the multiplication of cattle, I have ordered they should be utilized in the tithes, [and I] order the overseers of the ranches to promote the increase and procreation of calves. This my order will be executed without exception, and should it appear to me that my deputy or those who succeed him tolerate such sales, they will be punished severely and, furthermore, fined at my discretion; and [the deputies] are not to maintain any reservations against this mandate for any consideration of fear or other pretext.

And I thus further order and command that if they receive any complaints from the proprietors of ranches that the Indians are killing their cattle, they shall carefully investigate; and, identifying the culprits, they shall punish them severely, and report this to me; and if it is determined that some cacique or caciques have countenanced or tolerated, or taken part in it, that they shall be punished and make restitution.

And because I have understood that the Chacatos, who are under their jurisdiction, have inflicted some injuries and fatalities upon the pagans with whom we are trying to re-establish friendship, [to our] grave detriment and impediment, they shall be given warning and given to understand my order that when they meet with [these

Indians], whether in settled or unsettled places, they shall comport themselves in a friendly manner, with all civility and good will. And those of the said Chacatos who disobey this my said order will be punished with the greatest severity, as they will experience when the occasion offers; and this [disobedience] my deputy [governor] or his successors will not tolerate.

And, finally, he will see that in all the villages the natives are provided with all supplies necessary for operations of war, which they can and must arrange, and [that] the infantry likewise be supplied with munitions ready and prepared in such a manner that no misfortune might arise from lack of preparation. In this my Deputy Captain Jacinto Roque Pérez will behave, as he has to the present, with the watchfulness, foresight, and care which from his zeal, bravery, and experience he gave promise, evidencing himself a good vassal and servant to His Majesty.

This order will be made publicly known at the time it is issued. It is to be posted in the council houses [*bujos=bujios*]; and today, day of the date, I have sent it to him and simultaneously to the caciques of the entire province. And he will take one copy of the aforesaid order along with this original, and place them in the file of orders and papers in his custody, as a perpetual testimony to the zeal with which I have devoted myself to the promotion and preservation of the province and its natives, which is in the service of His Majesty. To that end I order the present sent, signed by my hand and countersigned by the undersigned notary for the public and government, given in Florida on November 5, of this year of Our Lord, 1700.

Joseph de Zúñiga y Zerda

By order of the governor and captain general. Juan Solana, notary for the public and government.

11. *Royal Cédula. Madrid, January 11, 1701.*[46]

THE KING

My governor and captain general of the Province of San Augustín of Florida:

Having very reliable news that the English and Dutch are planning an invasion and conquest of the Indies, for which purpose they have assembled a great number of war vessels with a large landing force, I desire to warn you of these plans so that you will be informed of them and make all preparations that may be necessary for defense and opposition of any invasion. For this purpose you will avail yourself of French auxiliary arms, not only of those found in the island of Santo Domingo and other places in the possession of that crown, but also of those which recently have been sent to those coasts by the Most Christian Majesty and my grandfather. And you will likewise avail yourself of every means afforded by the million in subsidy conceded by His Holiness [Pope] Innocent XII from the funds of the crusades and other resources designed for the expulsion of the Scots from Darien, since this [threat of war] is but the consequence of appeasement. And in the war against the enemies of the crown and of the religion, you will closely attend to this and will report whenever opportunities offer, after the receipt of this dispatch on whatever you do by virtue of its authority, being advised that in conformity therewith, orders are being sent to the viceroys of both kingdoms, and to the governors of all forts and ports of the Indies, and that the same advice is given to General Admiral Don Pedro Fernández Navarette, to the commanders of the windward fleet, and to the vessels of Cartagena, with the order that they are not to leave those coasts until they are so ordered; rather, that they survey those [coasts] in order to supply their fortifications with the necessities for their defense. Madrid, 11th of January, 1701. I the Queen; the Cardinal Porto Carrero; Fray Don Manuel Arías; Don Fernándo de Aragón; the Bishop Inquisitor General; By Command of the King, Our Lord; Don Manuel de Aperregui.

12. *Auto of the Inspector Relating to Apalachee. San Luis, February 22, 1701.*[47]

The Captain Don Juan de Ayala Escobar, deputy judge [*juez comisario*] and inspector general [*visitador general*] of both these Provinces of Apalachee and Timuqua by nomination and appointment of the Field Master Don Joseph de Zúñiga y Zerda, governor and captain general of the city of San Augustín of Florida and of these provinces by His Majesty:

Whereas in this village of San Luis de Talimali, today, day of the date of this inquiry [*auto*], there was delivered to the deputy Manuel Solana a letter from Field Master Don Joseph de Zúñiga y Zerda, governor and captain general, in which his lordship ordered that he very carefully investigate the peace [treaties] which the natives of these provinces have covenanted with those of Apalachicolo and other pagans of that territory, and which today are in effect, according to the report given by those who have come from these provinces. The said inspector is suspicious of the said treaties, of which he [already] has given account to the governor because of [the conditions] which exist today among the pagan villages influenced by the English, who have free commerce with them. In regard to the contents of the letter from his lordship charging him with the duty of enforcing what he commands in it, from now on the said inspector orders and commands the deputy and the remaining infantry, and existing settlers and inhabitants, as well as all the natives of this province, caciques and chiefs, that not for any motive or pretext [may] they continue to travel or go to the provinces of Apalachicolo to consult and trade with the said pagans, unless they go with the express permission of the said governor, except that on all occasions when the said pagans come to barter, they receive them with all good will, and only continue to buy from them the usual and customary goods that they bring, [so that] they may not purchase or trade for any kind of clothing, nor arms, nor anything which may have been introduced by the English under any pretext. Similarly it is prohibited that they leave this province, or give either horses or silver or other thing which might be marketable among the said pagans, and which were formerly traded [by] said natives among one another, with the warning that whatever of the contents of this *auto* may be violated, either in part or in whole, will be condemned with all severity on detection by the governor, as it is a matter of the greatest importance to the service of His Majesty. Of this *auto* there will be taken an affidavit to be delivered to the deputy of this province so that he may give notice of it in each village of the natives, as well as to the infantry and Spanish settlers present in this said province, in order that none may allege ignorance; and this *auto* [shall] be placed at the end of all of the *autos* of the inspection, so that it may be evident for all time.

Dated in this place of San Luis de Talimali on the 22nd day of February of this year of 1701, and Your Worship signed it in the company of the witnesses present and of I the notary, of which I swear. Don Juan de Ayala Escobar; Juan Solana.[48]

Fort San Luis

13. *Order from Governor Zúñiga y Zerda. San Augustín, March 14, 1701.*[49]

Don Joseph de Zúñiga y Zerda, field master of Spanish Infantry by the King Our Lord, governor and captain general of this city of San Augustín of Florida and its provinces by His Majesty:

Inasmuch as from the *autos* and depositions relating to the expedition and the operations which have resulted from the expedition that was made by my order to the province of Mayaca, because its inhabitants had been driven away, and from other reports given me, it appears that the *Ygnaja* [*enija, hinija*] and Timuquan Indians have done some killings without the consent of their leader on the occasion, to whom I had issued appropriate orders as to what they had to do; and they [failed to] manifest the peace and good will which their deportment should exhibit, by making the said Indians carry the scalps to the camps [*reales*] and places where the said leader went.

Thus I am obliged to invoke a suitable deterrent, because His Majesty has so pointedly charged me with the alleviation, good treatment, preservation, and increase of the natives of these provinces; and said abuse being so abhorrent in the eyes of God and such a bad example of the barbarity with which they perpetrated it, and very foreign to those who profess the evangelical law, I must abolish at once a custom so devilish as taking scalps, and the massacres they carried out in order to acquire them, without other motive or cause than to kill those they meet of different and distant tribes.

I order and command the adjutant Manuel Solana, my deputy [governor] in the Province of Apalachee, and the deputies in other provinces, that from now on, and in the future, they do not permit such practices as dancing with scalps in the council houses [*bujios*], that they should avail themselves of other means and identification to point out as *norocos* and *tascayas* those who have taken them in legitimate war and have occasioned some deaths, giving them to understand this by interpreters and the best means that you can, in a manner acceptable to the natives, so that they not persist in practicing such a diabolical custom, born of and developed in, their primitive paganism.

This order, or as much of it [as necessary], shall be posted after it has been proclaimed in the council houses, so that it reaches the attention of all; and to the caciques of each village [it is] ordered, that each, in his, should see to the execution and observation of this my order, with a warning from my said deputies that they observe this, and that they will proceed against those who conceal it or in any manner permit it.

And there be published as many [copies as may be necessary] to send an original to each deputy, leaving a record of this order in the *autos* made on this subject, each one acknowledging its receipt, proclamation, and posting, and each placing one of the originals in the archives of their province, which by *auto* of this day, day of the date, was decreed for the advancement of the service of their two majesties. Given in Florida, on the 14th of March, 1701.

Don Joseph de Zúñiga y Zerda

By order of the governor and captain general. Juan Solana, notary for the public and government.

14. *Governor Zúñiga to the King. Upon the raid into Santa Fé and the expedition upon which Captain Romo was sent. San Augustín, September 30, 1702.*[50]

Sir: I related to Your Majesty how in the past year of 1701 there came to the Province of Apalachee a *hinija* [*eneha* of American papers] and others of the principal chiefs of the pagans from the Province of Apalachicolo, offering to renew the peace with the Apalachians and reaffirm the submission previously given to Your Majesty. Since from the proximity of these places to Saint George, and the covenant which they have with the English since the year [16]85, as my predecessors have related to Your Majesty, there originated disobedience and the breaking of the peace which has recently occurred. Since the Apalachians have accepted the peace [treaty], I ordered my deputy [governor] to use every kindness and friendly practice with the *hinija* and Apalachicolos, which he did. Following this, four Apalachians went to the villages of the Apalachicolos, by whom they were seized. One of them escaped, and the other three were killed and sacrificed in a cruel and inhuman manner, without other motive than [resulted from the fact] that I have been able to prevent the Apalachicolos from removing horses out of the Province of Apalachee unless they reimburse the Apalachians with some of the guns which the English supply them for skins, clothing, and tools of their fashioning. Along with this agreement, I ordered the inspector to visit the said province, which proved to be advantageous, from his recognition that the peace which the said *hinijas* had come to re-establish was a subterfuge, since the pagans did not desire anything except pack horses which the English ask of them for their traffic. Thus, for vengeance, they treacherously murdered and caused the death of the three Christian prisoners, which occurred in 1701. Not being satisfied with the wickedness done, and deliberately laying waste the woods in an attempt to capture [the place] by surprise, they entered in the dawn watch and burned and devastated the village of Santa Fé, one of the principal towns of the Province of Timuqua, Saturday, the 20th of May of this year of 1702, making an attack on the convent with many firearms and arrows and burning the church, although not the images which with some risk were saved. Finally, the fight having lasted for more than three hours, our force repulsed them, after the hasty strengthening of an indefensible stockade which served as a fence to the gate of the convent. The enemy retired with some injury, and although our side had some killed and wounded, it would not have been large if the adjutant deputy, Juan Ruíz de Canicares, had not left, with small prudence and but few men, in pursuit of the enemy, whose number had increased. After pursuing them for six leagues, they overtook them the same day after dusk, engaging them briskly, and one soldier that got away [reports] that one and another up to ten of our Indians died in the skirmish, because the enemy received them in a half moon [a crescent] and, closing it, caught many of them in the center, only a few Indians escaping.

The Apalachee Indians are now fearful of the hostilities and injuries which their villages will have to suffer from the raids the Apalachicolos will make unless they are curbed and punished until they cease these invasions.

By letters of July 3rd and August 30th of this year, which they wrote me through my deputy, they have asked, amid noisy importunity, permission for eight hundred of them to set forth, including some Christian Chacatos, to avenge these slayings and hostilities, and at the same time asked me that I give them some soldiers and a leader to direct them, upon which, by *auto* of the 4th of the present month, I called a Council of War; and on the same day, observing the clamorous importunity of the Indians, because the said letters were read in council, and harkening to these and their arguments, and the charges that the cacique Don Patricio made in his name, it was deemed expedient to concede them permission, with some soldiers and the leader for whom they asked. I nominated Captain Don Francisco Romo de Uriza of the infantry, who has been deputy of Guale and of Apalachee, and who bears the orders of what they have to execute,[51] because if no attempt is made to restrain these pagans, their boldness, as it could not before, will gather strength and vigor, as they have from killing my deputy in Timuqua by reason of his blunder, in that he exercised little prudence in setting out in pursuit of the enemy after he had very well conducted the defense and repulse which he had given them, and [we are handicapped] by the aid that the English give them, to whose friendship they incline as barbarians because they do not impose upon them the law that we do; nor will they submit either to the parish church or clergy. Once they have achieved the destruction of the Christian provinces—in the midst of peace between the two crowns they burned and desolated Santa Cathalina de Ajoica and San Juan de Guacára, villages of Timuqua, during the terms of Don Juan Marqués Cabrera and Don Diego de Quiroga, my predecessors—and if [they are] not restrained by this projected expedition, even though he promised me favorable results through divine favor, it will be necessary to employ greater severity with larger forces against the pagans and the English who encourage them with arms and ammunition, and who even accompany them, for the opinion exists that an Englishman led the band which entered Santa Fé. And these Apalachians, Chacatos, and other nations under the protection of this government being Christians, it has been necessary for me, for the already expressed [reasons], and in order that the Indians may not be dismayed and take to the woods, to grant to them the protection they solicit and the expedition whose completion will require the entire month of October, of which I judge an account should be given to Your Majesty, whose Catholic and royal person may God protect for as many years as Christianity requires. San Augustín, Florida, September 30, 1702.[52]

15. *Proclamation by the Deputy of Apalachee. San Luis, December 20, 1702.*[53]

The adjutant Manuel Solana, deputy of the governor and captain general of this Province of Apalachee by commission and appointment of Field Master of Spanish Infantry Don Joseph de Zúñiga y Zerda, governor and captain general of the city and presidio of San Augustín of Florida, [of] this province and the others of his jurisdiction, by the King Our Lord, etc.:

38

Fort San Luis

Because the hardship [suffered] by the city and presidio of San Augustín of Florida is public and notorious, besieged[54] [as it is] by sea and land by the English enemies who came from Saint George, and being without [aid] even up to this date from any of the places whither the governor sent [for assistance], asking it with his dispatches, and finding myself on this occasion with an order from my governor in which he commands me immediately on its receipt to set out with the force that may have come from Pensacola and Mobile, joined with those from this garrison and the other Spaniards in it and whatever Indians who might be able to leave this province, this to be [done] in case that greater aid is not expected from any other quarter. And having arrived at this port in the felucca of Pensacola, to further [the order], the Ensign Diego de Florencia, whom my governor had sent with his dispatches and the request for assistance from Pensacola and Mobile; and having seen the aid which he brought from both places, which includes one hundred guns, forty arrobas of powder, and a thousand gunflints from Mobile, and similarly, from Pensacola, ten infantrymen and the Ensign Francisco de Montes, their leader; and seeing the scarcity of men; and it being necessary for me to execute this order and to see that his province is not left unprotected . . . , from which, and in the interests of His Majesty's service, I order and command the Captain Don Pedro Bilbao and . . . of the said felucca and the remaining crew of it, that for no reason whatsoever they should leave the province by sea or land until I return from my journey or other order is received from the governor, but that they participate in the garrisoning and safeguarding of this province under the orders of the leader who remains in my place, attending first to securing their vessel in the most convenient and secure position there is . . . in the interest of His Majesty's service, and for this . . . I command and sign in this place of San Luis de Talimali on the 20th of December of this year 1702.

Manuel Solana

16. Letter from Diego de Florencia to Governor Zúñiga. San Luis, January 25, 1703.[55]

Governor and Captain General:
Having gone to Pensacola to seek the aid which Your Excellency sought in the exigency of the invasion of that presidio, the winds were so contrary that the outward journey was extended to ten days

39

and the return to fourteen; the remainder of the thirty-four were spent in Pensacola and in a journey to Mobile, where [they] had the petition of Your Excellency and my authorization to ask as much, [in the face of] my duty and the great need of that presidio and these provinces, I was able to secure only ten men with an ensign from the governor of Pensacola, because that settlement is nearly without people. Of the few whom they have, the greater part [are] sick; and from the French governor of Mobile I secured one hundred new and good guns, one thousand pounds of powder—five hundred in fine [powder] for the guns, and the other five hundred coarse [powder] for cannon, but all good—and one thousand flints for guns. All this will be evident from those receipts I gave to the Sergeant Major of Pensacola. Because I do not understand French, His Grace of Pensacola added his entreaty, and simultaneously served to interpret that which the adjutant Manuel Solana gave me, in the presentation I made to him of all the aforesaid. Your Excellency will note the prices.

The Frenchman did not have men to spare, because he said he had very few and many ill, and he has the work of the fort on his hands, but they agreed to lend two hundred cartridge belts [cananaes]; and united with [those] of the province of Chicasa [they] will [attack] the Province of Apalachicolo in the spring. At the same time they were expecting their fleet from France, which is [composed] of two ships of the line and two others of moderate size, whose general is Monsieur de Heveruila, with which force they expect promptly [to respond] to any order from Your Excellency to aid you and to serve you.

I went with the force from the entire province which left for the relief of Your Excellency and your presidio, but our bad fortune[56] dampened our enthusiasm and the fervent desire with which we went to shed our blood for our King Our Lord, for God, and for our land.

I could not continue the journey as I had obligation [to do], to place myself at the feet of Your Excellency, because my nephew [had] an accident, which today detains me with much care and worry, and because there was no paper, I did not then do it [that is, write]. Now I only ask the Lord to protect the person of Your Excellency many and happy years, as the living wall of that city, and may it prosper with much increase. San Luis, 25th of January, 1703.

Governor and Captain General: I kiss the hands of Your Excellency, your servant and subject.

Diego de Florencia [rubric]

Fort San Luis

17. Manuel Solana to the Governor. San Luis, February 3, 1703.[57]

I have received two [letters] from the adjutant Fernando Nieto, which show they are [written] by order of Your Lordship. The first, dated the 10th of the past month, was received on the 29th at 7 of the night by the hand of Marcos de Reina, in which I was told that Your Lordship is found indisposed [*achacoso*], and that I should forward some chickens by the Indian carpenters. Your Lordship's poor health makes me grieve much. May Our Lord will that when this arrives it finds Your Lordship with it [that is, health] and that you enjoy prosperity. Immediately on receiving the letter, I sent to the village of Ivitachuco to detain the Indians who were to leave on the 30th, and sought fifty chickens, and brought them to Ivitachuco to forward them. Yesterday, the 2nd of the present month, I received the other letter from the adjutant by order of Your Lordship, its date being the 20th of the past month, in which you order me to secure forty tanned hides, thirty arrobas of tallow, [and] more or less six hundred skeins of coarse yarn. With regard to the hides to make shoes, these are not to be found in this province, because with the incursions of the enemy [we] have not had one who can tan. With regard to the tallow, I do not know what there is in the province, but I will go to San Luis and make search. And in regard to the yarn, this is being made and as much as can will be sent with the people of the *cava*. The bearer of this is Joseph Fuentes, who brings with him the five Indian carpenters and as many chickens as could be gotten together in the short time before the departure of the Indians, and there also go with them the caciques as I have advised Your Lordship.[58] While I am writing this, the Captain Jacinto Roque arrived at this Ivitachuco and left for San Luis without tarrying. He delivered to me an *auto* which he will put into effect immediately on his arrival in San Luis. I deeply regret not to be capable of that duty which Your Lordship assigned to me. My insufficiency for it, as well as [my] being so badly regarded in that presidio, and my having to impose justice, as I will, will end [with] all that presidio joined against me. But the only things which matter to me are the orders which I have from Your Lordship, in which I have not been remiss, as appears to me from the compliments you have given to them,[59] and from the care exercised to give account to Your Lordship of that which will offer itself, whom God protect many and for-

tunate years. San Luis, February 3, 1703. Field Master Don . . .
Your Lordship's hands, your servant.

Manuel Solana [rubric]

Endorsed: The leader of the squad, Joseph de Fuentes, carried one
of the King's guns, and the cacique of Ivitachuco and him of San
Luis and two others likewise, and say that they received them there,
and [that] another [was given] to the cacique of Escambé.

18. Captain Jacinto Roque Pérez to Governor Zúñiga. San Luis, May 25, 1703.[60]

Governor and Captain General:

I relate to Your Excellency how on Thursday, which they count
as the 24th of the current [month], I arrived at the port of San
Marcos, on [my] return from Pensacola and French [territory],
where I found nothing more than fifty guns and five hundred flints
for them, for which I gave them a receipt in the sum of 503 pesos
and 6 reals. I found the one as well as the other settlement deficient
in men and supplies, so that if their relief is delayed, they will suffer
much misery. For this reason they have not given me what I went
to seek, but they are under promise to give it immediately on the
arrival of their ships. I proposed to M. Berbila the great service that
they would make to the crown if, on the arrival of his brother
[*humano=hermano*], he would decide to go to that presidio, so that
from there he could go to Saint George. He replied to me that he
would do everything to promote it and that they much desired it.
I also proposed to him that in the interval he should see if, with the
Chickasas, Aibamos, and other neighboring tribes, they could make
war on the Apalachicolos, which would be very advantageous. He
replied to me that he lacked one essential to do it, since he had nothing
to present to the Indians, neither balls or guns to give them, and that
without some incentive the Indians could not be instigated to make
war, and that he much regretted he could not do it, but that he was
certain, that having the means, they would.

They did not overlook a smack which was in the port discharging
ballast, as an opportunity to send Your Excellency's letter to Vera
Cruz and another from the Sergeant Major Don Francisco Martínez
for the viceroy, to whom I also wrote, giving him an account of all

Fort San Luis

I had done on order of Your Excellency and [of] the meager resources to be found in the one or the other plaza, for their governors
find themselves so lacking in people, as well as [of] the very evident
danger in which are found that presidio as well as these provinces,
if His Excellency will not provide with promptitude the necessary
measures. It is very likely that the news is already in Vera Cruz,
because at this date it is twenty days since I left the fort of Mobile,
and the smack was to leave within four days of my departure. Don
Francisco Martínez promised me that immediately on the arrival of
his field master he will importune that those provinces should be
immediately aided with one hundred men of those available, and
that if possible he would come with them. I believe that he will do
what he can. Both governors wrote to Your Excellency letters which
I delivered to the deputy of this province.

The journey, Sir, in such a vessel is very slow, and urgency cannot
be assured; the coast is very wild and a slight wind raises a heavy
sea and it is necessary to shorten sail [*tirar a baxar*], as happened to
me on the outward journey, and the seams opened so it did not appear
the boat would serve. We fixed them the best we could and arrived
at Pensacola sixteen days after our departure from San Marcos, and
from there [to] the French five, and five on the return to Pensacola,
and eight from Pensacola to San Marcos. I was only two days in
Mobile and four in Pensacola, with which all of the time of my
delay was on the sea.

The French are settled sixteen leagues within land, seven leagues
from the villages of the Mobiles. In one year [they] have made a very
elegant fort of four bastions and have placed four cannons in each
one of them, and within the governor's residence, a very elegant
church, storehouse, and guardhouse, which are all joined to the
curtains, the parade ground being in the center, and the whole covered with oak shingles, one-third [yard] in length and one-half in
width. They have built more than a hundred very pretty houses in
the plaza, and the lands and forests are very good, [so] that if they
remain, these will make a great place. They lack only a good port,
because its bar has so little water that it only permits entrance of
small smacks. This is all that occurs to me to relate to Your Excellency, who will make me happy if he continues in very good health,
and I ask Our Lord to preserve him for many and fortunate years
with very good effect as I desire. San Luis, May 25, 1703. Governor

and Captain General: Your most affectionate servant kisses Your Excellency's hands.

Jacinto Roque Pérez [rubric]

19. Royal Cédula. Madrid, September 4, 1703.[61]

THE KING

Field Master General Don Joseph de Zúñiga y la Zerda, my governor and captain general of the Provinces of San Augustín of Florida, or the person or persons that govern them:

In a letter of the 30th of September of the past year of 1702, you give a detailed account of the deaths which the pagan Apalachicolos caused in the village of Santa Fé [by] burning the churches, and [you state that], as a consequence, you organized an expedition against them, and that in the repulse which they experienced a soldier of more than forty years of service, called Lorenzo Guerrero, fought valiantly against them. You request that I should grant to his wife and children the favors which they expect.

And having submitted [your letter] to my Council of War for the Indies, and having deliberated upon it, I will give general approval (as by the present I do) to the preparations you made [que disteis] to prevent the hostile acts of the pagan Apalachicolo Indians, in which I acknowledge I have been well served by you.

And as for that which touches upon the wife and children of Lorenzo Guerrero, I approve doing them the favors, which you will see from the dispatch bearing the same date as this.

20. Memorandum[62] [undated] by Governor Zúñiga.[63]

They have to finish the stockade of the blockhouse of San Luis and . . . the Indians [are ordered] to build the enclosure requested around the convent and church, with a stockade communicating with the said enclosure of the blockhouse.

The corn which is in the hands of individuals is to be collected and stored under lock in the blockhouse, with a record and an accounting, because it is for the benefit of all.

A ration of meat is to be given on the King's account to the infantry, and to the soldiers of Pensacola, should they remain there until the arrival of Captain Jacinto Roque from Pensacola.

A company of horse is to be organized in conformity with the order that I have given to Don Francisco Roitener; and further he is to give horses, either as pay or on loan, to all of the soldiers who do not have them [and] who were deliberately [detailed] for [this duty] in the present situation, and to exercise much care besides to ensure that they are not lent by those to whom assigned; and if there is difficulty in securing them on loan, they [are to] be taken for the King, and he will report the amount and to whom given, in order that it be repaid from their wages, with the obligation that even should it be lost, it remains charged to his account unless he restores a horse, except it already should be lost or killed in fighting.

The twenty-five horses which I asked of the caciques for this presidio on the account of the King should arrive shortly, with their saddles if possible, or without.

Whenever the alarm is sounded, a cannon should be discharged from the blockhouse, which will be the signal for all to gather in their enclosures and repair to their designated posts, those of the horse in conformity to the orders which the deputy may have given. . . .

Zúñiga

21. *Order from the Governor. [No place, no date.]*[64]

Instructions and regulations to be observed by all on the farms of the villages, Spaniards as well as natives. My deputies are to order their execution, as follows:

1. Firstly, they have to proclaim as lost and confiscated the cattle—bovine and equine—and swine left on the savannahs, as well as other things left by the Indians who voluntarily departed with the enemy; and if this should have already been done, to see if there are more to confiscate; and of all of these there is to be made an inventory and estimate of the actual property, in order that here may be decreed what may be divided, in compliance with what the occasion [renders] most necessary to the needs of the province and its defense.

2. All the properties of our dead or captured Indians are to be given to the legitimate heirs, and you are to do well [*haga bien*] for their souls in conformity [with] what is customary among the natives.

3. It is conceded that all the pagans whom our Indians capture may be retained by them as slaves, and they may sell them where it is convenient, except that my deputies may not take nor buy anything from them, being

prohibited from these purchases either directly or indirectly, since by reason of their deputyships the Indians might yield them gratis. As a consequence the Indians may flee in order not to be molested, and thus in no manner are my deputies to take or buy them.

4.   That all of the English or Irish, Catholics or non-Catholics, who wish to come to these provinces from whatever parts, either by sea or land, will be admitted under the royal pledge of peace with good treatment and transported by available vessels to Havana or such other places they may choose, as was done with the Irish Catholic who on a recent occasion went to surrender at the blockhouse of Apalachee.[65]

5.   That all of the Negroes of Carolina, Christians or non-Christians, free or slave, who may wish to come, will be given the same treatment and granted their complete freedom, so that those who do not wish to remain in these parts may pass to others which appear better to them, with formal certificates of their freedom granted them under royal pledge.

6.   That all the Indian vassals of the King who left voluntarily and now are repentant, and who wish to return under the Catholic law which they professed, will be permitted to do so, as from the present if they do, I give them [permission] in the name of His Majesty; and if they return, [I promise] to restore their ranches and lands or their value at His Majesty's cost.

7.   That those Indians who wish and may be able to spread this word in those regions, or who, being by accident captives, divulge it, and flee after the deed, will be rewarded in the name of the King, when it is learned that they have communicated these articles.

8.   That it is not permitted to export provisions from the province of Apalachee either by sea or by land to Pensacola or any other place, nor to make purchases of cattle or of other things, even though these be insignificant. Those who contravene this order are warned they will be punished, as will the deputy who may permit it by contrivance, according to the present regulations. To the greater service of His Majesty and the encouragement and preservation of this city and said province and its natives.

Joseph de Zúñiga y Zerda [rubric]

22.   *Memorandum and Accounting for 500 Yards of Jergueta That Your Excellency Sent Me. San Luis [no date], evidently by Manuel Solana.*[66]

Firstly, there were sent in the past year, by the sloop of which Joseph Antonio was master, 1202 measures[67] of corn and 150 of beans, in the delivery of which to the point of embarkation there were spent 60 measures, all of which together make 1,412 measures, which were purchased with 353 yards of *jergueta*. 0353

Further, for the journey made to the presidio there were spent 4 measures of corn which I have certified are owed to the adjutant Joseph Rodríguez, and which were bought with 12½ yards of *jergueta*. 0012½

Further, there were burned in the lodge of the Ensign Diego de Florencia during the raid of the enemy 80 measures of corn which had been purchased with 20 yards of *jergueta*. . 0020

Further, there were bought 15 measures of wheat which were shipped to Havana, and which were [valued at] 15 yards of *jergueta*. 0015

Further, there were bought two hogs which were carried to Your Excellency by Silvester Resio, and which cost 8 yards. . 0008

Further, there were spent in the purchase of thirty-two chickens that were carried to Your Excellency by Joseph de Fuentes, 8 yards. 0008

Further, there were spent to purchase eight [deer] skins, 4 yards. 0004

Further, there were spent to purchase eight arrobas[68] of tallow, which were carried to Your Excellency by Julio Domínguez, 8 yards. 0007

Further, by order of Your Excellency, I gave to the Father Fray Joseph Balero 12 yards of *jergueta*. 0012

Further, the interpreter of the King received 8 yards to be repaid in corn, and died without the means with which to pay it either in corn or other substance. 0008

Further, there remains owed by the Father Fray Domingo Criado,[69] 6 yards of *jergueta*. 0006

Further, there remains owed by Julio Hurtado 8 yards which were by his account burned at Ocuia, and [he] has not since had that with which to pay. 0008

Further, there was forwarded in the sloop in charge of Francisco Fuentes, master, thirty-six measures of corn, which are [valued at] 9 yards of *jergueta*. 0009

Further, there was requested of me by order of Your Excellency, the *jergueta* owed the deputy Juan Ruíz Mexía, which were 36 yards, and which were delivered to him. 0036

501½ [*sic*]

From Your Excellency's greatest servant, who kisses your hands.

Notation: By this it is permitted me to say to Your Grace that of my *jergueta* which you have, buy fifteen measures of wheat if it is worth 8 reals a measure, and if it is worth less, Your Grace will spend no more than 15 pesos; and whichever may be bought you will deliver them to the Reverend Father Domingo Criado, and on this let there be no lack from any reason. God protect Your Grace. San Augustín, May 14, 1703. Zúñiga [rubric] My deputy, Manuel Solana.

23. *Extract from a letter of Governor Zúñiga to the King. San Augustín, February 3, 1704.*[70]

. . . And now in a sloop which I have kept in reserve solely for emergencies, I am sending to Havana an appeal for supplies and reinforcements, in view of the news which I received yesterday at one o'clock, of how on the 25th of January of this year,[71] the enemy attacked Ayubale, one of the largest places in Apalachee, and captured it with a large force on foot, of English, Negroes, and Indians, with which they have invaded the province, to besiege the blockhouse. It was my desire to send assistance to the infantry and settlers found there, as well as to some natives who have joined them, but I find myself with so few people, and I am disconsolate that I dare not leave this place without some defense. . . .

24. *List of friars signing a petition to the King, soliciting relief following the Ayubale raid.*[72] *San Luis, February 6, 1704.*[73]

Fray Tiburicio de Osorio	Fray Domingo Criado
Fray Lorenzo Santos	Fray Ygnacio Cartabio
Fray Philipe Osorio Maldonado	Fray Angel Miranda

25. *Extract from a letter of Governor Zúñiga to the King. San Augustín, March 30, 1704.*[74]

. . . And since in two months of siege they could not accomplish their aim, they seek [now] to destroy the provinces and terrorize the Indians, pagan as well as Christian, and have this additional force to make hostile incursions in these parts as close as sixty leagues either by sea or land. In the incursions they have made since the siege, San

Fort San Luis

Joseph de Ocuia in Apalachee, Pilitiriva, and San Francisco have all
been destroyed and many Indians killed, and in all they have carried
off more than five hundred prisoners. All this has been related to
Your Majesty, but they have now returned to Apalachee, accompanied by the governor who here besieged me, with a force of fifteen
hundred Indians and fifty English, desolating the country, and
assaulting the place of Ayubale on the 25th of January of this year,
which was defended with all bravery by the Indians and the parish
priest Fray Angel de Miranda, who fought from morning until two
in the afternoon, when their munitions gave out. The enemy advanced to the stockade close by the church and convent, which they
set fire and captured. On the 26th my deputy [governor] in Apalachee, Captain Juan Ruíz de Mexía, with about thirty Spanish
soldiers and settlers, and four hundred Apalachee Indians, surrounded the enemy and killed six or seven of the English and about
one hundred of the pagan Indians, to say nothing of another fifty
killed by the priest Miranda and the Indians of Ayubale, and two
or three English more. But finally, for lack of munitions, my people
were defeated, [and] my deputy was wounded by a ball which toppled
him from his horse. They also killed the parish priest of Patale, who
wished to accompany them, and two soldiers and some Indians who
were roasted with much barbarity and cruelty by the abhorrent pagans,
who bound them to some stakes by the feet and hands and set them
afire until their lives were extinguished. This was seen by my deputy
and soldiers, whom they stripped and secured in stocks, except Fray
Angel de Miranda, who was unbound. During this cruel and barbarous martyrdom which the poor Apalachee Indians experienced,
there were some of them who encouraged the others, declaring that
through martyrdom they would appear before God; and to the pagans
they said: "Make more fire so that our hearts may be allowed to
suffer for our souls. We go to enjoy God as Christians, but when
you die the demons in hell will keep you eternally ablaze, at which
lamentable event Our Lord will not be moved to compassion." . . .
The enemy freed my deputy, the priest Miranda, and four of the
soldiers, on the supposition that they could exact a ransom of four
hundred pesos in reals, with five cows and five horses for each. But
Captain Don Jacinto Roque Pérez, whom my deputy had left in
command for the defense of the blockhouse of San Luis, sent word
to the English governor that he did not intend to give anything.
Finally, the governor did not attack the blockhouse, but turned away

at a distance of two leagues. On their withdrawal, they left five places destroyed, and of these, the entire population of two [places] accompanied them voluntarily. They carried off all that could be collected, including cows and horses, and that which could not be carried, they destroyed and burnt. The enemy carried off more than six hundred of the Christian Indians. Four of the Gallegan soldiers who arrived in the past year fled to the enemy from the blockhouse, carrying off their arms, carabines, pistols, and horses. An Irishman fled to the blockhouse of San Luis with a flag of peace. He was sent here for interrogation, and from his examination no cause to justify harsh treatment was found. He was liberated, as there is no opportunity for him to communicate with the English prisoners whom I have here, and he is to be sent to Havana, so that from there they may send him to those kingdoms, or to New Spain. . . .

26. Letter from the Deputy of Apalachee, Manuel Solana, to Governor Zúñiga, San Luis, July 8, 1704.[75]

Most Excellent Sir: I have related to Your Excellency of how on the 29th of the past month, the Apalachicolo enemies threatened this blockhouse and the village thereof from the locality of Escambé, which is a cannon shot distant, having had the day before news by a former captive who had fled from the enemy force which had entered the village of Patale. [I have also related] that on their departure they encountered another band, among whom they saw an Englishman and a Negro; that he overheard them say the Apalachicolos had six hundred men and the rebellious Apalachians fifty; and that they would that same night, without fail, seize the village of Escambé. With this news, which was an act of the Lord, I ordered the withdrawal of all the people of that place, who were occupied by a festival honoring Saints John and Peter, which was attended by the people of this place, men and women. As a consequence, they did not succeed in securing captives, except for some who were incredulous and remained on the savannah.

By another captive brought in after the first, I had word that the enemy was not so powerful as the former had told me. He had heard it said there were three hundred men. On the 28th I also had word that the felucca of Pensacola had arrived on the seacoast in sight of the port of San Marcos, for which reason I dispatched some soldiers to ascertain their motive for coming, since they did not come into the port. With the news of the presence of the enemy, I sent to recall the said soldiers, and with them the others on board the felucca, feeling myself closely beset by the enemy, who descended from Escambé to *a tal bona,* which belong to the houses of Captain Jacinto Roque, and from there did some damage in this place of San Luis; so that even had I sent out some of our people to repel them, we could do nothing as we were so few. I sent to call the men from Ivitachuco, so that joined with those I awaited from the felucca, we could go out to dislodge the enemy of whom I had news, and raising the royal [standard].[76] . . . He went to the village of Patale where he also captured the stockade, as had been done in [the village] of Escambé. Don Patricio, cacique of Ivitachuco, arrived at this blockhouse with his people, and immediately went to the meeting point with forty-five men; and observing that the enemy had retired to Patale, and not knowing his intention, [but] fearful that he might have gone to Ivitachuco and would capture the women and children who had been left with only a few men to protect them, he decided to return with his force, and asked that I let him have four soldiers who were in his company. These I gave, and they left from here by night to travel in greater security. On the road they captured four insurgent Apalachians of those whom the soldier Joseph Gutiérrez told me had informed him that the enemy numbered no more than two hundred Apalachicolos and fifty rebellious Apalachians who had very little ammunition. At this time I already had in the blockhouse the crew of the felucca, which numbered twenty-three men, only two of whom were left in the vessel, five having been sent in a canoe to San Marcos with the provisions and ammunition which they brought for the people who were to drive the cattle by land to Pensacola, which was the reason for the coming of the felucca. To these five men, and the two whom I had as sentinels [at the watchtower], I sent word of the enemy, and an order that together they should ascend the river in the canoe to a landing place which is three[77] [*sic*] leagues from here, and from there they might try to enter the blockhouse. This they did not do, but went from San Marcos on the royal road to San Luis, and before they arrived at this place, half a league away, the enemy captured them.

Finding myself, as I say, with twenty-three Spaniards from Pensacola, as well as those from the garrison, and numerous Apalachians, they all represented that, in view of the small size of the enemy's force, it would be a disgrace not to fall upon them [since we had] the same news we already had from the captives who had escaped, namely, that there were no more than two hundred Apalachicolos and fifty Apalachians. I proposed [this move] to the Indians, and they replied to me that if the Spaniards would fight afoot as they do, they would go, but if the Spaniards went on horses, they did not want to go. I told them that we would all go afoot to the number of forty-three Spaniards, among them twelve musketeers, ninety-three Indians with firearms, and sixty archers. I gave twenty balls with corresponding powder to all who had firearms, since they had also proposed to me that I should give them sufficient ammunition. Leaving Captain Jacinto Roque in the blockhouse with fourteen soldiers and numerous Indians, I set out towards the enemy by night. Arriving nearby, about half a league from the village of Patale, at a little later than five in the morning, I halted my force to await the arrival of the party from Ivitachuco, which I had ordered out to meet and join forces with me. All came. A troop of the enemy, apparently gone to hunt cattle, as there are none at that place, [passed] by the spot where we were; as soon as they were seen by my forces, and in disregard of order and without strength to detain them, some Spaniards threw themselves upon them and killed four, among them two rebels: one . . . Pedro, son of the cacique of Aspalaga the old; the other of Thomole, called . . . Francisco. The others having fled, they carried the news to the enemy, who immediately came out against us. Since, as related, I had placed the Spaniards afoot, thus encouraging the Indians, I attacked [the enemy], and we pressed them with much force. Since the district was a plain surrounded by woods, some of our people began to cry out, saying that they were encircling us, at which outcry our Indians retreated, without my having any who could detain them. On observing this, the enemy turned on us with a great deal of bravery, and finding myself with only the Spaniards, we went to make use of the horses, and already our Indians had seized some and loosened others. We were laboriously retreating; he that had found a horse [went] mounted, and he that had not [went] afoot. They finally defeated us; and those remaining in the skirmish were either those who made more of punctilio, or those obliged to retreat afoot [carrying] muskets, since of the twelve musketeers, only one was saved. Thus it is seen how, captured [or] defeated as we were, each went where he could. The Spaniards returned to the blockhouse. Most of the Indians took to the woods, while I exercised all the care that the occasion required in regard to all who came to the blockhouse that night. At dawn I sent at once to ascertain whether the enemy remained there or had retired, as I reasoned that he would withdraw during the night. As best I could I headed this force with the Spaniards who came out of the conflict.

This skirmish was on the 4th of the current month, and on the 6th I sent to search for the dead that might be found in the parish . . . of the enemy, so that they might be buried. Those that went said they found two dead bodies in the field, and in the square where the enemy was they found sixteen bodies bound and burned, from some of which the tongues and ears had been cut. They could not be identified because of deformation of the bodies from the sun, and they were buried. And there appeared a captive who had escaped from the enemy, whom they brought to my presence. He said that the other day the enemy left hurriedly and slept five leagues from there, [and] that they did not carry [off] munitions, as those left by the Spaniards who fled were divided among many.

He said that they burned eight Spaniards whom they had caught on the day of the skirmish—burned them alive and cut the tongues and ears from some. Of the Spaniards whom they carried off, bound and in thongs [*cuiros*], he did not know anyone except Domingo Gutiérrez, while it seemed to him that sixteen were carried away. He heard say twelve rebellious Apalachians and ten Apalachicolos were killed in the skirmish, and that six wounded were carried away. He also reported that he had heard said that this band came without permission from Saint George, and that they left hurriedly to meet in their villages with a very large force composed of all of the tribes and the English from Saint George. They expect to gather as many as three thousand men, and to come to settle in this province, since the lands appear good to the English, and there are many cattle and many fruits; and they will come to San Marcos after they have readied ten ships, to make a settlement there, and similarly thirty ships will go to San Augustín to seize the fort; and having done all this they will pass to Pensacola to drive out the Spaniards.

The soldiers missing from this garrison number twelve. The two taken from the lookout were Sebastian de Morales and Bartholomé Sebastian.

The ten that were lost in the fight are Luis de Granada, Balthazar Francisco, Alonso del Pino, Juan de Texada, Juan Antonio Crespo, Domingo Gutiérrez, Joseph Rodríguez, Simón de la Cruz, Francisco Arías, and Benito Garrido.

Those missing from Pensacola number ten, the five that had gone to San Marcos and five that were lost in the fight. The Englishman who remained here after the last voyage of the felucca fled to the enemy.

The Indians told the cacique of this place that the missing number seven, and that from the village of Escambé five [are missing]. The number of those who went forth from other villages is not known, nor whether any are missing. The prisoner said that [the enemy], for lack of Indians to burn, burned the Spaniards to equalize the deaths which were inflicted on them, and that this was urged by the rebellious Apalachians.

As a consequence of this event and the news mentioned, the Indians are hastily fleeing to the woods. I made them a speech in which I asked them where they were going, and whether they did not know that they were going forth to perish, and [said] that if they wished to leave their lands and their property, it would be better to go to the presidio where they would not lack lands to plant; that if they wished, I would write to Your Excellency; and that if I proposed it, that without doubt His Excellency would send permission for them to leave and drive the cattle, which to me appeared more suitable, and not to go to perish in the woods. To all of which they replied to me that they were weary of waiting for aid from the Spaniards: that they did not wish merely to die; that for a long time we had misled them with words, [saying] that reinforcements were to come, but they were never seen to arrive; that they know with certainty that what the pagans say, will happen as they say, because all that they have said up to now has been done, and because they have believed us, they have [now] finished [with] us; and that if we do not believe what the pagans say, that we who remain in the blockhouse, they well know, remain to die; that if they go, it will not be to the Spaniards, and if they remain until the return of the enemy, it will be in order [to go] against us, and they will burn us within the blockhouse, while they escape with their lives. And that in the matter of going to the presidio, they neither wish that, for they would have there the same risk should the English surround the fort, and they care not but to go to the woods or to the isles of the sea, each one to where God will aid. This is the decision with which they have replied to me.

The priests also say that they do not wish to remain here, that they would go to the isles, they know not where, and that already they have written to their prelate. I cannot pacify them, and thus only await the decision which Your Excellency will take in [the matter]. On the final departure of all, [I ask] should I then enclose myself in this blockhouse with the infantry which remains to me, or is it to accompany me? I await a reply as soon as possible. For which, notwithstanding, I feel that I will be corroborated by sending this letter by Joseph del Pozo, to whom Your Excellency can give entire credence to everything of which he may inform you, as a witness who has seen what has happened here. If it be possible, he will leave on the return [journey] with the reply as soon as possible.

The families of Spaniards here have made many demands on me, either to allow them to embark in the felucca or to save their lives. I have permitted the embarkation of women and children who could [go], and [ordered] the return of the felucca to transport the images and ornaments so that they may not be burnt here. The commandant of the felucca, who is the adjutant, Juan Joseph de Torres, delivered to me twenty-five skeins of *casiamo* [matches] for which I gave him a receipt, which is sent by the Sergeant Major Don Joseph Guzmán who governs that plaza of Pensacola, and for which I gave him a receipt. I received your letter in which you told me to forward the [letter] of Your Excellency to Mobile, and on receipt of the reply will dispatch it. From Don Andrés de Arriola I have not [had a] reply. There remain here at this moment six men from Pensacola to drive the cattle, if there be any left.

It is impossible to defend this blockhouse with fewer than fifty soldiers, in addition to those who are [here]; and this is for its security, not to go forth or to throw at the enemy of the province. And thus, excepting the best opinion of Your Excellency, my [opinion] is that those who here remain should be transported to that presidio, and that all of the cattle be driven, for if not, all will be lost. This is all that requires the attention of Your Excellency, from whom I await all help and who [I hope] will view this with mercy and as expedient. San Luis, July 8, 1704.

Most Excellent Sir, at the feet of Your Excellency, your humble servant,

Manuel Solana

27. *Auto by Governor Zúñiga. San Augustín, July 12, 1704.*[78]

In the city of San Augustín of Florida, on the 12th of the month of July of 1704. His Excellency the field master, general of the armies of His Majesty, Don Joseph de Zúñiga y Zerda, governor and captain general of this city of San Agustín of Florida and of its provinces, and governor designate and captain general of Cartagena of the Indies, by the King Our Lord:

Who said that inasmuch as at about six o'clock this morning, there arrived in the presence of His Excellency, Joseph del Pozo, soldier of the garrison of Apalachee with a letter from the adjutant Manuel Solana,[79] his deputy, dated the 8th of the current month, in which he related that the pagan enemy and the English descended upon the village of Escambé on the 29th of the past month; that on the 4th of the present month he had an engagement with them in which our forces were defeated, and further, how . . . on the 23rd and 24th of June they entered in Patale and Aspalaga, killing on the 23rd the religious teacher, Reverend Father Fray Manuel de Mendoza, the present *definidor*, and carried off many prisoners; that on the 24th [they took as prisoners] all those of Aspalaga; and that he was informed by an Indian, Estevan, that for another incursion, similar to that experienced in the past month, there is being readied an enemy force of perhaps three thousand, whose purpose is to destroy the province. They are to be supported by ten vessels that will [take them] to that province, and will come to this presidio in thirty, and will immediately go to Pensacola to dislodge the Spaniards from that place. Since Your Excellency desires the greatest prudence [exercised for] the good of their two Majesties, I order and command that at 8 o'clock in the morning there be convened a Council of War of the officers of the royal treasury, the sergeant major, the captains of the infantry and artillery, and retired officers of this presidio, to whom will be read in its entirety the said letter of the 8th of the present month, so that in their presence may be decided that which is most practicable, and by this warrant I decree, order, and sign.

Don Joseph de Zúñiga y Zerda
Juan Solana. Notary [for the] public
and for the government.

28. Council of War. San Agustín, July 13, 1704.[80]

In the city of San Agustín of Florida on the 12th [*sic*] day of July of 1704, being present in this royal house of residence of His Excellency, Field Master General Don Joseph de Zúñiga y Zerda, governor and captain general of this said city and its provinces, and designate of Cartagena of the Indies by His Majesty, Captain Don

Francisco de Florencia, treasurer and storekeeper of supplies for His Majesty, and Don Juan de Pueyo, auditor *ad interim* during the absence of the proprietary official, judges of the royal treasury and coffers of these provinces; Sergeant Major Don Enrique Primo de Rivera, by [commission of] His Majesty; Captains Don Joseph de Begambre and Don Francisco Romo de Uriza, of the infantry by [commission of] His Majesty; Diego Dias Mexía, [acting] for the infantry during the absence of the commissioned officer; Don Joseph Primo de Rivera, incumbent by nomination of His Excellency; Captain Don Joseph de Beneditt Horrutiner of the artillery by [commission of] His Majesty; and the retired Captains Joachin de Florencia, Bernardo Nieto de Carvajal, and Don Juan de Beneditt Horrutiner—all assembled—was read by me, the notary, the letter contained in the preceding *auto*. It was heard and understood by all, and the contents were discussed at length and wisely by one and another. What attracted attention was the circumstance that in the said Province of Apalachee there are no people remaining, in comparison to the number when there were fourteen villages, in which were a total of eight thousand persons, of whom not two hundred remain; and these are prone to leave, some to the woods and others to the enemy. It appeared most advantageous to the service of God and of the King to destroy the blockhouse and the palisade walls, not only of Ivitachuco but of the other places, for if they afforded shelter it is to be expected that whenever the enemy returned with sufficient force, they could readily capture everything, as the blockhouse lacks supplies as well as troops. Nor could it be furnished with one or the other from here, since the presidio does not have [spare] infantry, and the defense of this presidio must receive first consideration, as much by reason of the present threat as because of the command of His Majesty given in various royal cédulas. If this is lost, all the provinces are lost. Thus it would be better to withdraw without the few Indians who remain with the cacique, Don Patricio Hinachuba, who sent a verbal message to His Excellency by Joseph del Pozo, a soldier, who brought the said letter, indicating that he would willingly come with his people to this city to die as a good vassal among the Spanish, and that the statues, ornaments, and other objects of the Divine Cult, and cattle, horses, cannons, pedreros, arms, and ammunition would be very advantageous. All should be withdrawn to this presidio, or to the site of San Francisco Potano thirty leagues away, with which is incorporated the population of Santa Fé. These could be joined by those from San Pedro and San Matheo, thus serving as an outpost, with some infantry, in the said village of San Francisco. Notice should be given to Pensacola of this decision and of the threats posed to that bay by the enemy. If the felucca should have returned with some news, another needed suggestion may be for them to make port at San Martín with a pilot, and at the same time lend a boat to be sent the Havana fleet to give notice of this decision. If some boat or sloop is ready to sail to the port of San Marcos, it should be stopped, as should the said felucca of Pensacola, because of the risk of their capture by some rebellious Apalachee Indians and other enemies who may be settling there. This decision is to take immediate effect, not [only] because, [even] should the situation improve, it would not suit our interest to return and occupy that province and port of San Marcos, but because for the present it is impossible to protect it. It has also been found that the Indians have been justified in saying they have been expecting one confusion after another, as a consequence of the promises made to them that help would be sent them shortly. Up to this time none has arrived, for none of the promises made them could have been fulfilled. In the repeated invasions made in this region during three years, there have been more than three thousand killed, and a great number of captives have been carried off. Another large group, fearful of what might happen, have voluntarily gone over to the enemy, so that now, as was seen in the last incursion of the enemy, many of the rebellious Apalachians have increased the size and strength of the enemy forces with their presence, whereas ours have diminished. In view of this, His Excellency, though he could not do otherwise, after viewing things as they are in this presidio, so destitute of all resources, concurs in everything with the members of the council with whom he has conferred. For its execution His Excellency will issue the required orders and inform His Majesty and the viceroy of New Spain of the last [mentioned], and of the miserable condition of the said Province of Apalachee and of that of Timuqua, as well as of the perils with which this presidio is beset. He has ordered, and commands, that the said *auto*, letters, and council [minutes], and the last letters cited in said *auto* describing the two raids next to the last, be placed first, and that all relevant testimony be extracted, and furnished to His Majesty, the said viceroy, and to other parties concerned. With this formality the said council was closed, and the minutes signed by His Excellency and all the participants. *[Signatures of the twelve participants]*

Compared with the *auto*, council minutes, and other deliberations of the date mentioned, sent to and retained in my office, so that the commands of His Excellency, the said governor and captain general, and the official royal judges may be evident. Given the present in Florida on the 13th of July, 1704. Written on four sheets with this my signature and on ordinary paper, since stamped paper is not available in this presidio, and in faith thereof, I affix my signature in testimony of truth. Juan Solana, notary [for the] public and for government.

29. *Royal Officials to Viceroy. San Augustín, July 16, 1704.*[81]

. . . And now, Most Excellent Sir, by the latest report from the deputy of Apalachee, the warnings so often given of the desire of the enemy to possess that province are seen justified through the destruction of the native Christians, which they have been accomplishing since the date of the [last] dispatch sent to Your Excellency up to the present. Those unfortunate soldiers, settlers, and natives experienced death, burning, captivity, and the desolation of the few places that remain, after they were reduced to four; and the repeated and frequent raids have left very few people in two [of these]. In one, they even killed and burned a priest and his sexton in their convent, and are so daring as to come within sight of the wooden blockhouse with a garrison that His Majesty has in that province to protect those places. The deputy set out with some foot soldiers and Christian Indians to oppose and dislodge the enemy. During the skirmish he was abandoned by those Indians who accompanied him, and who joined their own kind, whereupon those who were mounted fled, leaving behind those who were surrounded by the enemy. Twenty-two of the infantry, killed or captured, were lost. Among them were those who had come from Pensacola to drive back cattle for the subsistence [of that place], of which they are now deprived. The Indian alcaldes were barbarously burned alive, and sixteen Spaniards were killed. The remainder were ignominiously carried off naked. For each death of a wounded enemy Indian, they retaliated by burning a Spaniard or Indian, as will be evident to Your Excellency from the enclosed letters.

It is learned from captives who have escaped from these raids that these adversaries are planning to join with a band of three thousand pagans raised by the English, and with other rebels, to descend again and ravage the few remaining people in Apalachee, capture the block-house, and burn the infantry. With this news and the events already experienced, the Indians are quietly passing to the enemy unopposed, as they have no desire to see themselves killed or captured; they are leaving their families, who are Christian and loyal to the King, to be supported by the Spanish. They intimate that even [were they given] aid and encouragement of future assistance, that because of their need and the injuries they have received, and in order not to experience them further, they would quietly desert to the enemy, for otherwise they would be burned by them. In view of this, and seeking as a last resort to save the lives of those few soldiers and settlers who at the price of their ranches and lives have defended the blockhouse to gain His Majesty's good will, and [to save] the few vassals who, reduced to only two localities, have remained there, and to maintain them as friends before they become alienated—since now because of the meager resources, they could not be aided from the presidio with men and supplies at a distance of eighty leagues, sixty of which are depopulated, and only traversed with much risk, as they are already occupied by the enemy, and a river which cannot be forded—and since the women and children of some few Spanish families, as well as some priests, have already fled from the danger, some to Pensacola, others to some islands, and because of the uncertain subsistence and loyalty of the Indians—it was decided by a general council that all would be withdrawn to the presidio, the blockhouse dismantled and burned, and the cattle that the enemy had left driven in. [This is done] in order to deprive them of this sustenance—they have no other—and so that the Indians who can be assembled be also withdrawn to this place, as was proposed by a chief himself and his village of Ivitachuco. It is hoped that God may restore this province and that it may again be garrisoned.

And in this manner, Most Excellent Sir, as a last resort is the province deserted and abandoned. The enemy will eagerly settle it, and will go on, as is known and expected, to besiege this place which is so desired by their royal power, [because it offers] a situation so convenient to their operations on the mainland through its connection with the settlements to the north, and with ports on the Gulf of Mexico, which they much desire to obtain, since now it is free from the Apalachee. It is known that they are preparing eighteen vessels for Pensacola and for this place thirty vessels, with men and bombs that they bring from Europe. This we submit for the serious consideration of Your Excellency, so that the condition of this garrison may be clear. It is exposed to a misfortune (may God not permit it) from a lack of troops, provisions, and munitions that obliges us to have recourse to the mercy of Your Excellency, to whom we represent the foregoing in order that now, from the solicitude of Your Excellency in that kingdom, we may expect of you the help that necessity requires in this exigency to protect the defenseless lives of this presidio and free them from the barbarous cruelties of the Indians, and especially of the rebellious Christians, so that His Majesty will not lose [the territory] which is now the Province of Apalachee, of Guale, and part of Timuqua. Of what remains there can be some doubt because of its vulnerability, and the fear of the natives that God may withdraw His law from them. Of all of this we are confident, from the great piety of Your Excellency, on whom alone depend our hopes and aid today, as now there is no other [recourse] than the aid which we ask and this place expects of Your Excellency. Our Lady protect Your Excellency many happy years in the dignity which you merit. San Augustín, July 16, 1704. Most Excellent Sir: At the feet of Your Excellency: Your humble servants.

> [Captain Don] Francisco de Florencia (Treasurer and
> Storekeeper of Supplies)
> [Captain Don] Juan de Pueyo
> Judges of the Royal Treasury and Coffer

30. *Royal Officials to Viceroy. San Augustín, August 18, 1704.*[82]

Most Excellent Sir:

. . . We related in the dispatch to Your Excellency, how as soon as some of the apparently loyal Indians who remained in Apalachee learned of the withdrawal of the garrison and the retreat of the natives and cattle, they informed the enemy, who immediately descended in a large band, in addition to those which were already in the neighborhood, both groups arriving in the places while our forces were still in the province. The English immediately occupied San Luis, whose chief, with his people, sought shelter at Pensacola, as did those from other villages, pagan and Christian; only the chief of Ivitachuco, with some few of his people, sought this presidio. It was impossible to secure cattle, because the Indians, on order of the enemy, had driven all of them away, as well as all the horses of the Spaniards. For lack of [these horses] everyone, even the women, came afoot, leaving behind, because of the length of the journey, their scanty possessions, ornaments, bells, and some arms, all of which were either burned or buried. At the same time, a considerable quantity of cattle were driven to Pensacola, but they were intercepted by the enemy, who killed the drovers. These adversaries are more cruel than the rebellious Christians. In this manner, Your Excellency, was the province of Apalachee overcome and conquered by the enemy. And this presidio, in lonely isolation, lacks supplies and defense, and has no other recourse than the magnanimity of Your Excellency, to whom we express what is described and the condition in which one finds this presidio, all of which will be more evident from the more extensive dispatches included. [We trust] that Your Excellency, with great foresight, will give that [attention] which the case and occasion require, and by virtue of this hope, will assist this place in the siege which we expect. May Our Lady protect, for many fortunate years, the person of Your Excellency, with the dignity you merit and your servants desire. Florida, August 18, 1704. Most Excellent Sir: At the feet of Your Excellency, Your humble servants. Francisco de Florencia. Don Juan de Pueyo.

31. Commandant at Pensacola [Joseph de Guzmán] to Viceroy. Santa María de Galve, August 22, 1704.[83]

Most Excellent Sir: Having received an order from General Don Andrés de Arriola, governor and commander in chief of this presidio, to dispatch the felucca to transport a needed supply of matches requested by the deputy of the Province of Apalachee, I executed the order by sending them on the 22nd of June in charge of the adjutant Juan Joseph de Torres, who immediately on his arrival at the *Río de Lagneus* [Ocklocknee River] had news of how the enemy was committing a thousand excesses in the village of Escambé, on which notice he dispatched the matches, which arrived in time. There being no one in the blockhouse of San Luis, the deputy, on learning of his arrival, sent a detail of four soldiers, asking that he aid him with the crew of the felucca, for the sake of God and of the King, as he was in grave straits. On learning this, the adjutant set out with his force and arrived on the 3rd day of July, the enemy having already withdrawn to the village of Patale. With this assistance, and in anticipation of being joined by three hundred Indian warriors and four Spaniards from the village of Ivitachuco, the deputy proposed to set out in pursuit of the enemy on the 4th. He departed with forty Spaniards from both forces, and one hundred and thirty-six Indians, departing by candlelight to the place where they expected to unite with the force from Ivitachuco. But in the middle of their way they met a band of the enemy who began firing on our force, and who were soon reinforced by a great multitude of pagans. At this [juncture], more than one hundred and twenty of the one hundred and thirty-six Indians of our force deserted to the enemy. When this was observed by the deputy and adjutant, who were engaged in the midst of the enemy, they charged upon them and fought them for more than an hour, after which they retreated to the moat of the village of Patale, where our force could not make use of their horses. When our force attempted to retire in order to improve their position, the enemy fell upon them, killing and capturing twenty-three of the forty. Of the men from this presidio, eight were killed, three captured, and three wounded. Following their victory, the pagans burned seventeen in the village of Patale, after they had previously tied them to stakes and cut off their tongues, noses, and ears. The others succeeded in retreating to the blockhouse of San Luis. The adjutant arranged for his return to this presidio, which was begun on the 23rd of July, and for transportation of the families of Captain Jacinto Roque Pérez, and Ensigns Diego de Florencia, Juan Sánchez, Miguel Salinas, and many others who had come to favor this post.

Seeing that I had become responsible for so many people, that such a multitude of Indians had arrived,[84] and that they could not be maintained here except from the royal supplies, I explained to the Spanish families, and to the chiefs and principal Indians, my plan to reduce the half-pound ration of bread from the 1st of August, under which control the supplies should last to the 6th or 8th of February. I beg Your Excellency to supply us quickly, as we are expecting many more people from the neighborhood of Apalachee, since the Spaniards have abandoned that province and withdrawn the garrison to San Augustín on order of their governor, burned the blockhouse, and carried off the artillery if at all possible, as described in the letter which the deputy wrote me on July 23rd, requesting the protection of our arms. This is the reason which prompts me to solicit the benevolent attention of Your Excellency to the repeated reports which I have had, namely, that in Saint George they are preparing various vessels in order to occupy and fortify the Province of Apalachee, and to attack, by sea and land, this presidio, which they desire as an anchorage for their vessels.

On the 22nd of July there arrived at Massacre Island a French frigate of fifty-six guns, commanded by Captain M. Ducondresi, who advised me of his arrival. [He stated] that on his departure from the port of Rochelle on the 19th of April, he left their Majesties in good health; that our King was in Portugal with seventy thousand Spaniards and French; that His Christian Majesty has prepared a heavy fleet which will shortly depart in command of the Admiral, Count of Toulouse, to impede the designs of the enemy; and that he will return to France on the last day of this month, stopping at the port of Havana. At that time I will avail myself to give Your Excellency this news, hoping that with your great forethought you will provide for this presidio and the helpless poor who have come and are coming to its shelter. God protect the most excellent person of Your Excellency many years in your greater dignity. Santa María de Galve, August 22, 1704. Most Excellent Sir: I kiss the feet of Your Excellency: Joseph de Guzmán.

32. Royal Cédula. August 22, 1704.[85]

THE KING

Field Master and General Don Joseph de Zúñiga y Zerda, my governor and captain general of the Provinces of Florida, and elect of Cartagena:

In letters of the 3rd of February and 30th of March of this year, you reiterated the news previously transmitted of the condition of that plaza and provinces, and of the perils to which they are exposed from inadequate relief and lack of provisions and men. You reported that in January of this year the English of Saint George, accompanied by the governor who, in October of 1702, placed your presidio under siege, with some Indians and English, attacked the village of Ayubale, one of the larger of the Province of Apalachee, and captured it, although [it was] valiantly defended by the Indians and the missionary Fray Angel de Miranda from morning until two in the afternoon, when their ammunition was exhausted. [You also stated] that on the following day you sent Captain Juan Ruíz Mexía, deputy of Apalachee, with some thirty mounted Spanish soldiers and settlers, accompanied by two hundred Indians; that they encountered the enemy, many being killed as you describe in detail; and that, finally, for lack of ammunition, our force was routed and the deputy wounded, while Fray Juan de Parga, missionary of Patale, as well

64

as two soldiers and various Indians, were killed. The deputy, Fray Miranda, eight soldiers, and some Indians were captured, and were cruelly treated by the Indians, as you described. You also tell how they withdrew, their disappointment in failing to secure a ransom for the prisoners, and how they left four villages destroyed, carrying off the people from them, their cattle, and everything else they could carry. There was an Irishman who remained behind with his weapons and horses and surrendered under a flag of peace, and whom, you say, you obliged to appear in your presence and found no cause to subject to rigorous treatment, although he was deprived of the opportunity to communicate with the English prisoners who are there. [You state] that you have decided to send him to Havana, so that from there he may be sent to these kingdoms or to New Spain; and [you also mention] other topics to which you broadly refer, relating to the lack of support experienced in that presidio, of the desirability of putting it in a position for the defense and security of those provinces, and regarding the dislodgment and depopulation of Carolina, which should be again repeopled by us.

Having submitted this to my Council of War for the Indies, and taken council upon all the points which suit our interest as you desire, I have sent to command my viceroy of New Spain and the governor of Havana to furnish that plaza and presidio with as much as they can to relieve the need from which you say they suffer. For other measures, you may prepare the necessary dispatches. In this [connection], I desire to express my gratitude for the zeal and vigilance which you have given to my greater service, and I commend you as I approve your disposition of the Irish prisoner. I direct you to inform me of what you can do for the relief of those soldiers and Indians who were engaged at Ayubale, and for the children of those who perished in it, encouraging in my name the missionaries who you also say are discouraged by the lack of aid. So that neither for this nor other reasons should their fervent zeal for the aid and relief of these natives, and of the Holy Catholic faith falter; and I also thus charge the commissary general of the Indies who resides at this court. Dated on. . . .

33. *Governor Zúñiga to the King. San Augustín, September 3, 1704.*[86]

Sir: I relate to Your Majesty how the continued raids and hostilities of the pagan enemy have continued on the villages of Apalachee, from large bands of pagan Indians led and aided by the English of Saint George. They were compelled to demolish the blockhouse of San Luis de Talimali, as was decided upon in general council held on July 12th of this year. This was held to be an expedient act, so that the enemy might not seize the artillery and other supplies there stored; moreover, because of its strong construction, it would require much effort to dislodge them. It would have been of great concern should they have captured the infantry and settlers there situated. All of these, together with the principal chief of Ivitachuco and his people, and with the church ornaments and silver ornaments,[87] were brought to this presidio for the best security. As best they could they fled rapidly, with the expectation that the enemy would return in still greater force, as they did indeed on the 2nd of August, when a large body entered San Luis, while the infantry were only sixteen leagues distant in San Pedro de Timuqua. They did not consider pursuing them, although they sent a band to pursue those who went toward Pensacola with a few cattle which they had bought, and who were all killed and the cattle taken. This Province of Apalachee would be of great use settled, which would be easy were Your Majesty to issue an order that there be brought from the Canary Islands two hundred laboring families, with which encouragement there might be collected the Indians who have gone to Pensacola, and those who have fled to the woods, as well as many of those who willingly went over to the enemy, or those who were carried off as prisoners, some of whom are already escaping. I have not exerted any effort to prevent the Indians from marauding, or from going with the enemy, or to Pensacola or to the woods, because of the fear produced by the three raids which occurred on the 23rd, the 24th, and the 29th of June; or awareness that they had burned alive some Indians and soldiers in the last skirmish which they had with my deputy and soldiers on the 4th of July, which obliged them to abandon the province without awaiting further atrocities. And this exodus [of Indians] has been under way, I believe, since the end of January, when the governor of Saint George attacked Ayubale, the same who came here to besiege me, and permitted burning alive in his sight, and carried off the deputy and Spanish prisoners and a large number of Indians, of which I have given an account to Your Majesty. And the reason I do not send the depositions I am now collecting is so as not to subject them to risk, for we still have enemies in these waters, as they captured from me a sloop which I had sent to Havana to secure supplies, and the leader was obliged to throw in the water the dispatches which he carried for Your Majesty, who reviewing all will decide and order that which is your royal pleasure, whose Catholic and royal person may God preserve many years for the service of Christianity. San Augustín, Florida, September 3, 1704. Joseph de Zúñiga y de la Zerda [rubric]

34. *Governor Zúñiga to the Viceroy. San Augustín, September 10, 1704.*[88]

Most Excellent Sir: In compliance with my obligation, I formally communicate to Your Excellency how the hostilities of the pagan Indians, led by the English have succeeded in depopulating the Province of Apalachee, together with the greater part of Timuqua which had remained of some consequence. They killed some and captured others, including some Spaniards, in the last encounter, and the remaining Indians have fled to Pensacola, according to the reports I have had, so that the blockhouse which was in that province was left with only some Spaniards who did not attain thirty in number and who were of very unproved quality. Consequently, should the enemy return [to the province], they could readily take it; and their finding it fortified and with artillery would be sufficient motive for them to occupy the province. In the light of [these circumstances], it was decided in council, to destroy the blockhouse and withdraw the few Spaniards there stationed, since we have not had relief and there are not sufficient forces for its maintenance, and because it is situated eighty leagues distant from this presidio. This was executed with considerable danger, since two days after their departure, the enemy returned again to the province.

At the moment I believed that the ships of the Windward Fleet which were in Havana might come to aid this port, even though they might return shortly after arrival—it would have comforted this presidio and dismayed the enemy—I received a letter from Don Antonio de Landeche, commander of the said fleet, in which he said to me that should I find myself besieged I should inform him, and that he would not await a reply from me longer than the 15th of August. You may imagine, Your Excellency, what form this aid would take, since, should I find myself besieged, I would be prevented from sending my notice; although everything considered in view of the present state of affairs, His Excellency should have to perform that which is most advantageous to His Majesty. I am only responsible for the effort, which in view of what has passed, I should bring to the attention of Your Excellency, to whom obedience coincides with my desire that God will protect Your Excellency many years. Florida, September 10, 1704. Most Excellent Sir: I kiss the hands of Your Excellency: Your humble servant,

Don Joseph de Zúñiga y Zerda

Eximo Sr. Duque de Albuquerque

35. *Governor Zúñiga to the King. San Augustín, September 15, 1704.*[89]

Sir: Although I have expected [aid] from those kingdoms, and Your Majesty has ordered that there be sent to this plaza, with the Sergeant Major Don Juan de Ayala, some infantry and provisions, not even the least relief has arrived at this presidio, from New Spain or elsewhere. And although I applied to Havana that they send me two hundred men, in order to put one hundred in Apalachee to relieve the Indians, the governor sent me only forty-seven, with orders to Captain Don José de Santa Cruz, who brought them, that he should return immediately, as he did, with more than one half of them in a sloop which I was sending to Havana in search of supplies, and which the enemy captured. This afforded me some opportunity for delay, [when] the said governor repeated the order for the return of the soldiers whom I had here, so that I ordered the royal officials to inspect those I had here, and advise me about their return, and other matters pertaining thereto, which was decided in council, as Your Majesty will see from the testimony of *autos*, which I remit with this report. This presidio and province, Sir, finds itself in a miserable condition, as I have informed Your Majesty. On the 3rd of the current month, and later, my deputy in Timuqua advised me how they were tricked by the enemies of Apalachee, who defeated, laid waste, and burned alive the caciques of San Pedro and San Matheo and their vassals, and in the Lachua cattle ranch, four leagues from the village of San Francisco, they killed a Negro and captured four. These inhumanities and atrocities which the pagan Indians inflict are the causes which dismay the Christian Indians, and for the fear they have of them, they remove to their lands. And should they invade[90] the provinces of the south—Rinconada, Jororo, Mayaca, Tisimea, Tocuime, and other populations—which although extensive, enjoy peace, I have no doubt that they will succeed also with these, because I am without any force, not even that needed for this plaza. And unless specific orders come from Your Majesty for the depopulation of Carolina, and the resettlement of Saint George and its farms, this presidio and these provinces will not enjoy peace and quietude. And this, Sir, will be very easy, for in Saint George there is no fort or any formal defense works, and the English inhabitants are few, since the war they make on these provinces is with the [aid of the] Indians whom they incite to conflict. These must be driven out and [either] obliged to come of themselves, or be brought, to the obedience which for a long time they gave to Your Majesty. The Apalachicolos and other nations have effected this dislodgment. Seeing that by myself I could not [do this], I tried to [secure aid] from the governor of Petit Guave, on authority of the royal cédula of Your Majesty of January 11, 1701.[91] And M. Auger replied to me that he would aid with supplies and men, which response and promise was effected by means of Monsieur Francisco Tristan, privateer, who with another, came at my call from Havana. I do not know the effect which this will produce, and although they may make some raid, not for [fear of] this should we refrain from effecting the dislodgment of the English from Saint George and its plantations, and resettle all, because if we do not make one kingdom of all of this, nothing is secure, . . . as Your Majesty will accordingly see. And informed of all, you will decide what may be most [advantageous] for the royal service of Your Majesty, whose Catholic and royal person may God protect many years, as Christianity requires. San Agustín, Florida, September 15, 1704.

Joseph de Zúñiga y Zerda

36. *Don Andrés de Arriola to the Viceroy. Havana, December 7, 1704.*[92]

Most Excellent Sir: On arrival at this port I found a soldier who had come from the garrison of Santa María de Galve, and from whom I received the news that the felucca of that bay had gone to the Province of Apalachee in compliance with orders. I advise Your Excellency so that assistance may be given that province and the garrison of the blockhouse of His Majesty be reinforced, and I will order them to resist the hostilities which the enemy will attempt. Having departed, they encountered the enemy in increased numbers in a skirmish, in which one of those from the felucca was killed and eight more were carried off as prisoners, as a result of which the governor of that province decided to demolish the blockhouse, to which fire was set, upon the execution of which the felucca and its crew returned to this garrison accompanied by all of the families of the said Province of Apalachee. Your Excellency will learn of this in greater detail from the letter of Sergeant Major Don Joseph de Guzmán, I having discharged my obligation to inform Your Excellency, whose most excellent person may God protect in enhanced dignity the many years which I desire, and is required. Flagship *Our Lady of Guadelupe* anchored in this port of Havana, December 7, 1704. Most Excellent Sir: Your Excellency's servant, L.S.P.B. With all submission. Don Andrés de Arriola. Most Excellent Sir, Duke of Albuquerque, my Lord.

37. *Declaration of Bartholomé Ruíz de Cuenca before the Governor of New Vera Cruz. January 20, 1705.*[93]

New Vera Cruz, January 20, 1705. Declaration taken by the governor of New Vera Cruz: Bartholomé Ruíz de Cuenca, native of Arcos de la Frontera and settler in the city and garrison of San Augustín, Florida, where he was located for sixteen years, says that two years after the siege of [San Augustín], Florida, he with his family left for Pensacola, where he located and where he remained two years, during which period he fell sick. The Sergeant Major Don Joseph de Guzmán gave him permission to leave for treatment, and with this permission he left for [San Augustín], Florida, departing on the royal felucca in which he travelled to Apalachee, which they found had been invaded by the enemy on Saint Peter's Day of the past year 1704. The deputy of Apalachee ordered the commander of the felucca to join forces with him to pursue the enemy. This [order] was obeyed and, leaving the felucca secured, they went inland to San Luis, and from there all left in search of the enemy, who was two leagues distant. Forty Spaniards, one half from the felucca, and one half from Apalachee, and two hundred Christian Indians of that province faced the enemy. They fought with the foe, whose force approximated two hundred pagan Carib Indians and a few English, for about two hours, in which battle our Indians fled, leaving the forty Spaniards in the fight. Of this number they captured twenty-three men, two of whom were burned alive: One of the pair was from Pensacola and was called Don Pedro Marmolejo; the other, from

Apalachee, Balthazar Francisco. They sacrificed them, tying each one
to a cross of fagots rich in rosin, and securing them until they burned.
[The enemy also] carried off twenty-one prisoners to Saint George:
of eleven captives from Pensacola, three were wounded; and twelve
from Florida were included in the twenty-three. They went below
in search of the felucca, and the commander of the felucca decided to
return to Pensacola and give an account of his deeds to his sergeant
major, which he did. Then the declarant remained in Apalachee, and
there came an order from the governor of Florida that the blockhouse which was in Apalachee should be destroyed, and that the
garrison which was in it should retire to the presidio of Florida and
abandon the post. This they did, spiking and breaking three pieces[94]
and four pedreros; and they went to the said Florida, and this
declarant accompanied the said people. And the village of San Luis,
which consisted of two hundred families, was abandoned by them,
and they retired to Pensacola, accompanied by a Frenchman of Mobile
called Joseph Belinda, who had been carried [off] as a prisoner by
the enemy. Eight days after their arrival at San Augustín, there
arrived a French sloop commanded by a Captain Tristan, and a Spanish brigantine commanded by a Captain Joseph Pimienta. These were
sent by the governor to Saint George, a settlement of the English who
had invaded and burned the town. Having reached an agreement,
the two captains separated, Captain Pimienta pursuing a different
course, while the French captain sought the port of Saint George,
where he raised the English flag. The pilot at the bar came aboard
the sloop and was made captive, as were two Negroes and two youths.
These were examined, and related that the place had fewer than one
hundred men, as most were on their plantations. And seeing that there
were few men about, they raised anchor and went to a plantation of
the said Saint George, which they robbed of everything upon it, and
[where] they were joined by two other Negroes; whereupon the
alarm was sounded and they returned to San Augustín to give an
account of these events to the governor, who then sent the vessel to
Petit Guave, whose governor had previously offered to supply men
and munitions to the former. Eight days after the departure of this
vessel, a sloop was sighted to the north of San Augustín. The sloop
of that port was sent forth to reconnoiter, and found [the other sloop]
to be an English vessel from Saint George, having on board an
emissary of their Parliament, who said that he brought a dispatch
from the Queen of England, which he must deliver personally into

the hands of the governor of San Augustín. The commander who made the reconnaissance related all this to the governor, who ordered that they bring him [that is, the emissary], alone, one league from the plaza to the locality called N. S. de la Leche, and that the vessel lie to a dozen leagues distant. He was brought [in] with two Franciscan friars who had been made captive at the time of the siege. The emissary delivered the dispatch responsible for his visit, but the declarant does not know the nature of its contents. When asked if he did not know what the said dispatch of the Queen contained, he replied that he did not from personal knowledge, but that he had heard that a treaty had been made stipulating they should not raise a force against Saint George, and that likewise Saint George should not do it against San Augustín. This was believed to be nothing more than a pretext to enter San Augustín in greater security in order to acquire news of what they meant to do as a consequence of capturing the pilot, and to learn as well if we had some expedition in preparation to invade them. The friars who had been prisoners said that the Frenchman, Belinda, who had fled, had been subjected to torture, under which he revealed that the garrisons at Pensacola and Mobile were small, and that a force of fifteen hundred men was being readied to go in the spring to Mobile and Pensacola. The declarant left San Augustín in a sloop for Havana, where he embarked on a brigantine for Campeche on the same day that Don Andrés de Arriola and Diego Sánchez left, the 12th of December. All left port together, arrived at Campeche, and revealed to the governor of that province all that is related herein, and from there passed to this city.

38. *Extract made by Don Miguel de Horue, royal notary, from an anonymous letter for submission to the Viceroy, New Vera Cruz, February 2, 1705.*[95]

Two of our privateers, Joseph Pimienta and Francisco Tristan, arrived at this port with the idea of attacking Saint George by surprise with one hundred and forty men. Upon leaving this port, Pimienta, who had the stronger vessel and the most men, disobeyed the order of the governor of this place and went elsewhere. Tristan obeyed the order, and having arrived at the bar of Saint George, anchored his vessel and hid all of his men except five who were dressed as Englishmen. A boat arrived with the pilot of the bar with a crew of two youths and two Negroes, who told Tristan to weigh anchor and follow him. Tristan feigned to raise the anchor, and as he could not raise it with the five men, he began to upbraid them. When the pilot observed this he came on board to aid, and was then given a kick, and his men brought up and made prisoners. The pilot said that if they were to go up to the place, they would be faced by only one hundred men, who would be obliged to flee to the woods. Tristan did not dare to undertake this because he had no more than forty men, for which reason we lost an opportunity to sack and burn them in tranquillity. He also seized the sentinel of the bar and raided a plantation; and through the people there he sent a threat to the governor of Saint George, [indicating] that if he did not return the prisoners of this presidio, he might be expected to return shortly and put all to the knife. This produced among them such fear and confusion that they sent an embassy to this city in the person of a gentleman of the Queen of England, who came from Saint George to investigate them, and who was well received by our governor. They agreed upon a truce, because we are not in a condition for anything else, as neither upon sea or land could I defend myself, since Apalachee, Timuqua, and Guale are already devastated, and we do not have much more territory than extends to San Francisco Potano, whither the people of Ivitachuco have retired with some Timuquans and our garrison. Although Tristan arrived at this port and in a few days left for Petit Guave and Cuba with letters and orders of our governor to secure men [here several words blurred] destroyed this thievery of Saint George. The pilot of that port was brought back a prisoner in order that he might lead us into that port, which was a matter of great consequence for the ambassador, who was sent to recover him more than for any other reason, after it was learned that he had been carried off by Tristan.

Compared with the title of the letter cited, which was sent on the mentioned date, and which for the purpose of extracting evidence was shown to me by the said general, in whose defense it is attested by the treasurer, for submission to the Most Excellent Duke of Albuquerque, viceroy, governor, and captain general of this New Spain, which [letter] I communicate in compliance with the order of the previously mentioned commission in the city of New Vera Cruz on the 2nd of February, 1705: I make my sign in testimony of the truth. Don Miguel de Horue, royal notary.

39. Extracts from the auto of an inquiry into the deaths of the Fathers in Apalachee, conducted in the convent of San Francisco in San Augustín, upon order of the Most Reverend Father Fray Lucar Alvarez de Toledo, retired reader of the secret council of the Inquisition, by the Licenciate Don Ignacio de Leturiendo, Curate, Vicar, and Ecclesiastical Judge of the city and provinces, in June, 1705.[96]

Testimony of Juan de la Cruz:

In the city of San Augustín on the 9th day of the month of June of this year 1705, before . . . Don Ignacio de Leturiendo, curate of the holy parochial church of this city, and interim vicar and ecclesiastical judge in it and the provinces of its jurisdiction, appeared Juan Baptista de la Cruz, soldier of this presidio and of the garrison of San Luis de Talimali, seat of the Province of Apalachee, who before me the notary, swore by God Our Lord, and [was given] the sign of the cross in legal form, which the aforesaid returned, and was charged with the promise to tell the truth; and being asked the questions required by the tenor of the interrogatory, . . . said and declared the following:

(1) To the first question he said that for many years he had seen in this province of mission villages the Reverend Fathers Fray Manuel de Mendoza and Fray Juan de Parga, and does not know of what place they were natives, and has much information concerning the wars in Apalachee. In reply to the general [questions] of the law[97] [he] stated that they do not concern him and that his age is 35 years. In reply

(2) to the second question, he said that he had seen the said fathers in different villages setting a good example and teaching the natives. In reply

(3) to the third question, he said that the witness was in Apalachee on the occasion of the attack on Ayubale, to which the question refers, and was one of those who accompanied the deputy, Juan Ruíz Mexía, and all the soldiers and Christian Indians whom he led. They spent the night before the battle in the village of Patale, and at dawn the teacher of that village, who was the said Father Fray Juan de Parga, preached a sermon in the Apalachian tongue which lasted more than an hour, saying many things to the natives: that they should go to fight against [illegible] and pagans that came to disturb the law of God and destroy the Christian provinces; that all those who may die in that conflict will go to enjoy God, having engaged in defense of his holy law, and thus they could

go content; and that he was going gladly with them for the encouragement
of all. These and many other things he told them in the said sermon,
and gave absolution to all Spaniards and Indians; after this he left to
accompany them; and though the deputy once and many times urged that
he not go with them, as he already had given them a good example and
teaching, he replied "No," [and added] that he had to go with his children
and accompany them to the death. Having left on the Ayubale road, by
chance they met the enemy, with whom they began to fight, and twice
the Spaniards and Indians drove back the pagans and English in such a
manner that they retreated to the council house; and the fate of the
English might have been [illegible] the Indians disposed themselves in
such a manner that [they] rapidly regained [the ground]; and our Indians,
being already somewhat short in ammunition because of much firing, had
to retire, because the enemy, who were fifteen hundred, launched some
charges, with which they cut our people and captured the deputy who
had been wounded, and killed a religious, Father Marcos Delgado[98] and
a soldier, Juan Solana, and captured others. As it relates to the deaths
of the Indians, whom they burned, he knows their number exceeded forty,
who, tied to stakes, were set afire, until they died. They cut off the head
of Father Fray Juan de Parga, and the pagans brought it to the council
house. This he heard told by the captives, because he was not there, having
withdrawn with other soldiers. He heard say that to an Indian of San
Luis, called Antonio Enixa, they applied fire slowly from morning until
his death nearly at sunset, and that the said Indian exhorted the pagans,
telling them that they should kill him, [for] he would die consoled, in
that as a Christian he would go to enjoy God, while they would go to
hell, and that the Most Holy Virgin was helping him and appeared near.
Thus it was that he was helped [illegible word] courageously to tolerate
the martyrdom which they inflicted upon him. The [illegible word] *cuipa*
Feliciano, principal [cacique] of San Luis, also preached much, and with
great bravery himself taunted the pagans so that they would torture him,
saying to them that the body would die but that his soul would go to
enjoy God eternally. The body of another man from San Luis, called
Luis Domingo, was slashed with knives, and they stuck burning splinters
into the wounds they had made, but nothing of this could prevent him
from preaching until he died. In reply

(4) to the fourth question, he said that it is true that the missionary
[*doctrinero*] Father Fray Angel de Miranda was in Ayubale, and that
when the munitions gave out, he fell into their hands and they seized the
said teacher. He was heard to say that as he had seen the martyrdom
experienced by the Indians from their being burned alive, he asked the
[English] governor how he could permit it, as it was not the usage of
war to maltreat prisoners, because the torture was regarded as inhuman,

and that the governor had said to him that the English were eighty and the Indians were one thousand five hundred, and he could not prevent it. The Father then went and untied the Indians, and said to the pagans they should not do that with Christians, nor before them, for which reason they were taken farther away, according to what the captives said; and of the captives they made, not one is today in this presidio; and in response

(5) to the fifth question, he said that he knows that on the day of San Juan there was another raid by a small band of the enemy at midnight, and that they killed the Reverend Fray Manuel de Mendoza, whom they found below the wattle and mud wall of the completely burned convent, according to what he heard said, and that the metal of a small crucifix which he carried about his neck was half melted by the fire. In reply

(6) to the sixth question, he said that he knows very well, as it is public and common knowledge, as he has seen, that the said Father Fray Manuel de Mendoza was very charitable with all the poor Spaniards and Indians, giving them as much as he had; and on the occasion referred to in the question, this witness remembers very well that there was much need in this city, and he gave many alms, in general dividing all that His Majesty had supplied for his maintenance. In reply

(7) to the seventh question, he said that he was also found in the last battle fought in Patale in the early part of July; that the adjutant Manuel Solana, who was deputy, set forth with some soldiers and Indians, and there were many killed and many captured by the enemy, who also were many, two or three soldiers and some Indians; and that [in retribution] for the seventeen pagans who were killed, they burned another seventeen captives, and among them two soldiers—one who had come from Pensacola, called Don Pedro Marmolejo, whom they found burned at the foot of a cross, and another soldier of those of the garrison of Apalachee, called Balthazar Francisco, native of the Canary Islands. Immediately following his capture, they cut out his tongue and eyes, cut off his ears, scalped him, and put a crown on him, which in Indian style is placed on the Indian warriors when they dance, and which they call *tascayas*. And they tied him to another cross, and slashed him all over and placed burning splinters in the wounds; and as soon as they set him afire, they mocked and insulted him, laughing on hearing what the said Balthazar Francisco told the pagans in the Spanish and Apalachian languages, [while] he called on the Most Holy Virgin to help him, for she would carry him to God with much pleasure from knowing that he would go to enjoy his holy glory. There were related many other things which the Indian prisoners who escaped stated they had heard from the said Balthazar Francisco until he died. And after the departure of the enemy, the witness and other soldiers went to search the locality and found the Crosses of Calvary tied to the aforesaid and fallen to their feet. He replied

(8) to the eighth question, saying that everything he had said and declared is [a matter of] public truth and notoriety, public opinion, and fame in this city and all of these provinces, and [that he] will repeat it if asked under oath, which has been done. So that it is asserted and affirmed, and [he] does not sign it because he says he does not know [how] to sign. His Grace the said Vicar: Don Ignacio de Leturiendo.

Before me, Manuel de Quiñones, notary public in the said city on the said day, month, and year, and immediately before His Grace, the vicar and ecclesiastical judge, appeared Don Francisco de Fuentes de Galanca, soldier of this presidio, and one of the Apalachee garrison, who before me, the notary public, swore before God Our [Lord] and [was given] the sign of the cross in legal form, which the aforesaid returned, and [expressed] his obligation to tell the truth, being asked by the tenor of the questions of the interrogatory, and said the following:

(1) To the first question he said that he was well acquainted with the Reverend Father Fray Manuel de Mendoza and Fray Juan de Parga; that he believes the said Reverend Father is from Rio Seco and Father Parga a Gallegan—he does not know from what part of Galicia; and that he has knowledge of the battles in Apalachee as a soldier and participated in some of them. In reply to the general [questions] of the law, he said that they did not affect him, and that he is thirty-seven years of age. He replied

(2) to the second question, saying that he had known the said Fathers in various places as teachers who gave a very good example and teaching to the Indians and soldiers; that the said Father Parga gave long sermons in Apalachee in the language of the Indians as well as in Spanish, preaching during one Lent in this city in the holy parish church and in the Church of the Soledad many sermons which were fruitful; and that he had also seen the Reverend Father Fray Manuel de Mendoza preach to the Indians. In reply

(3) to the third question, this witness said that although he was not in the battle of Ayubale, because he was below by the sea as a sentinel, he heard of the matter referred to in the question from the soldiers and Indian captives; that the Father was killed in a canebrake and found with one leg gone and a leather boot on the other, [his body] naked, swollen, and half decomposed; and that they had carried [the corpse] away for burial at the village of Ivitachuco as soon as the enemy had left. [According to the witness], the soldiers who had gone to Ayubale to bury the bodies of the Christians also found many Indians burned while tied to stakes and trees, and he heard said that two in particular—one the

enija of San Luis, and the other principal of the said place, [the former] called Antonio, [the latter] *cuipa* Feliciano—had also preached long sermons to the pagans while they were burning. [There was also] another Indian called Luis Domingo, and these three they burned with fire. It was related that the others died more rapidly because they applied the wood all at once, but that all called on God and on His Most Holy Mother, Our Saint the Virgin Mary. The deputy did not wish the Father to go to battle, and [the latter] replied that he must go to exhort and encourage the Indians who were his children, so that they would fight with bravery in defense of the law of God. He replied

(4) to the fourth question, saying that all that relates to this matter he heard from the soldiers. In his reply

(5) to the fifth question, the witness said that he went with the party seeking Father Fray Manuel de Mendoza, who was the missionary [*doctrinero*] in Patale, and who was killed during the enemy's raid, and that they were in doubt as to whether or not he had been taken away captive, because he was not found. [Finally,] they discovered him beneath a fragment of mud wall and burned wattle. Half of his body was burned to ashes, and the beads of the rosary which he had at his neck, as well as the body, were charred. A crucifix which he always carried with him was almost entirely melted, and the body of the Father had been so burned that when they went to carry it off it fell to powder. He does not know the manner in which he was killed, and he heard said that the Indians called on him; in particular, one Apalachee Indian of the same village, who had rebelliously joined the enemy, called him, saying to him "Good, you may open, Father, I am Fulano; you do not know me; but look, we will not do you harm." [Finally, he said] that the Father had opened the window, and they killed him with a shot, which they discharged as soon as he opened it; that they immediately set fire to the convent; and that as the enemy were few, they quickly left. In replying

(6) to the sixth question, he said that all the substance of the matter is public and notorious in these provinces and that the witness had seen him many times, because the said Father was a great almoner and friend of the poor. In reply

(7) to the seventh question, the witness recalled the last battle, in which they were defeated, because the Indians would not fight for fear of the past tortures in Ayubale, and because the number of the enemy was great. Nevertheless, some were killed on the one side or the other. They captured some soldiers, among them some from Pensacola, and they burned Don Pedro Marmolejo, and Balthazar Francisco and . . . a soldier of Apalachee. These, according to [what] the captives who escaped say, preached much, [suffered] with great martyrdom, and died calling on the Most Holy Virgin. In reply

78

(8) to the eighth question, he reaffirmed his statements and declared [them] to be the truth, under oath, which is made public and notorious, asserted and affirmed; and he signed it, and His Majesty's vicar rubricated it.

Don Francisco de Fuentes: Before me, Manuel Quiñones, notary public:

In this city on the said day, month, and year, there [appeared] immediately before His Grace the said vicar, curate, and ecclesiastical judge, Manuel Solana, soldier of this presidio, son of the former deputy [governor] of Apalachee, who before me the notary, was sworn by God, Our Lord, and was given the sign of the cross according to law, which the aforesaid repeated; and I charged him to promise to tell the truth, and being questioned by the list of the questions of the said interrogatory, he said the following:

(1) To the first question he said that he was acquainted with the Fathers, Fray Manuel de Mendoza and Fray Juan de Parga; that he does not know from what places they came; and that he participated in the battles of Apalachee. And he replied to the general [questions] of the law, saying that they do not affect him, that he is twenty-one years of age, a little more or less. He replied

(2) to the second question, [saying] that in the time when this witness was in Apalachee he saw the Fathers giving very good examples and teaching to all. He replied

(3) to the third question, [saying] that the witness did not go along when the deputy Juan Ruíz Mexía went to fight the battle of Ayubale, but that if things went well he was to carry munitions, and that in Capola he encountered some retreating Indians and Spaniards, and they gave him account of how the [enemy] had killed the Father Fray Juan de Parga; that he heard [that the] other Indians had thrown him in a canebrake and heard him ask them to aid him; and that Marcos Delgado and Juan Solana—a brother of the witness—went to his aid, and both were killed; and that they had captured the deputy and the Father Fray Angel de Miranda who was stationed in Ayubale. On the departure of the enemy, the deputy sent Jacinto Roque Pérez to reconnoiter the vicinity of Ayubale and bury the bodies of the Christians, and the witness and three [other] soldiers went along. They were accompanied on this detail by [some] Indians, and they found many burned bodies and [those] of some women pierced by sticks and half roasted, many children impaled on poles, and others killed with arrows, their arms and legs cut off. The Christians were buried, and of the pagans who died they left many [unburied] because the entire vicinity of the plaza and council house [bujio] was

foul smelling. And concerning the Father, he heard it said that the Reverend
Father Fray Juan de Villalva, deceased, who was then missionary of
Ivitachuco, [already] had sent in search of the body of Father Fray Juan
de Parga; which the pagans had carried off minus a leg, and this was
identified by a sandal and a boot; and [also heard that] the soldiers, four
in number, who escaped to the enemy, fled while [they were] searching
for some cows. They also set at liberty the deputy Juan Mexía. The
witness heard all speak of the burning of the Indians and the great torture
inflicted on a leader [*hinija*] of San Luis, Antonio Acuipa Feliciano, and
on Luis Domingo, natives of San Luis, whom they burned little by little,
and [then] scratched their bodies with spines, and placed burning splinters
in the said wounds [*regoaladuras*]. And during the time this lasted, the
pagans made great ridicule and mirthful mockery, because they were heard
to call on God and Our Lady the Most Holy Virgin. And they would
say to the pagan Indians: "See what brave men we are become from the
strength and courage which God gave us, so that we can undergo this
martyrdom, and we will be transported with pleasure before God, because
His Divine Majesty suffered more for us"; [they would also say] that
their teaching fathers had taught them all the law of God, and made
them many sermons, but that the soul would not die, but would go to
enjoy God eternally, while they [the pagans] in dying would be carried
off by devils because they did not believe in God nor in the commandments
—all this and many other related things [they said]. The captive soldiers
may have been discoursing to them during the whole day their martyrdom
endured, from what the Christian Indians said, because they [the pagans]
burned them with a straw the Indians called *pico*. And when they ceased
speaking and did not complain, the [pagan] Indians lost their inclination
[to torture], as they did not have the desire to hear them [further] or
to mock what they said and preached. They left them with a flame under
them, and in this fire [the Christians] expired. The Captain Don Juan
Ruíz Mexía, who went to the Kingdoms of Castile, could give a better
or longer statement, as he was the deputy who went to the battle of
Ayubale and was captured. In reply

(4)   to the fourth question, he said he heard that the said captive
soldiers told everything the said question contains, and that the said Father
Manuel de Miranda is today a missionary in Abasaya, with the people
of the village of Ivitachuco, which is the only one of the eleven in Apalachee
that escaped; of the others, some were destroyed by the enemy, while
others, from fear, went tranquilly with them. He replied

(5)   to the fifth question, saying that [on] the day of the battle of
Patale or destruction of this village, which was small, when they went
to give report [of this] to the father of this witness [word blurred]
Manuel Solana, who was deputy, he mounted a horse and with ten soldiers

went to Patale, and they found the convent burned, all fallen in, and did not find anyone who could give an account of the Father. And his father followed the enemy for ten days with the said soldiers, among them the witness, and at three or four leagues they found an infant of two years all pierced and cut to pieces with knives, and it was presumed they had done it because it could not walk fast and to avoid the labor of carrying it. Farther on, they found near a pond an Indian female dying with many holes in her head, which had been made with a stake; and his father left her a loaf of bread which he carried and ordered her given water, and [then] continued in pursuit of the enemy, a small body of people who travelled rapidly, and hid themselves in the thickets of the woods. Since [his father's party] did not carry anything to eat, they returned, and the Indians bore the Indian female on a stretcher to San Luis, [where] she confessed, and said that because she could not walk, they had left her there for dead [after] giving her many wounds on the head; she died from these wounds on the third day. And as the Indian female had said that they did not carry off the priest captive, his father ordered that they dig beneath the convent, and they found he had been burned after he had been killed by a shot on opening the door. He replied

(6)   to the sixth question that he knows the continued alms which the Father Fray Manuel de Mendoza dispensed and had given were public and notorious. And in reply

(7)   to the seventh question, he said that the witness participated in the last battle which they had with the enemy in the village of Patale, to which his father went forth, as he was deputy, with about thirty Spaniards, soldiers of Apalachee and others of Pensacola, and two hundred Indians. And as the Indians did not fight, the enemy defeated the Spaniards and took some captives, and they burned Don Marmolejo, soldier of Pensacola, and Balthazar Francisco, an islander, and cut out his tongue and eyes, cut off his ears, slashed him all over, stuck burning splinters in the wounds, and set fire to him while he was tied at the foot of a cross. The Indian captives who had escaped [from] them, related all this, and said that the said Balthazar Francisco cried out to call on God and to Our Lady; that he spoke with an able tongue to the Indians, as he knew them well as an old soldier, who had been more than fourteen years in garrison in Apalachee; and that he wished it recorded, he heard him say, that he was from the Island of Teneriffe, of the region of Los Silos. These men died, according to general opinion, [as did] many other Indian martyrs, by being skinned alive. The [savages] put them in stocks and there cut off the scalps from the heads, and the breasts from the women, and dried them on some long sticks; and even *le parese* heard it said [by] the [escaped] captives that the Indians of the Chichemeca and Chisca nations cut off pieces, which they half roasted and ate, in the battle at Ayubale;

and in this last [battle] at Patale, he was also sent to bury the dead, and they found as many as seventeen burned, most of them upon the Crosses of Calvary of the *Via Crucis* which was around the plaza of Patale. And the said Balthazar Francisco had a crown [made of] the beaks of parroquets, deer hair, and wild animal hair, such as are much used in the dances which the pagans have for *tascayas* or *norocos,* names which are given to the courageous Indians. He replied

(8) to the eighth question that all he has said and declared is the truth, under obligation of the oath, which he took; and he asserts and affirms [this statement], all of it being public and notorious; he does not sign because he says he does not know how, and His Grace the said vicar signed it: Don Ignacio de Leturiendo: Before me, Manuel de Quiñones, notary public.

In the city of San Augustín of Florida, on the 16th day of the month of June of this year 1705, His Grace the Vicar Don Ignacio de Leturiendo, curate, vicar, and ecclesiastical judge in this city and all the provinces of its jurisdiction, said that since the 9th of the present [month] there were examined the foregoing three witnesses and that he has been awaiting the arrival of Diego Pablo de Villalva, who is thirty leagues from here in the garrison of the village of San Francisco, and Joseph del Pozo, soldier, who is in a *piragua* of war to the north on guard along the paths of the enemy on the bars of Santa María and San Juan. [These witnesses] were captives and were liberated by the governor of Saint George. There are no others, because the adjutant Manuel Solana, who was deputy, is now captain of a brigantine of this city which left on the 2nd of February, to secure supplies in Havana. It is suspected that he is prisoner because to date there has been no news of him; the deputy Juan Mexía is in Spain. . . .

40. *Admiral Landeche to the Viceroy. Havana, August 11, 1705.*[99]

Most Excellent Sir: Upon closing accounts after the delivery of arms, munitions, and supplies in the village of Santa María de Galve, and [having] effected the payment of its garrison, as I have related to Your Excellency in a letter of this date, I arranged to call a council on the 20th of June with the leaders of that presidio, my captains and the administrators of the merchant vessels, their pilots, and those of the fleet and other persons familiar with the coast of Apalachee, to inform myself of the state of that province, and plan the reconnaissance that Your Excellency had ordered me to execute in its territories.

Fort San Luis

Having discussed the manner of that navigation, it was the decision of the pilots and experienced persons that this frigate and the two large merchant vessels should be left in the Bay of San Joseph, which is situated forty leagues to the windward of Santa María de Galve and as many more to the leeward of the port of San Marcos, and that the two merchant brigantines of this port (that came with my protection), the felucca of this presidio, and the launch of this frigate, would sail from there to convey the landing party, in view of the bad weather which may be expected in the month of July on those coasts and their bays. In this judgment I concurred for the reasons expressed, for the two laden frigates were short of sufficient cables to anchor as far from the coast as was necessary, or, once anchored, to resist whatever disaster that might arise from bad weather. With that conference I set the date for our departure, which was effected on the 20th of the same month, proceeding to the Bay of San Joseph, where we arrived on the 29th of the said month, the tedious voyage being due to the calms and contrary winds experienced in that crossing. Immediately on anchoring, I arranged for the transfer to the two brigantines of the arms, munitions, and supplies destined for the force detailed for the march. The felucca of the presidio arrived on the 30th, with its commander, Captain of Infantry Don Pedro de Vilas, with forty men of the veterans of that presidio, and the launch of this frigate was prepared. Leaving that vessel in charge of its captain of sea and war, Captain Don Sebastian de Moscoso, with appropriate orders for what he should do in my absence, I embarked in one of the brigantines, distributing the force on both, and in the launch; and accompanied by the felucca, I left on the 2nd of July for the port of San Marcos, sending the aforesaid felucca and launch ahead by one of the narrow channels to await our arrival at that anchorage, while I navigated outside with the two brigantines. I arrived at the said port on the 6th, and finding it reconnoitered by the said Captain Don Pedro de Vilas, and observing that there was no opposition that could impede the march, I set out on the 8th of July with one hundred and eighty armed men, who were all that I could assemble, including those seamen of the crew of this frigate, as well as those from Santa María de Galve and some adventurers from the merchant vessels. We travelled, with all vigilance, the eight leagues to be covered from the port of San Marcos to the village of San Luis de Talimali, which was the principal settlement of the province of Apalachee, where the blockhouse was situated. We arrived at that locality on the 10th, notwithstanding the mired roads due to the rains which never ceased, as it was the time for them. No trails of people or of cattle were found in the entire region; the blockhouse was demolished in such a manner that there remained only some portions of the stockade, which, from the scarcity of rosin, the flames that consumed the rest did not reach. It was, according to our reconnaissance, a very regular fortress, capable of any defense, as Your Excellency will recognize from the plan which I ordered made, and which I will transmit to Your Excellency as soon as I arrive at the port of San Juan de Ulúa [Vera Cruz].

We remained there two days, although with great discomfort to the people because of the rain, as we had nothing in which to shelter ourselves, and we could protect only the arms and powder. During this time I dispatched various details of infantry in charge of retired officers, accompanied by persons familiar with the region, who guided them to the villages adjacent to San Luis, of which were found no more trace than the statement of the guide that in those spots they were situated; nor were any tracks of Indians or of cattle found. With these reports I interrogated those who had accompanied me and who had been settlers in Apalachee, concerning the manner in which its re-establishment could be effected. They informed me that a garrison of five hundred men was necessary to protect the natives who remained friendly, and who with their families have retired to the region between Pensacola and Mobile, and to San Augustín, from Apalachee, for these would return and build their houses and plant their fields, cultivating again even the fruit trees which they had, for the region is wooded. Since the number of pagans and rebels of the province is, from my reconnaissance, considerable, it appears to me necessary to ascertain their attitude in case you are disposed to a re-establishment. I assume Your Excellency is aware of the concern I felt from the destruction of this province, stimulated by what I learned of the goodness of its natives as well as by the fertility and beauty of its lands.

It having been necessary to disembark the prisoners who were destined for San Augustín for the purpose of bearing the supplies and munitions that the vessels brought, six of them fled on the night of the 11th, which was set for the return to the port of San Marcos; their names are presented to Your Excellency in the enclosed note. They had the notion of communicating with the English who accompany the pagans, into whose hands should they fall, I suppose they will perish. I informed the governor of Florida so that, in case they appear there, he can add them to his prisoners.

I arrived on my return at the port of San Marcos, on the 13th, and readying the brigantines which were obliged to navigate outside, I embarked in the launch of this frigate, accompanied by the felucca. I hastened my journey to the Bay of San Joseph, to prevent the departure of the frigates immediately following the arrival of the brigantines, which was on the 19th; and on the next day, having previously sent off the felucca, I sailed for this port. It is my hope that I have exactly complied with the orders of Your Excellency, whose most excellent person may God protect many years in greater dignity. Frigate *Our Lady of the Rosary*, flagship of the fleet anchored in the port of Havana, August 11, 1705. Most Excellent Sir: I kiss the feet of Your Excellency: Antonio de Landeche: Most Excellent Señor, the Duke of Albuquerque.

41. *Extract of a letter of Don Antonio de Espinosa to the Viceroy. Mexico, February 26, 1706.*[100]

The galley prisoners for San Augustín of Florida that fled and escaped in the province are listed in this manner:

Manuel Chaves	Pablo de Rosas	Antonio Marcial
Pasqual de la Cruz	Joseph Molina	Domingo Bermúdez

42. *Summary of the Martyrdoms experienced in Florida by the Franciscans. Letter of the Franciscan Fathers to the King. San Augustín, May 7, 1707.*[101]

Sir: The provincial and chapter master of this Holy and Apostolic Province of Santa Helena of Florida, at a convocation in these West Indies of Your Majesty, prostrate at your royal feet, ask and supplicate that Your Majesty may be pleased to give consideration to the following indispensable representations:

This province of Your Majesty in the spiritual realm has always, since the beginning, been administered in its conversions and administrations by the religious of our seraphic religion, the first cultivators of this evangelic vineyard. The first laborers that sowed the seeds of this church of Florida were the sons of Our Seraphic Father San Francisco, who have continued with great labor, [despite] obstacles, nakedness, hunger, and even the shedding of their blood on occasion, sacrificing their lives in the apostolic employment of evangelic preaching, without being intimidated by the tyranny and severity of the idolatrous enemies of the faith, and continuing their labors at the sight of hardships and threats by which they were terrorized at the beginning of the conversions: By the years [15]50 and [15]97, in the Province of Guale, one of the provinces of this government, there had died at the hands of pagan Indians and some of the recently converted who had forsaken the faith, in defense of the Catholic religion, five missionary fathers and one lay brother. One other priest, son of that Holy Province of Castile, escaped with his life by divine intervention, although he suffered a prolonged martyrdom, since they had him for a slave, stripped of his holy habit. He served them for about two years by carrying wood and water to their pavilions [*bujios*], which are their community houses where they have their meetings, dances, and feasts, and [he] attended [the Indian occupying] the seat near the fire, when they made their cassina, the usual drink of the Indians, which they make from some leaves of a small tree[102] that is [placed] in a small vessel, roasted at a strong fire, and then boiled. This poor professor and priest tended the fire and served the dais on his knees according to the custom of the country, where he suffered intolerable hardships, which is submitted to the exalted comprehension of Your Majesty. When Divine Providence was pleased to liberate him from heavy and continuous labor, full of labors and years, he retired to that Province of Castile, where he finished his life in one of its convents.[103]

In the year [1]647 three other professed priests, missionaries in the Province of Apalachee, died a violent death at the hands of pagans and of some recent converts who were incited to revolt against the Spaniards and Fathers at the beginning of the conversion of the said province, although they shortly returned *(reluxeron)* to the faith. These [Christians] have prevailed, although nearly annihilated by the many plagues and illnesses which have consumed them, and by the continued incursions of the pagan Indians, their enemies, until, since the year [1]702 and subsequently, the said province was destroyed from the continued persecution of the pagan enemies. Of the few that have remained in the said province, some are refugees in the vicinity of this presidio; these are the fewest; others [have gone] to the shelter of the presidio of Pensacola, and others to that of Mobile, presidio of the Most Christian King, most illustrious progenitor of Your Majesty. Still others, as is known, are settled in the vicinity of the pagan enemy, giving obedience to force and violence, until the Divine Majesty may be pleased to give them liberty. Many others of the said province, [as well as of] Timuqua [and] Guale, as has been learned from captives who have escaped from Carolina and villages of the pagan enemies, have surrendered and passed to the islands of the dominion of the Queen of England. In the year [1]696, the rebellious of the mission of [J]orroro took the life of a missionary priest, the minister of those villages, of which an account was given to Your Majesty.[104] In the past invasion of the enemy in the year [1]702, the English of Carolina and the pagan Indians, their confederates, captured three missionaries, who for nearly three years had been in the power of the said English before they were restored to their liberty, where they suffered many penalties, some of them being obliged for their decent subsistence to accept menial service, according to their account.

With the continued incursions of the enemies in the said year of [1]702 and subsequently, [there furthermore] have suffered and died at the hands of the said enemies, the Fathers Fray Juan de Parga Araujo, and Fray Manuel de Mendoza, professors, priests, and evangelical ministers and apostolic missionaries, as has been related to Your Majesty by the Field Master General Don Joseph de Zúñiga y Zerda, formerly governor of this province. The first of the said priests was a son of the Holy Province of Santiago; the second, of the Province of Concepción in those kingdoms; and the last had participated in these conversions, administrations, and teachings [for] about twenty-six years, and the first nearly ten, having shown much zeal, the one as well as the other, in preaching and in teaching the Indians, and, during the invasion of the Province of Apalachee, in stimulating and encouraging the soldiers and Catholic Indians, marching with much bravery among them until he was killed by the enemy. Father Mendoza, encouraging and stimulating the Indians of the mission of his charge, was wounded by a shot, and was burned half alive within the *Conventico de Su C . . . taz.* We are hoping that because of their lives and professed conduct, both are enjoying the Divine Presence, as is also Fray Augustín Ponce de León, professed priest, native of this presidio, who at the beginning of September [1]705, went in company with Captain Don Joseph Begambre, who was acting governor of this presidio by Your Majesty, with a group of infantry and Christian Indians with their arms, in pursuit of the enemy Indians that carried off as captives all the women with all their children and others of minor age of the village in charge of the said Fray Augustín Ponce. The said captain and his force having encountered the enemy at dawn on the 3rd of September, [Fray Augustín] fought with them until several shots made him surrender his soul to his creator, as the others of his force also did. Fighting with all bravery and effort, they defeated the enemy, although at the sacrifice of their lives; by this means he [thought he] might liberate the women and infants, except for a few who did not have the fortune to escape; and the said Fray Augustín, who went along to encourage the Spaniards and Indians of his force, seeking [the places] where the need to administer the sacrament of repentance to the wounded might exist, without exhibiting fear that they might kill him. As a good shepherd, he surrendered his soul in defense of his sheep and children of the mission in his charge, because, although he lost his life in pursuit and redemption of his children, as a consequence of his admonitions he succeeded in the recovery of the greater part of them, even though he could not effect it for all.

Three other priests in the said year of [1]705, wandered in the forests, experiencing much hardship, need, want, hunger, and punishment, because they would not leave the sheep in their charge; they followed the poor Indians, their children, who wandered in the woods fleeing from the continuous incursions of the enemies wherever they went, until one of them, called Fray Domingo Criado, was captured. Nearly all the Indians of his village, who were settled in a wood on the banks of a rapid stream, a matter of ten or twelve leagues from this presidio, were killed; and [Fray Domingo was] carried off a captive. It is supposed by some captives who have escaped from the enemy [that], stripped of his holy habit and experiencing much inhumanity and mockery, [he was carried] to their village, where in prolonged martyrdom he served the enemy Indians as their slave; at the end of some months he died, according to accounts from Christian Indians who have escaped from the said enemies and returned to this presidio, and who have given individual reports.

The other two Fathers, seeing the continued dangers and realizing they could not persevere in such prolonged wanderings, because even in the most hidden woods or most tangled undergrowth they did not find security, returned in the past summer to this presidio, with the few Christian Indians they could collect, who in the shelter of this presidio are now gathered. These are, Sir, the labors and hardships, reduced to a summary, which the poor professors, sons of the wounded angel, stationed in this part of Florida, have suffered and will suffer, if the enemy continues his incursions in accordance with his obduracy.

But always, Sir, all the fervent chaplains of Your Majesty, and with indescribable bravery, [are ready] to suffer other greater hardships, even to exposing their lives to death and sacrificing themselves in the joy of obedience in the service of Our God and Lord. And of Your Majesty, who, with so much charity, protects, maintains, and sustains us from his royal means in these vast countries of his Province of Florida, where the Catholic Kings, predecessors of Your Majesty, without seeking any temporal gain, but only for the spiritual welfare of the poor natives of these provinces, have spent many allowances of your royal means. Your Majesty, in imitation of them, continues to maintain and protect these few Indian natives who remain, as well as their evangelical ministers; to protect, favor, and shelter the one and the other; and to spend a large amount to maintain this presidio, for which all of us must give to God, Our Lord, due thanks, as these we give, in order that Your Majesty may be preserved and protected for long years, with all prosperity, and be granted felicitous succession, for the comfort of all your vassals. And to Your Majesty we give humble veneration and compliant obedience as we should, again presenting [ourselves] to the protection of Your Majesty as humble and submissive vassals and chaplains, declaring with entire veracity that we will persevere to the last moments of life, as to the present we have done, in obedience to Your Majesty and in the government and instruction of the few Christians that remain, without shrinking from the severity and tyranny of the enemy. If in the future the Divine Majesty should open a road for new conversions and settlements, [may he] employ us in them with the fervor and charity [manifested] to the present. That Our Lord protect Your Majesty many years, as all Christianity needs, is the desire of all your humble subjects and chaplains, gathered together in the provincial capital of this your apostolic Province, in this convent of the presidio of San Augustín, Florida, on May 7, 1707. We kiss the feet of Your Majesty, your humble subjects and chaplains

Fray Claudio de Florencia
   Provincial Minister

Fray Simón de Salas
   Father of the Province

Fray Manuel de Urisas
   Definidor

Fray Antonio de los Angeles
   Definidor

Fray Domingo Vásquez
   Custodio

Fray Francisco de León
   Definidor

Fray Andrés de Oramos
   Definidor

43. Governor Francisco Corcoles y Martínez to the King. San Augustín, January 14, 1708.[105]

Sir: My principal concern, since I entered upon the government, has been to try by all possible means to prevent the enemy from destroying all at once these provinces and the few natives who remained when I took possession. This prompted me to call a Council of War, at which it was judged advantageous to withdraw the garrisons at the village of Santa Fé, in addition to that at San Francisco and the infantry which was stationed at the passage of the Salamototo River, as I completely informed Your Majesty on the 30th of November, [1]706. [Thus] we could resist [the enemy] with a larger guard and the inhabitants of this city have some tranquillity after the construction of the heavy line of palisades which on the 30th of September, [1]706, I reported were completed, permitting organization of a company of horse to operate beyond these limits, which might leave, as has been done, to accompany the master carpenters and laborers who go out to labor in the cutting of logs for the royal construction. Nothing of all this has sufficed to prevent the enemy from continuing his constant killings and hostilities, which since the siege they are doing, departing for this purpose from the Indian villages adjacent to Carolina, being aided by the English with guns, ammunition, cutlasses, and pistols, and even being accompanied by some English who urge, incite, and encourage them to these assaults, until they have desolated the entire mainland and the coast of the south and of Carlos, and have carried off, as each day they are carrying, a growing number of these barbarous Indians, for there are not now left any of the Christians which were in Apalachee, Timuqua, Guale, and parts of Mayaca and Jororo. Altogether those they have carried off to sell as slaves must number more than ten or twelve thousand persons. From the aforesaid provinces there will be here gathered about three hundred persons, including men, women, youths, and infants, and even of these they are carrying off and killing some each day while on the excursions they make to procure wood and palm [hearts] for their subsistence. The Indian women fish, and hunt for some wild roots for their use, to which they are tempted, for they could not have sustained themselves alone with the aid and help that I from the royal stores furnished them. Today, day of the date, they cried out to me to report that of those of Jororo and Mayaca who had gone in search of roots, there were carried off some twenty-eight persons, of whom four escaped to give the news.

When fatigue produces the desire to have some stipulation of peace, it will be greatly to the service of God Our Lord, and of Your Majesty, [and to the] comfort and relief of these wretched Indians, if Your Majesty will order that all those of these nations and provinces that are found to have been sold, made captive, or detained in Carolina, be restored to these provinces, and if, in the future, the English neither trade nor barter arms and ammunition with the Indians, as it is by means of these that they have continued to make war on us to the present; and they have become so expert in the handling of arms that they use them as if they were born in this service. And if [peace is] not stipulated, then the consequence follows that they are so excessively given to these hostilities that, although in other parts of Europe and America they make peace, simulated war is always breaking out here, which the English always incite, having the natives on their side. They protect and support them in the use of arms, which, from what is observed, hurts us with them. For which reason the safest [course] is the destruction of this settlement and its re-occupation, as Your Majesty has ordered the viceroy, without regard to the sufficiency of the motives that will have been communicated or will be communicated to Your Majesty, to revoke this order. Since it is a subject of the highest importance to the royal crown, which is of consequence to the future of all these provinces for the propagation of the Holy Evangels, as I have informed Your Majesty by *autos* on the 28th of February, [1]707; and since I am desirous that you gain from this service, I have discussed it at length in this report, because it is my duty from the satisfaction that Your Majesty has given my person by this employment. God protect the Catholic and royal person of Your Majesty many years, as Christianity requires. San Augustín, Florida, January 14, 1708.

Don Francisco de Corcoles y Martínez

44. *Colonel Moore's Letter to Sir Nathaniel Johnson, 16 April, 1704.* [*This date is improbable.*][106]

May it please Your Honour,

To accept of this short Narrative of what I, with the Army under my Command, have been doing since my departure from the Ockmulgee, which was on the 19th of December. On the 14th of January[107] at the Sun rising we came to a Town, a strong and almost regular Fort, called Aiavalla [Ayubale]: At our first Approach the Indians in it fired, and shot Arrows at Us briskly, from which we hid and Sheltered Ourselves under the Side of a great Mud Walled House, til we could take a View of the Fort, and consider of the best way of assaulting it, which we concluded to be by breaking open the Church Doors, which were a part of the Fort, with Axes.

I no sooner proposed this, but my Men readily undertook it, run up to it briskly (the Enemy at the same time shooting at them) were beaten off, without effecting it, and 14 white men wounded. Two hours after that we thought fit to attempt burning the church, which we did, three or four Indians assisting us in it we burnt it. The Indians in it obstinately defended themselves and killed us two men, viz., Francis Plowden and Thomas Dale. After we were within their Fort a Fryar, the only [white] within it, came forth and begged mercy: In this we took 26 men alive and 58 women and children, the Indians took about as many more of each sort. The Fryar told us we killed in the two storms 24 men.

The next morning the Captain of St. Lewis's Fort with 23 Whites and 400 Indians came to fight us, which we did, beat him, and took eight of his men prisoners. And as the Indians (which say they did it) tell us, killed 5 or 6 whites. We have a particular account of 168 Indian men killed and taken in this fight and flight. The Apalatchee Indians say they lost 200, which we have reason to believe the least. In this fight Captain John Berringer, fighting bravely in the head of our men, was killed at my foot. Captain Fox died of a wound given him in our first storming of the fort.

Two days after I sent to the King of the Attachookas [Ivitachuco] (who with 130 men was in his strong and well-made Fort) to come to me to make his peace with me, he did it, and compounded for it with his church plate and led horses leaden with provisions. After this I marched thro' two towns, which have all strong Forts and defenses against small armies [sic],[108] they all submitted and surrendered their Forts to me without conditions. I have now in my company all the whole people of three towns, and the greatest part of four more; we have totally destroyed all the people of two towns, so that we have left in Apalatchee but that one town which compounded with me, part of St. Lewis's and the people of one town which run away altogether, their town, church, and fort, we have burnt. The people of St. Lewis's which remain, come unto me every night. I expect, and have advice, that the town which compounded with me, are coming after me. The waiting for these people make my marches slow; for I am willing to bring away free, as many Indians as I can, this being the address of the commons to order it so. This will make my mens parts of plunder (which otherwise might have been £100 per man) but small, but I hope with your Honour's assistance, to find a way to gratify them for their bold and stout actions, and their great loss of blood. I never saw, or heard, of a stouter or braver thing done than the storming of the fort; it hath regained the reputation we seemed to have lost under the conduct of Captain Mackie, the Indians having now a mighty value for the whites.

Apalatchee is now reduced to that feeble and low condition, that it neither can supply St. Augustine with provisions, or disturb, damage or frighten our Indians living between us and Apalatchee, and the French. In short, we have made Carolina as safe as the conquest of Apalatchee can make it.

If I had not had so many men wounded in our first attempt, I had assaulted St. Lewis's fort, in which is now but 28 or 30 men, and 20 of these came thence from Pensacola to buy provisions the first night after I took the first Fort.

On Sunday the 23rd of this month I came out of Apalatchee settlement, and am now about 30 miles in my way home, but do not expect to reach it til about the middle of March, notwithstanding my horses will not be able to carry me [to the] Cherokee Nations.

I have had a dirty, tedious and uneasy journey, and tho I have no reason to fear any harm from the enemy, thro the difference between the Whites and the Indians, between Indian and Indian, bad way and false alarms, do still labour under hourly uneasinesses. The number of free Apalatchee Indians, which are not under my protection, bound with me to Carolina, are 300; the Indians under my command killed and took prisoners in the plantations, whilst we stormed the Fort, as many Indians as we and they took and killed in the Fort.

I am &

Ja. Moore

45. *Extract of Colonel Moore's letter to the Lords Proprietors, 16 April, 1704.*[109]

I will not trouble Your Lordships with a relation of the many hazards and difficulties I underwent in my expedition against Apalatchee, but beg leave to let you know what I have done there.

By my own interest and at my own charge I raised 50 whites, all the Government thought fit to spare out of the settlement at that time; with them and 1000 Indians, which by my own interest I raised to follow me, I went to Apalatchee: The first place I came to was the strongest Fort in Apalatchee, which after nine hours I took, and in it 200 persons alive, and killed 20 men in the engagement. I had killed 3 whites and 4 Indians; of the last there were but 15 ever came within shot of the Fort. The next morning the Captain of the Fort of St. Lewis and Governor of the Province of Apalatchee, with all the force of Whites and Indians he could raise in the Province came and gave me battle in the field; after half an hour's fight we routed them and in the fight and flight killed six Spaniards, one of which was a Fryar; took the Captain and Governor and Adjutant General and Seven men Spaniards prisoners, and killed and took 200 Indian men. In this fight my Captain was killed and 11 of my Indians. I lay in the field of battle four days, some of my wounded men not being in a condition to march, or to be carried any way in this time. The next strongest Fort was surrendered to me upon conditions. On the 5th day I marched to two more Forts, both which were delivered up to me, without conditions, and the men, women and children of the whole town, which were in it, prisoners at discretion. In one of these Forts I lodged one night; the next day I marched to two more Forts, both [of] which with the people that were in them were delivered to me without conditions, as were the two other Forts. In one of these I lay two nights, here I offered freedom of persons and goods, to as many Kings, as with all the people under their government would go along with me, and live under and subject themselves to our Government. On these terms four Kings and all their people, came away with me, and part of the people of four more Kings; which I have planted among our Indians, and put them out of a capacity of returning back again alone[.] In this expedition I brought away 300 men, and 1000 women and children, have killed, and taken as slaves 325 men, and have taken slaves 4000 women and children; tho I did not make slave, or put to death one man, woman or child but what were taken in the fight, or in the Fort I took by storm. All which I have done with the loss of 4 whites and 15 Indians, and without one penny charge to the publick. Before this expedition we were more afraid of the Spaniards of Apalatchee and their Indians in conjunction the French of Mississippi, and their Indians doing us harm by land, than of any forces of the enemy by sea. This has wholly disabled them from attempting anything against us by land, the whole strength of Apalatchee not exceeding 300 Indians and 24 Whites, who cannot now (as I have seated our Indians) come at me that way, must they must [*sic*] March thro' 300 Indian men our friends, which were before this conquest of Apalatchee (for fear of the Spaniards and their Indians) every day moving to the Northway of us.

That colony of the French which is situated on the River Mississippi, are not the French we have reason to fear; they have seated another colony on a river called Coosa six days journey nearer us than Mississippi, and not above 50 miles from us than Apalatchee. These French and their Indians (if suffered to live where they are now) will be no less a dangerous enemy to us in peace than in war, it being much easier for them to cut off our settlements from this place, than it is for the Canada Indians to cut off the inland towns in New England.

Notes

Introduction

1. In the William L. Clements Library, University of Michigan.
2. Pittman, 1934.
3. Boyd, 1938.
4. De Lacy, 1801.
5. Trunnions.
6. Williams, 1908.
7. Boyd, 1935.
8. Probably no farther than to St. Marks.
9. An explanation of the identifying numerical designations of the Spanish documents may be in order. These indicate their position in the files of the Archivos de Indias (abbreviated as A. I.) in Sevilla, Spain. The first three numbers separated by dashes refer respectively to the *estantes, cajones,* and *legajos* where a document reposes, or (1) the case or cupboard, (2) the shelf thereof, and (3) the number assigned a tied bundle of documents lying thereon. The number to the right of the colon indicates the document, or more usually a package of documents in a *legajo*. In the latter case the pages are numbered.
10. Geiger, 1937.
11. Wenhold, 1936.
12. See Leonard, 1936, 1939; Dunn, 1917; Boyd, 1937.
13. Bolton, 1925.
14. Crane, 1928.
15. Geiger, 1937.
16. Boyd, 1939.
17. Wenhold, 1936.
18. Document 28.
19. Document 42.
20. Leonard, 1939.
21. Document 26.
22. Documents 44, 45.
23. Document 25.
24. Document 44.
25. Wenhold, 1936.
26. Swanton, 1946. Swanton treats of the Apalachians and Yamassees as separate tribes, a distinction which appears to be well grounded. It is therefore singular to observe that the former inhabitants of Apalachee appear to have been inclusively referred to as Yamassees by the elderly Indian informant of Williams and Burch.
27. Smith, 1866.
28. Documents 6, 7.
29. Document 9.
30. Documents 10, 12.

Documents

31. A. I. 58-1-22: 306. 2 pp.
32. This letter of Don Diego was published in Spanish by Buckingham Smith in 1860, in a small folio volume without title page. This letter is notable in that it transmitted to the King, letters written in the Apalachian and Timuquan languages, with accompanying translations into Spanish, from the caciques of Ivitachuco and San Matheo. Both of the letters from the caciques are reproduced in facsimile. See also Gatschet, 1880, page 495.
33. A. I. 54-5-13: 72. 2 pp.
34. A. I. 54-5-13: 73. 4 pp.
35. Governor Torres y Ayala here refers to his transit of Apalachee made in May and June of 1693, when governor-designate. On this occasion he commanded the overland expedition from Apalachee to Pensacola, which was a part of the Pez-Sigüenza operations of that year. See Dunn, 1917 (p. 158, p. 169); Leonard, 1939.
36. See Boyd, 1936. This affords an approximation of the time when the first fort at San Marcos was built. Don Pablo de Hita de Salazar was governor in 1679, although succeeded in 1680 by Don Juan Marqués de Cabrera.
37. A. I. 58-1-26: 136. 5 pp.
38. A. I. 58-1-22: 439. 2 pp.
39. A. I. 54-5-19: 138. 4 pp.
40. For a discussion of the significance of Muscogean terms of rank, see Hawkins, 1848, page 69. The Spaniards refer to the leading Indian of a Christianized village, to whom had been given a Christian name on baptism, as *cacique*, which is probably the equivalent of *mico* or *mic-co*, although several persons in one town might bear the latter title. According to Hawkins, the *mico* superintends all public and domestic concerns, receives all public characters, hears their talks, and presents them to the consideration of the town. He is always chosen from some one family and remains for life, and is usually succeeded by his nephew in the female line. The *mico* generally bears the name of the town, and is by the traders called "king." Next in rank are the *hinijas (ygnaja, enija, eneha, e-ne-hau)*, who are second in command, and have direction of public works and buildings and cultivation of the fields, and are also in charge of the "black drink" ceremony. The title *tus-tun-nug-gee* (tustennuggee) signifies warrior rank.
41. A. I. 58-2-14: 43-43. Pp. 5, 6. This letter was forwarded by Father Antonio from Havana in 1702, with the covering letter of the same year which is presented out of chronological sequence, immediately following. May Father Antonio have considered it necessary to exercise discretion in transmitting this complaint?
42. A. I. 58-2-14: 43-43. Pp. 1-3.
43. Document 12.
44. A. I. 58-1-23: 4. 2 pp.
45. A. I. 58-2-8: B³. Pp. 39-42.
46. A. I. 58-2-2: 84½. 2 pp.
47. A. I. 58-2-8: B³. Pp. 3-6.
48. See comment on this visit in Document 8.

49. A. I. 58-2-8: B³. Pp. 43-45.
50. A. I. 58-2-8: B³. Pp. 7-10.
51. By chance a counteroffensive was in preparation. Almost simultaneously with the departure of Captain Romo with a force of Spaniards and eight hundred Apalachian Indians from Bacuqua, an Englishman, Captain Anthony Dodsworth, set out with a force of several hundred Apalachicolos from Achita. Fortuitously they became aware of each other's presence somewhere along the Flint River. Suspecting that the Spaniards would attempt a surprise attack at night, Dodsworth set the stage and prepared an ambush for the attackers, who were ignominiously routed. See Bolton, 1925, p. 58.

In the topographical memoir on East and West Florida by Captain Hugh Young (1934, p. 83), who accompanied General Andrew Jackson in the latter's raid into Apalachee in 1818, is the following paragraph:

"The ancient possessors of the country now held by the Seminoles were, as stated in the table, the *Palaches* [Apalachees], *Eamusses* [Yamassees], and the *Kalusas*. These tribes were dispossessed by the vagabond Seminoles some time after the first settlement made by the Spaniards. A decisive battle was fought in the fork of Kichafone [Kinchafoone] and Flint in which the three native tribes were defeated and driven to the Spanish Fort St. Rose on Okalokina[;] here they were followed by the Muscogees who after a long siege drove the Spaniards and Indians with great slaughter from post to post out of the country."

It is likely that Young secured his Indian data from John Blount, a Tuckabatchee Indian who served as Jackson's guide. He and his band were given a reservation on the west bank of the Apalachicola River by the Treaty of Moultrie Creek on September 18, 1823, in which is comprised the site of the present town of Blountstown, Florida. Although it is to be regarded as garbled Indian tradition, the above quotation is of interest as affording (1) approximate localization of the site of Captain Romo's defeat, and (2) evidence of garbling in the mention of *Fort St. Rose on Okalokina*. The battle site would be just north of Albany, Georgia, in northern Dougherty County or southern Lee County. The fort on the Ochlockonee River could have been only San Luis, which was within five miles of that river, while it is likely the name St. Rose is derived from the tradition of the second Pensacola located on Santa Rosa Island.

52. The letters reporting the disastrous outcome of this expedition have not been encountered. According to Bolton (1925, page 59), the following pertinent reports are found in A. I. 58-2-18, *Demanda Puesta* (Manuel Solana to the King, October 22, 1702; and Francisco Romo de Uriza to Zúñiga, October 22, 1702).

53. A. I. 58-2-8: B³. Pp. 51-52.
54. For Governor Zúñiga's account of the siege of San Augustín by Governor Moore from November 11 to December 26, 1702, see A. I. 58-2-8: B³. Pp. 22-29, translated by Boyd (1948a). Zúñiga conducted a gallant defense and had successfully repulsed Moore, who ignominiously retreated on the appearance of a Spanish fleet.
55. A. I. 58-2-8: B³. Pp. 47-48.
56. No explanation of this has been encountered.
57. A. I. 58-2-8: B³. Pp. 55-56.

58. See Document 22.

59. Although Manuel Solana's letter (Document 17) is dated at San Luis, all, or at least the last part, was evidently written in Ivitachuco. He becomes quite despondent after his mention of Captain Roque's passing. One may surmise, from Document 18, that the despondency may be attributable to the disclosure by Captain Roque of his mission to Pensacola, an assignment which Don Manuel evidently coveted.

60. A. I. 58-2-8: B³. Pp. 81-83.

61. A. I. 58-1-23: 253. 2 pp.

62. A. I. 58-2-8: B³. Pp. 85-87.

63. The illegibility is insuperable in the case of certain key words in the first and last paragraphs, which deal with stockades. As a consequence, the complete sense of these paragraphs cannot be rendered, and hence the last paragraph has been omitted. The first paragraph does suggest that the bastioned stockade shown about the blockhouse in Figure 4 was constructed at a date much later than the blockhouse proper, probably not until shortly before the evacuation. It also appears that the church and convent were similarly enclosed.

64. A. I. 58-2-8: B³. Pp. 65-68.

65. See Document 25.

66. A. I. 58-2-8: B³. Pp. 59-61.

67. It may be inferred that the measures of corn, etc. referred to are *fanegas*, approximately a bushel or slightly more. *Jergueta* is a rough, coarse fabric, probably woolen.

68. Twenty-five pounds.

69. See Document 42 for an account of the fate of Father Criado. During the course of the excavation of the Jefferson County mission site tentatively identified as that of San Francisco de Oconi by Mr. Hale Smith, Assistant Archeologist of the Florida Park Service, there were encountered two matching sherds of a *tinaja* with the following incised inscription (incomplete) "Pᵉ Pʳᵉ Cria" and a broken letter, evidently a "d" at the right edge of the second fragment. The original vessel undoubtedly belonged to Father Criado.

70. A. I. 58-1-27: 64. 4 pp.

71. Carroll (1836), in reproducing Moore's letter to the governor of South Carolina, as copied from the *Boston News* of May 1, 1704, gives the date of the attack on Ayubale (Ayaville) as the 14th of December, while the transcript of this letter contained in "Spanish Papers" MSS, Library of Congress, VI, 892-6, later presented as Document 44, gives the date as January 14th. The January date, rather than that of December, is regarded as correct, which is corroborated in effect by Zúñiga's letter. The discordance between the 14th and 25th of January in the two accounts is due to the calendars observed by the respective nations. Although Pope Gregory XIII introduced the Gregorian Calendar, or New Style, in March 1582, which was immediately introduced into Spain, the English continued to observe the Julian Calendar until 1750 (Old Style), and during the eighteenth century the accumulated difference between the two calendars amounted to eleven days. Hence the 14th of Moore is the 25th of Zúñiga. The English did not initiate use of the New Style until 1752, when it was decreed that the day following the 2nd of September be counted as the 14th. (*Encyclopaedia Britannica*).

72. A. I. 58-1-20: 65. 2 pp.
73. Of the priests who signed this petition, Fray Domingo Criado, who evidently had been *doctrinero* or missionary at San Francisco de Oconi, experienced martyrdom (see Document 42), and Fray Tiburicio de Osorio is stated by Geiger (1940) to have been reported as killed in Apalachee during the troubles of 1704, although he is not elsewhere mentioned in these documents. He may have been the priest mentioned as carried off as a captive, in a supplemental document listed in the introduction, during 1706. Fray Lorenzo Santos, according to Geiger, was stationed at San Luis in 1704. He and the others not specifically mentioned survived the disasters.
74. A. I. 58-1-20: 92-92². (*Cf*. Documents 44, 45). 6 pp.
75. A. I. 58-2-7/2. Pp. 65-72.
76. The facts expressed in the following document (No. 27) are based on the present letter of Manuel Solana. It is evident that in the early Spanish transcript of this letter which we follow, there has been an important omission from Document 26 at this point.
77. The capture of the seven men who had disregarded the order of Manuel Solana to "ascend the river (from San Marcos) in a canoe to a landing place which is three leagues from here [i.e., San Luis]" affords an interesting problem in present-day topography, as there is now no water channel in communication with St. Marks which approaches within seven and one-half or eight miles of the site of San Luis. Neither is there any reason to attribute the statement of three, as the number of leagues, to a copyist's error. San Marcos (present-day St. Marks) was, and is, located at the point of the confluence of the Wakulla and St. Marks rivers. It is interesting to note that on Brasier's map of the fort at this site, made shortly after the British occupation, the Wakulla River is called the Guacára, and the St. Marks River the Detacabona (Boyd, 1936, p. 10). The word Wakulla is evidently an orthographic variant of Guacára. The Suwannee River was known to the Spaniards as San Juan de Guacára (*vide ante*). While the meaning of this word is obscure, it may be significant that both streams exhibit characteristics of solution topography, being largely fed by numerous springs. Be that as it may, it would appear that compliance with Solana's order would require ascent of the Wakulla River, which today would end at its source in Wakulla Spring, distant from San Luis in an almost north-south line a matter of fifteen miles, or about six leagues. If one refers to the map sheets of the Arran and Tallahassee quadrangles of the United States Geological Survey, it will be noted that about two miles below Wakulla Spring, the river receives, on the north side, a small, swampy stream known as McBride Slough, the open channel of which does not extend for more than a mile and one-half above its mouth. Near the mouth, and for about two miles above, its margins are delimited by the ten-foot contour. At about this distance the twenty-foot contours converge toward it from the east and west, and extend northward in a sinuous but roughly parallel course, at a distance of from one-half to one-eighth of a mile apart, until they unite in the channel of Bradford Brook, just a short distance below its origin as the outlet of Lake Munson. Bradford Brook now runs about two and three-quarter miles directly south from Lake Munson, to discharge into and terminate in a group of ponds without

surface outlet, which lie below the twenty-foot contour. It is obvious that the twenty-foot contour marks the course of an abandoned and poorly eroded stream bed, which once discharged the water of Lake Munson into the Wakulla River. The headwaters of this stream, marked by the present-day Bradford Brook, have been captured for subterranean conduction by the sink ponds into which the brook now discharges. In my opinion, in which I am permitted to say that Dr. Herman Gunter, Florida State Geologist, concurs, in the year 1704, when Manuel Solana was writing, this capture of the headwaters of this stream had not been effected, and canoes from the Wakulla River actually could ascend Bradford Brook a mile or more above the present ponds, to a landing place at about the three leagues' distance Solana gives. It is well known that the limestone formation of Florida is extensively honeycombed by unexplored underground solution passages, and that from time to time new surface connections with these passages are established. The sinkhole, marked by one or more of the ponds mentioned, which through capture of the waters of Bradford Brook desiccated the greater portion of McBride Slough, must have opened subsequent to 1704. It is likely that tree trunks and other obstructions made the navigation of this channel difficult and slow. Perhaps for this reason, as well as in order to keep knowledge of its existence a secret, it was not likely in common use. It is probable that for these reasons these men disobeyed, with consequent capture, the order of Manuel Solana.

78. A. I. 58-2-7/2. Pp. 60-61.
79. This trip of Joseph del Pozo from San Luis to San Augustín is something of an epic. Nothing is said of the hour of his departure from San Luis, nor whether he was afoot or mounted, although the latter may be inferred. In order to reduce risk of detection, it is likely that he left San Luis after dark on the night of the 8th. He made the approximately 200-mile journey in less than three and one-half days.
80. A. I. 58-2-7/2. Pp. 62-65.
81. A. I. 58-2-7/2. Pp. 10-13.
82. A. I. 58-2-7/2. Pp. 13-14.
83. A. I. 58-2-7/2. Pp. 15-17.
84. See also Documents 33, 34, and 42. Many, if not all, of these Apalachian refugees finally settled adjacent to the French at Mobile. According to Peter J. Hamilton (1897, Chapter XIII), they were furnished a missionary and had a chapel of their own, the records of which still survive. The earliest baptism of an Apalachian recorded was in the fall of 1704. While Apalachians are mentioned in Mobile parish records as late as 1751, it is likely that many had earlier returned to their original home.
85. A. I. 58-2-23: 305. 7 pp.
86. A. I. 58-2-2: 83½. 3 pp.
87. In A. I. 58-2-8: B289 (not seen) is a list of the silver brought from the church at Apalachee when it was abandoned, dated August 19, 1704, and signed by Manuel Solana. It will be noted that Moore claimed (Document 44) that the chief of a village, apparently referring to Ivitachuco, compounded by the surrender of the church plate.
88. A. I. 58-2-7/2. Pp. 44-45.

89. A. I. 58-2-2: 84½. Pp. 3-6.
90. This came to pass.
91. See Document 11.
92. A. I. 58-2-7/2. Pp. 17-18.
93. A. I. 58-2-7/2. Pp. 19-22.
94. The following data may throw some light on the fate of the three pieces of artillery mentioned. John Lee Williams visited the site of San Luis on October 31, 1823, and left three descriptions of the site. At that time he observed two pieces. The first was written in his journal (Williams, 1908, p. 22):

> "It is situated on a commanding eminence at the north point of a high narrow neck of highlands nearly surrounded by a deep ravine and swamp. The moat, parapet and bastions are strongly marked. The south front is 70 paces in length, the north 55 paces. Near a spring in the east ravine two old six-pounders were discovered; the breach of one and the muzzle of the other were broken off. They were very long and rough cast; we could not discover on them either letters or figures."

His second reference (Williams, 1823) is contained in a letter written to R. K. Call on November 1, 1823, while still in the Tallahassee country:

> ". . . an old Spanish Fort on a commanding hill about half way from Oclockney to Tallahassee. The south line of it measured 71 paces, the north 55, the east and west ends about 46. It had bastions near the angles, and in a spring about 50 feet down the ravine east of the works we discovered the breach of a six pound field piece, and near it another piece of the same dimensions, from which the muzzle was broken."

His third description (Williams, 1827) is as follows:

> "Fort St. Lewis was situate 2 miles west of Tallahassee. Its form was an irregular parallelogram; the eastern and longest side was 52 paces [sic]. Within the moat, 2 brick edifices had been erected, one 60 by 40 and the other 30 by 20 feet. There were bastions at each corner. The outward defenses were extensive. A covered way lead to a spring, in a deep ravine, under the northeast wing of the fort. Here were discovered two broken cannon, one of them having only the muzzle broken off; this has been removed to Tallahassee. . . . "

What may have been a third piece is mentioned under "Miscellany" in the *Pensacola Gazette* of February 26, 1825, as follows:

> "Tallahassee, Jan. 8, 1825. A dinner was served by Mr. Wyatt at his hotel, in honor of the anniversary of the victory of New Orleans. A cannon of a six-pound caliber, which had been found in July last, covered with rubbish in old Fort St. Louis, and had probably been silent for ages, performed its function in the celebration of the day."

95. A. I. 58-2-7/2. Pp. 41-43.
96. A. I. 58-2-14: 54-54'. 18 pp.
97. For the significance of this expression, see Haggard, 1941, p. 45.
98. One may speculate whether the religious of this name is the same individual who led the expedition of 1686 into the Upper Creek country (see Boyd, 1937). Although he is listed by Father Geiger (1940), nothing is stated of

his rank in the order. He is not given any ecclesiastical title when later mentioned in this same document by Manuel Solana, *hijo*. If actually a *lego* or lay brother, it would seem likely these names refer to the same person.

99. A. I. 58-2-7/2. Pp. 138-144.
100. A. I. 58-2-7/2. Pp. 137-139.
101. A. I. 58-2-14: 61. 6 pp.
102. *Ilex vomitoria*, Yaupon.
103. This refers to Father Francisco de Avila (personal communication, Father Geiger).
104. The year should be 1697, and the priest was Father Luis Sanchez (personal communication, Father Geiger).
105. A. I. 58-1-28: 32. 5 pp.
106. From "Spanish Papers," MSS, Library of Congress, VI, 892-6. *(Cf.* B. R. Carroll, 1836, Vol. II, pp. 375-6).
107. The account in Carroll (1836) says they came to Ayavalla on December 14th, a very evident misprint. The Carroll version states that the Captain of St. Lewis's Fort was made a prisoner, and gives the name of the English captain killed as Bellinger. This version gives the name of the town whose cacique compounded as *Ibitachka,* suggestive of Ivitachuco. In the Carroll version the claim is made that he marched to five towns and gives Robert Macken as the name of the leader under whom prestige with the Indians was lost. This also speaks of the point on the return route as Cheeraque's Mountain, and finally gives 1300 as the number of Indians under his protection, with 100 slaves. According to the Carroll version this letter was "Dated in the woods 50 miles north and east of Apalatchia." From the chronology of the letter to the Lords Proprietors, it would appear that the date 23rd given, relates to the month of January (O.S.).
108. Arms.
109. "Spanish Papers," Library of Congress, VI, 888.

SECTION II.

A Spanish Mission Site in Jefferson County, Florida

by

HALE G. SMITH

The Site and the Excavations

DOCUMENTARY studies on the Spanish missions of Apalachee, particularly the preceding paper by Dr. Mark F. Boyd, have cast considerable light on this important phase of the history of Spanish Florida, but prior to the excavation which is to be described in this report the archaeological remains of the period were unknown.[1] The finding of the probable site of San Francisco de Oconee, about 23 miles southeast of Tallahassee, disclosed the material culture of a mission destroyed in 1704 and led to the definition of the Leon-Jefferson Period. Evidence from the excavation supplemented knowledge based on the written word.

Before discussing the actual excavations at this mission site, it might be well to insert some brief notes on the mission period in this part of Florida and on the Indians who lived in the area, even though the latter part of the mission period is fully covered in Boyd's portion of the present volume.

Between the Ochlockonee and Aucilla rivers, and from the Gulf of Mexico into the present state of Georgia, was the territory of the Apalachee Indians in early historic times, although other groups such as the Oconee were also found in the area. The mission site investigated falls near the eastern boundary of this area, the Aucilla River, beyond which was Timucua territory. The Apalachee were a Muskhogean group about which relatively little is known.[2] Most of the information on the ethnography of these people is of a secondary nature or is mentioned casually by the narrators of the journeys of Narváez and De Soto. The Apalachee, who were primarily agricultural, grew maize, squash, and beans—a diet which they supplemented by hunting and collecting. They put up a very strong resistance to the first two Spanish expeditions into their territory—those of Narváez and De Soto. However, by 1607 they had seemingly changed their attitude toward the Spaniards and were asking for missionaries to come to their area to baptize them.

Missionary work among the Apalachee was begun in 1633. The missionization was not totally altruistic, as the Spaniards found that the fertile soil of west Florida could supply a surplus of corn, sorely needed for the inhabitants of St. Augustine. Foodstuffs from the province of Apalachee were shipped by sea from St. Marks to St. Augustine, or were carried on the more difficult overland route. During the mission period there were native rebellions in 1638 and 1647.[3] The Timucua rebellion of 1656 also involved the Apalachee. These uprisings were aimed against Spanish rule and the Church, which was itself a symbol of European dominance, and were apparently not participated in by the whole Apalachee group, but by reactionary factions within the tribe or confederation. After the native revolt in 1647 had been suppressed, the Apalachee were compelled to furnish laborers annually for the building of the fort at St. Augustine. Although the Indians made many unnoticed appeals to be freed from this work, this servitude was maintained until 1704.

In 1704 James Moore of South Carolina, with fifty British soldiers and about thirteen hundred Creek Indians, raided the province of Apalachee, burned the missions, and took as slaves many of the Indians. Those who were not killed or taken as slaves moved west to the Mobile area and never returned to their original homeland, but resettled in the Pensacola area at a later date. The story of this destruction of the Apalachee missions is told in detail, by the actors themselves, in the documents translated by Boyd in the first portion of this volume.

As is so often the case, the archaeologist did not set out deliberately to find this site, nor did he even stumble upon it. Information concerning the location came from Boyd, whose long interest in the Spanish mission period made him invaluable throughout the period of excavation and analysis of the site. Boyd had published a paper on the probable locations of Spanish missions in west Florida, based on documentary sources and supplemented by a knowledge of areas on which items presumably of Spanish times had been found.[4] The excavated site was one of the areas on which Boyd knew that the presumptive mission period materials could be found. His own knowledge of the site came originally from J. Clarence Simpson of the Florida Geological Survey, who had discovered that the owner of the site, Scott Miller, had plowed up five complete *tinaja* vessels.[5] Two of these vessels survive, Boyd and Simpson each having one. Simpson had also found that nails, pottery, and burned clay were prolific on the surface.

A Spanish Mission Site

With this information at his disposal, Boyd visited the site in 1940 and conducted a small test excavation in what developed to be a very rich section of the site. In this test operation he obtained an iron lance head (Pl. VI, 11), a sword or dagger guard (Pl. VI, 10), part of an iron hoe (Pl. VI, 13), an iron spring lock (Pl. VIII, 12), a large key (Pl. VIII, 11), an iron chisel-shaped pin, and an ornate wrought iron slide bolt (Pl. VIII, 2). About sixty hand-wrought nails were found in one small test trench, and a small fragment of a marble slab, possibly part of the altar stone, was also found. Materials from other collections at this site included a few potsherds (Willey, 1949, p. 301) and a small section of chain mail found by Montague Tallant.[6] These artifacts, which showed a blending of Spanish and aboriginal cultures, were sufficiently different from other known artifacts to indicate a new complex. In view of the number and nature of the specimens found, and the presence of burned clay indicating structure, the site was a logical one on which to inaugurate archaeological studies of the Spanish mission period. The excavation substantiated surface indications and led to the definition of the Leon-Jefferson complex.

Surface material which came largely from the area to the west and southwest of the mission buildings was found during the excavation. Spanish and aboriginal artifacts were so numerous in several places that the surface indications led to the belief that there were other habitations in this area, but testing revealed no remains of floor, walls, posts, or firepits. If such habitations had existed, they were evidently of such a nature as to be destroyed by plowing. Some obviously later materials, such as a section of iron kettle with a handle and four pieces of cut glass, were found on the surface and undoubtedly date from the plantation period. A complete listing of surface finds is included in Appendix B.

This Spanish mission site is located approximately 23 miles southeast of Tallahassee, in Jefferson County, Florida.[7] It is situated on a hilltop, or plateau, in the Tallahassee Red Hills,[8] 2.1 miles south and 1.1 miles east of the town of Waukeenah. The hills of this area are irregular and the valleys display some discontinuity and apparent lack of a drainage system,[9] but the area has numerous limestone sinks, several of which are within 500 yards of the site. Its elevation is between 250 and 300 feet, making it one of the highest areas in this section. Some 9 miles to the east is the Aucilla River, and 3 miles to the southwest is the Wacissa River. Lake Miccosukee lies 10 miles

to the north. About 2 miles south of the site the Red Hills drop off
sharply into the low, swampy, and sandy area bordering the Gulf of
Mexico on the west coast of Florida. Previously this would have
been an area of hardwood and pine forests, with occasional clearings
for aboriginal agriculture, but today most of the land is planted in
tung-oil trees or agricultural crops.

The identification of the particular mission which was excavated
might be of considerable significance in interpreting the ceramic relationships, for it is known that various tribal groups besides the
Apalachee inhabited the region in mission times. Since a complete
survey of the mission sites, particularly those in the eastern part of
the Apalachee area, has not been undertaken, it is impossible at this
time to make a positive identification. A probable identification as
San Francisco de Oconee can, however, be made.

The excavated mission falls between two points on the mission chain
which can be identified today: San Luis to the west of Tallahassee;
and the Aucilla River. In a direct line these two points are 31 miles
apart, and according to Bishop Calderón's list of 1675, there were
nine missions in this area, including San Luis.[10] Part of the difficulty
of positive identification lies in the exact boundary between Timucua
and Apalachee territories. This is always stated to be the Aucilla
River, and if such is literally the case, San Miguel de Asyle, the last
mission in Timucua territory, would be on or near the east bank,
while San Lorenzo de Hibitachuco, the first mission in Apalachee
territory, would be on the west side. There is, however, the possibility,
which must be borne in mind, that the actual boundary fluctuated
somewhat and that the Aucilla River was merely taken as a convenient
marker by the early writers. If this were the case, either San Miguel
or San Lorenzo might be on the opposite side of the river from their
customarily interpreted positions.

The total distance from San Miguel to San Luis is from 15 to 16
leagues, depending upon the informant used (see table 1).[11] This
is a remarkable correspondence. Since Calderón rounds his leagues to
whole numbers, while Fernández de Florencia gives half-leagues, it
may be assumed that the latter's figures are more accurate. On the
basis of 2.6 miles to a league, the distance from San Miguel to San
Luis is between 39 and 42 miles. This is considerably more than the
31 miles measured from San Luis to the Aucilla River, but it must
be remembered that the missions were not located on a straight line.
Even taking the circuitousness of the route into consideration, it is

probable that the distance to San Miguel would place it to the east of the Aucilla River, which lends support to the contention that the river actually was the tribal boundary between Timucua and Apalachee.

It will be recalled that the Aucilla River lies about 9 miles east of the excavated mission site, or, transferring the measurement into Spanish leagues, about 3.5 leagues. Site M-1 is located 11.75 miles, or 4.5 leagues, southeast of the excavated site and to the east of the Aucilla River. As this site yields material similar to that from the excavated site, it may be presumed to be another mission.[12] If this site is San Miguel, and it may well be, it is 1 league east of the Aucilla. About 2 miles south of Lamont, some 9 miles from the excavated mission site, a cache of about forty small bronze bells was unearthed.[13] This is about the right distance from site M-1 to have been San Lorenzo, if the former were San Miguel. If the mission trail were a straight line, 3 leagues from the postulated San Lorenzo would bring us to the excavated site, at which distance it should be San Juan. As the route was not straight, however, the excavated site might more reasonably be assumed to be San Francisco de Oconee.

To the west of the excavated site there are two other known sites which produce materials of the mission period, within about a league of one another. This fact strengthens the identification of the excavated site as San Francisco, for it will be noted in table 1 that these could

TABLE 1
THE MISSIONS OF APALACHEE IN 1675

Mission	Calderón Distance	Fernández de Florencia Distance	Population
San Miguel de Asyle (Timucua)			40
San Lorenzo de Hibitachuco	2 lgs.	1½ lgs.	1,200
La Concepción de Ayubali	1 lg.	1½ lgs.	800
San Francisco de Oconee	1 lg.	½ lg. plus	200
San Juan de Aspalaga	1 lg.	1 lg.	800
San Joseph de Ocuya	2 lgs.	1½ lgs.	900
San Pedro de Patali	4 lgs.	4 lgs.	500
San Antonio de Bacuqua	2 lgs.	2 lgs.	120
San Damian de Cupahica (Escambi)	2 lgs.	2 lgs.	900
San Luis de Talimali	1 lg.	1 lg.	1,400
Totals	16 lgs.	15 lgs.	6,860

readily be San Juan and San Joseph, but could not very easily be San Joseph and San Pedro, as the latter is 4 leagues from the former. A study of the locations of the known sites that contain mission period materials thus suggests the tentative identification of the site as that of San Francisco de Oconee. This conclusion is further strengthened by the population data from Florencia. La Concepción, San Juan, and San Joseph all have more than four times the population of San Francisco. The excavated site is much more in keeping with a group of two hundred than it is with a group of eight or nine hundred.[14]

Only when all mission sites have been located and studied can positive identifications be made. It must be borne in mind that it was possible for a mission to move its location yet retain its name, which complicates the problem by introducing the possibility that two archaeological sites may actually be the same mission at different periods of time. Our listings and distances are as of 1675. The end date of 1704 ascribed to the excavated site is based upon the assumption that the destruction by burning was the result of Moore's raids—an assumption that is strengthened considerably, almost to the point of certainty, by the finding of sherds incised with the name of Father Criado, a priest known to have been in the area at that time.

The importance of determining which mission was excavated is inherent in the name of the one which we believe it probably to have been. The Indians who occupied San Francisco were Oconee rather than Apalachee.

In February of 1947, the writer, accompanied by Dr. Mark F. Boyd and John W. Griffin, visited the site and made arrangements for excavation. The area had been freshly plowed, and the locations of the two mission buildings, in the form of red burned clay wall rubble, were quite evident. The surface of the ground yielded many nails, Spanish and aboriginal sherds, and other objects.

Actual excavation began with the establishing of a central axis which would approximately bisect both of the areas containing building refuse.[15] The site area was then staked out in 50-foot squares, each of which was designated by a capital letter (see site map, fig. 2). A system of 5-foot squares was laid out within each of the larger 50-foot areas. Sections A and D were the sites of the two mission buildings found, whereas Section E was a borrow pit from which the clay for the construction of the buildings had been procured, and which later became a refuse pit. It was discovered that Miller, who had

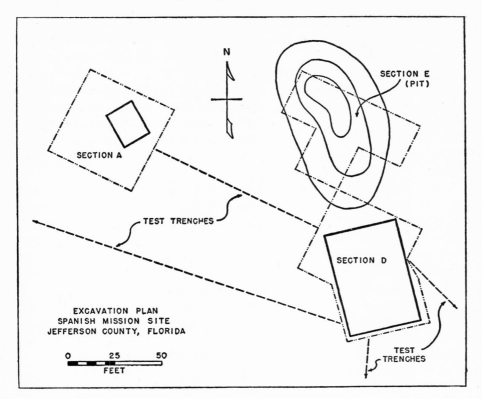

N

SECTION E
(PIT)

SECTION A

TEST TRENCHES

SECTION D

EXCAVATION PLAN
SPANISH MISSION SITE
JEFFERSON COUNTY, FLORIDA

0   25   50
FEET

TEST
TRENCHES

FIGURE 2

started clearing the land and planting corn from the time of acquisition in 1917, had cut into the packed clay floor of one of the buildings with his plow. Until 1946 he had plowed only to a depth of 6 inches, but in the winter of 1946-47 he deepened the zone to 8 inches. This slight additional depth of plowing cut into the building badly.

Initially, in Sections A and D, the top 8 inches of the surface burden, which was disturbed soil, were removed, with materials from each square being kept separate. This procedure was followed because it was obvious that the plowing would cause a certain number of the surface artifacts to drift; those artifacts in the top 6 to 8 inches would be displayed both laterally and forward with the direction of the plowing. Below this disturbed area was a level averaging 2 to 4 inches in thickness immediately above the floor. The cultural items at this level and those on the floor were placed together. In the borrow pit, Section E, the greatest depth of which was 8 feet 4 inches, a vertical slicing technique was used. Most of the cultural materials found in the excavation came from this area because, as stated above, after the clay was removed it was used as a refuse pit.

After excavation of the above areas had been completed, trenches were extended in all directions in an attempt to locate other buildings or features. The whole 20-acre field showed surface evidence of occupation, but trenching did not disclose any more buildings. It had been assumed that the mission was palisaded, but the excavations did not substantiate that belief.

The Buildings and Their Contents

FROM THE EXCAVATION OF THIS SITE, tentatively identified as San Francisco de Oconee, it has been possible to reconstruct the probable appearance of the mission settlement at the time of its occupancy. A conjectural restoration constitutes the frontispiece of this volume. Prior to this excavation, the floor plans of Spanish mission buildings in Florida were unknown. The excavation uncovered the floor plans of two buildings (figs. 2-4), both of which were basically similar, although they probably had served different purposes. The floors of the buildings rested on a light sandy soil, and were made of packed red clay or red clay mixed with sand and then packed. Destruction of the buildings by fire had partially baked the floors and the daub walls.

The wattle and daub technique used in the construction involves a framework of poles (wattle) covered with clay (daub). The framework was composed of vertical posts set in the ground at irregular intervals of from 3 to 18 inches. The horizontal wattles, which were interlaced through the vertical wattles and tied with thongs of leather, seem to have been placed closer together than the vertical posts. The daub, which was obtained from a red clay pit (Section E) 50 feet north of the larger of the two buildings, was made of a mixture of puddled clay and a dry fibrous medium, probably dry grasses, and was plastered over the wattles on both sides until the wall was from 6 to 8 inches thick. Both sides of the walls were then smoothed and the interior was coated with white plaster 1 to 3 mm. thick. This plaster was probably made by burning sea shells, thus reducing them to a powdered lime which was mixed with water.

Nails and spikes were used in fastening together the hewn beams and rafters, and a tie beam was placed along the top of the wall and secured to the vertical upright posts by nails. The square, hand-wrought nails which had large heads and which were apparently the work of local blacksmiths, varied from 3.5 to 29.5 cm. in length (Pl. VIII, 8). Of the 680 nails found at this site, 74.4 per cent formed a group between 6 and 11.5 cm. in length, and may be regarded as the "standard" nails. Shorter and longer specimens were probably made for specific purposes. Available evidence would seem to indicate that on the gabled ends of the roof, and on the crossbeams down the center line, king posts supported the principal rafters. The rafters formed 4-foot eaves which protected the daub walls and lessened their weathering. The roof was lathed with small light material, such as saplings, and thatched with palmetto leaves or tree bark.

The most common variety of aboriginal pottery at the site is tempered with grit and sand in small to abundant amounts which yield a paste that is moderately to coarsely grained. This is here called Jefferson Ware.[1] While the vast majority of the sherds of Jefferson Ware are plain, four types of complicated stamped designs are found (Pl. XI, 7-11). Many of the complicated stamped specimens are too obscured by scraping to permit identification of motif. The rims are frequently pinched or punctated (Pl. XI, 12-16). The next most common pottery type is called Miller Plain. It is characterized by a smooth surface and a black core, and is found most frequently in shallow bowl or plate forms, often with an annular ring base (Pl. XI, 5-6).

The technique of decoration by stamping is found in Jefferson Complicated Stamped and in one other type. This is Leon Check Stamped, characterized by large checks (Pl. XI, 18-19). Incision as a technique is used on four types, only one of which, Aucilla Incised, is a new type defined from this site (Pl. XII, 1-2). The other three—Pinellas Incised (Pl. XII, 6-9), Ocmulgee Fields Incised (Pl. XII, 3-5), and a type close to Lamar Bold Incised—have been found in other sites and areas. Perhaps the most interesting new type is Mission Red Filmed (Pl. XI, 1-4), which is red painted, either in zones or overall, and which usually exists in a plate form with annular ring base showing European influence. A plain ware with a gritty paste was not too uncommon at the site, and a few sherds of Alachua Cob-Marked, defined from central Florida, were found.

Although over 65 per cent of the pottery is aboriginal, the remaining sherds, of non-aboriginal derivation, form an important part of the Leon-Jefferson complex. The vast majority of these non-aboriginal sherds are from Spanish jars, or *tinajas*, and are mostly unglazed (Pl. X, 10-12). A very interesting group of material is formed by the glazed majolica-like pieces which we have called Hispano-Mexican (Pl. X, 1-7). Louis R. Caywood believes that these sherds were made in Puebla, Mexico, in the colonial period. The non-aboriginal ceramics also include two sherds of Chinese porcelain, and four fragments which can probably be attributed to the later American plantation period.

The distributional summary of all pottery types is given in table 2.

TABLE 2
POTTERY FROM THE SCOTT MILLER SITE

Type	Section A	D	E	Surface	Total	Per cent
Mission Red Filmed	29	6	33	7	75	0.87
Miller Plain	40	38	480	25	583	6.75
Aucilla Incised	36	6	80	10	132	1.53
Pinellas Incised	0	0	6	0	6	0.06
Ocmulgee Fields Incised	0	6	6	0	12	0.13
Lamar-like Bold Incised	0	1	1	0	2	0.02
Leon Check Stamped	11	4	49	5	69	0.80
Alachua Cob-Marked	0	2	0	1	3	0.03
Jefferson Ware						
Type A Complicated Stamped	116	36	34	12	198	2.29
Type B Complicated Stamped	4	0	11	0	15	0.17
Type C Complicated Stamped	0	0	7	0	7	0.08
Type D Complicated Stamped	0	1	13	0	14	0.16
Plain Body	990	850	1,028	585	3,453	40.09
Pinched and Punctated Rims	51	19	104	30	204	2.36
Residual Complicated Stamp	398	54	312	129	893	10.37
Unique Complicated Stamped	2	3	10	0	15	0.17
Gritty Plain	29	24	93	56	202	2.33
Hispano-Mexican	22	23	88	13	146	1.69
Spanish *tinaja*	322	1,789	221	95	2,427	28.18
Chinese		2			2	0.02
Lusterware		2			2	0.02
English porcelain				151	151	1.75
Totals	2,050	2,866	2,576	1,119	8,611	99.87

The artifacts, other than pottery, are discussed in the portion of the paper dealing with the area in which they were found.

Mission Building, Section A

The building in Section A was the smaller of the two excavated and appears not to have been so substantial a structure as the building in Section D. The floor was of red clay 1 to 3 inches thick, but only in the northwest quarter of the building did a hard-baked clay floor exist (fig. 3). This baked clay area had a basin form and was roughly oval in shape, its longest diameters being 3 feet 9.5 inches by 2 feet 10.5 inches. This area might have been either the site of a fireplace or the remnant of a more extensive baked clay floor area destroyed during plowing, although if more of this baked clay floor area existed prior to plowing, other scattered areas should have been in-

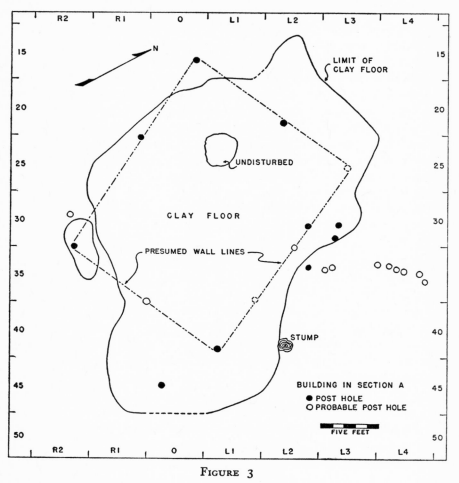

FIGURE 3

tact, as the plow marks that occurred on the floor were 1 foot apart and "bit" into the floor at a maximum depth of not over 1.5 inches.

The red-clay floor area extended out from the floor plan of the building to a distance in some areas of 9 feet, but it is believed that this extension was the result of erosion of the walls after destruction.

As this area was not very extensive, it could not indicate walls of any great height. If walls had existed up to the eaves, they would have been baked during the conflagration and the baked pieces would have come to light during the excavation. No sections of the baked wall rubble showed evidence of plaster, and only a few pieces had any wattle impressions.

From the centers of the corner posts the building measured 19 feet 10 inches by 16 feet 3 inches (fig. 3). The actual measurements for the four sides vary by a few inches, the east and west sides varying .5 inch and the north and south sides varying 8.5 inches. The vertical posts used to support the roof and walls were of pine, 6 to 8 inches in diameter; some were split logs, whereas others utilized the total diameter of the trees. The distance between the upright posts varied from 2 feet 2.5 inches to 11 feet 3.5 inches when measured from the center of the post. The posts not charred during the burning probably rotted away or were consumed by termites, and the holes subsequently became filled with white sand.

The walls of this building were low, not over 2 feet in height, and probably occurred only on two or three sides. This conclusion was reached because of the very small amount of wall rubble on the surface and at floor level. The wall lines themselves could not be traced because of deep plowing. It is believed that the wattle and daub walls that did occur were not burned intensively during the fire and were subsequently weathered and dissolved by rains and washed outward from the building. If they had been burned and baked into a brick-like texture like those of the larger mission building, there would still be evidences of them in the immediate area. Aside from the charred posts, there was little evidence of charcoal of any type over the whole of Section A. The majority of the nails were in or near the northwestern quarter of the building and gave the impression that the structure collapsed in that direction. For the most part, they were in debris 2 to 6 inches above the floor. Very few were found in comparison to those found in and around the other building, thus supporting the theory that this building was less substantial.

Most of the Spanish and aboriginal artifacts found at floor level in this section were within the limits of the building, although some did occur throughout the excavated area. Potsherds, always the most numerous of artifactual materials, were of both Spanish and aboriginal types and were found in the same proportions to one another throughout the building area and its immediate surroundings. The tooth of a domestic pig and very small fragments of unidentifiable bone were found at floor level.[2]

Several unique Spanish pieces were found in this area, including a flintlock striker (Pl. VI, 7), an eight-pointed spur rowel (Pl. IX, 1), and a blue glass bead with thin white vertical lines, the only one found at this site. Of particular interest was the brass figure from a crucifix (Pl. V, 3), found in the top 8 inches of soil, 10 feet from the west wall of the building.[3]

Also of great interest were Spanish *tinaja* sherds with incised markings. Most of these bore incised "X" marks, either singly or in pairs, but one sherd had two complete letters and sections of two others scratched on its surface, which could be recognized as part of a word beginning with *Cria*. In 1940 Boyd had found an inscribed sherd bearing the letters *Pe Pre* and a segment of the arc of yet another letter. Amazingly enough, the two sherds fitted together perfectly, the segment on Boyd's sherd being a portion of the *C* on the other one (Pl. V, 1). The *Pe Pre* probably stands for *Padre Predicador* or "Preaching Father,"[4] while the *Cria* is an unusual combination of letters in Spanish. Boyd soon found a reference which cast further illumination on the specimen, for there was a Father Criado present in Apalachee who died as a result of the raids of the British and Indians in 1704.[5] The finding of the name of a man actually known to have been present at that time provided proof that the site dated from the end of the Spanish mission period in Apalachee.

A number of stone artifacts, including a small triangular projectile point, were found in this area, as well as eighty-eight iron nails, molten brass fragments, and four flat pieces of green glass. For a complete listing of the artifacts found in Section A, see Appendix B.

Mission Building, Section D

The building in Section D was the larger of the two structures excavated and probably consisted of two adjoining structures with a walled area enclosing the rectangle on the west and half of the north and south sides (fig. 4). The whole building complex, two adjoining structures and patio, covered an area 58 feet 4 inches by 39 feet 3 inches, with the orientation of the building being in a north-south direction. The larger of the two rooms was in the southeast corner of the area, with the smaller room being situated in the northeast corner.

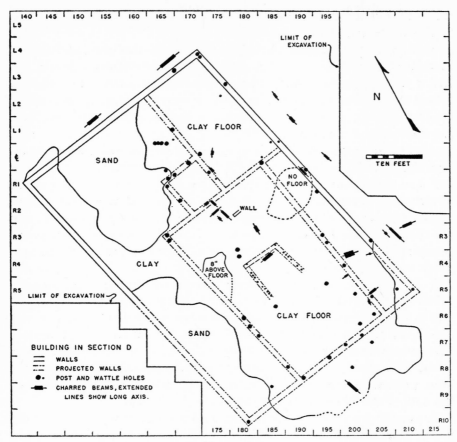

FIGURE 4

The charred beams found on the floor of the larger room were all parallel to the walls. A feature of a puzzling nature was the occurrence of two rows of wattles, 7 feet 2.5 inches apart, which extended for 5 feet in the approximate center of the room. On the third, or north, side, remnants of a wall were found. Evidently there was a low wall here that formed a **U** or square that might possibly have been planked over to serve as an altar. No evidence of a wall was found on the fourth side.

A hard-baked floor extended over most of the room, with an average thickness of 2 inches. In the northeast corner of the building there was a roughly oval fire-blackened area, devoid of any floor, 9.5 by 7 feet in diameter. This area might have been an optional site for an altar entirely constructed of timbers which were completely consumed by the fire, leaving nothing but ashes which subsequently were leached away by rain. In various small areas of the floor hard-baked clay did not occur, but red clay was encountered. It is probable that for some reason during the fire these areas were free from the intense heat that affected most of the floor, and so were unburned. The floor area, as a whole, was varicolored: red, brown, black, blue, and gray. It was noted that these areas had no significance other than that they were colored by the gases given off in the burning of different materials either in an oxidizing or in a reducing atmosphere.

There are two possible interpretations as to how the floor area of the larger room might have been divided. If the whole southeastern section made up the larger room, it would have been 26 feet on the north wall, 26.8 feet on the south wall, 36.5 feet on the west wall, and 37 feet on the east wall. If this were the floor plan, the thirteen vertical posts spaced throughout the interior of the building were probably auxiliary roof braces placed in areas where the heavy roof beams, probably of green timber, were weakened or warped. However, if another wall existed a few feet inside the eastern wall, the room would have measured 21 feet on the north wall and 19 feet on the south wall, with the east and west walls of the same length described above. This alternate interpretation would infer that the outermost limit was a low-walled or porched area. The second interpretation seems more feasible, as it would make for easier construction and give the building better proportions. It should be noted, moreover, that the low-walled "altar-like area" would then be approximately centered in the room.

The room in back of the one just described had dimensions of 21.5 by 13 feet. The west wall of this room was a continuation of the wall of the larger room. The southern section of this room had a good, hard-baked clay floor, whereas the northern section was red clay. A portico, or small storage room 7 feet square, extended out into the patio at the juncture of the west wall of the smaller room and the north wall of the larger room. The hard-baked clay floor extended outside the building area on the south and west sides. At the time of occupation this was probably a red-clay area produced by clay dropped during the manufacture of the walls. The south side, probably the entrance, purposely had a prepared red-clay entrance area. These areas, which were burned or fired during the conflagration, had the same appearance as the interior floor.

A Spanish Mission Site

In the northwestern section of the building complex an area was found that lacked red clay, hard-baked clay floor, wall rubble, and postholes of any kind. It was evident, therefore, that this area had not felt the effects of the burning and that the evidence of walls and other features had been weathered away. As no baked wall rubble protected the original ground level, any evidence left was destroyed by the various plowings. The walls of this building were plastered inside with a white-lime admixture. There were no evidences of frescoes found on any of the wall fragments.

The cultural materials, for the most part, occurred on and above the floor of the building, but certain artifacts had a distribution beyond the limits of the building proper. Plowing, as well as pitting by treasure hunters, would account for this distribution. The most widely distributed objects were aboriginal sherds, pieces of Spanish *tinaja* vessels, and nails. The majority of the aboriginal sherds found at floor level were concentrated in two general areas: the floor of the northern section of the larger room; and the southern section of the larger room extending out beyond the building 5 to 6 feet. Outside these two areas of concentration, the sherds occurred in an irregular distribution which, however, included most of the floor area. Extending out from the floor plan of this building complex no sherds, other than surface sherds, were found on the western, northern, or northeastern sides.

The surface sherds had an even distribution over this section, except in the extreme southeastern and southern squares excavated where no surface sherds were found. In all probability, the surface sherds that did exist in the peripheral squares were moved into the building complex area in plowing. The owner of the land stated that in his twenty years of occupation he had always plowed this field in a counterclockwise fashion. In this area the plow would be moving from east to west, thus gradually moving materials in a northwesterly direction. The various types of aboriginal ware followed the general distribution pattern outlined above. There was no concentration in any one area of a particular type.

The Hispano-Mexican sherds at both the surface and floor levels, although fewer in number, generally followed the distributional pattern of the aboriginal sherds. It was found, however, that the *tinaja* sherds at floor level, although following the same pattern, were concentrated in the larger of the two rooms, with only a few appearing sporadically in the smaller room. In the larger room there were three areas where complete *tinajas* had been broken *in situ*. One of these areas was between the the two problematic rows of wattles in the center of the room. The others occurred near the middle of the northeastern side of the room. The surface *tinaja* sherds followed the same distributional configurations as the aboriginal sherds. The white or gray glazed *tinaja* sherds were found only in this section and were concentrated around the south side of the building.

The 345 nails, for the most part, were concentrated on the floor of the larger room and beyond the south wall for a distance of 12 feet. It is of interest to note that there were no nails in many of the squares where there were no aboriginal sherds. The general distribution, therefore, followed that of the surface and floor levels of the aboriginal sherds.

All fragments of glass, shell, and metal other than nails, occurred at floor level within the larger room or in an area 5 to 10 feet southeast of the building complex. Only in the larger room were found such items as a curved chest handle made of a square hand-wrought iron rod (Pl. IX, 10), projectile points (Pl. VI, 4-5), a chisel (Pl. VI, 15), a double L shaped wrought-iron bracket, an oval keyhole plate with two nail holes (Pl. IX, 12), a gunflint (Pl. VI, 2), molten lead with matting impressions, peach pits, and Chinese porcelain fragments. Unworked chert nodules were found in both rooms, although more occurred in the larger of the two rooms. A charred corn-cob came from the patio area just west of the central portion of the wall of the smaller room.

From the distribution of the artifacts, it is evident that the larger of the two rooms and the area outside and along the south wall was the center of the activity of the building complex. For a complete listing of all artifacts found in Section D, see Appendix B.

Borrow Pit, Section E

From the surface, before excavation, this section was an oval basin-shaped area whose greatest depth was 22 inches. Upon excavation it was found that this feature went down to a depth of 8 feet 4 inches (fig. 5). Seven strata were encountered during the excavation, and these were numbered from top to bottom.

The top stratum (Level 1) was black humus with laminations or streaks of white sand, with a maximum depth of 3 feet 11 inches. The streaks of white sand were unevenly spaced and had an irregular pattern. The bottom 6 or 8 inches were composed of a darker black humus which was not laminated or intermixed with the white sand. A firepit, lined with charcoal, but with no artifacts in association, was encountered 4 inches from the base of the black humus. Level 1 contained the only burned daub found in the borrow pit, as well as the only iron artifacts. Many interesting items occurred among the

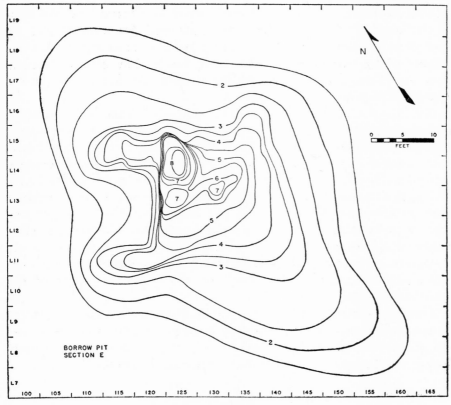

FIGURE 5

iron objects, including a large heavy anvil of unusual type (Pl. VI, 12), barrels of a musket (Pl. VI, 1) and a pistol (Pl. VI, 8), the haft portion of the axe found in Section D (Pl. VI, 14), two interesting locks (Pl. VIII, 13-16), a chest handle (Pl. IX, 11), and a large wrought-iron hinge (Pl. VIII, 5-6). Other smaller and more common iron items, including nails, were also found. The pottery, both

Spanish and aboriginal, represented most of the types found at the site, and in quantity surpassed any of the levels underlying it. The thirty-one Mission Red Filmed sherds found constituted the greatest concentration of this type at the site.

The second stratum (Level 2) was a brown-clay layer from 2 to 6 inches thick. In quantity of sherds this level was surpassed only by Level 1. Artifacts included two limestone discoidal stones and a cinder-like fragment of metal. Of interest were the animal bones in this level which included the teeth of the domestic pig and cow or ox.

Level 3 was a thin, yellow sand stratum, 2 to 3 inches thick. Although this level contained most of the pottery types at the site, the numbers were less than in levels above and below. A lip fragment of a green glass bottle, cinder-like metal fragments, three limestone discoidal stones, and bones (including ox or cow teeth) were found. Unique to this level were flat pieces of limestone with smooth-worked sides and four smooth granite pounders with pit marks on their pounding surface.

The remaining levels may be briefly described. Level 4 was another brown-clay stratum, ranging from 8 to 26 inches in thickness. In addition to Spanish and Indian pottery, a ceramic gaming disc, a limestone discoidal stone, and a limestone awl-sharpener were found. Just as under Level 2 a yellow sand stratum was located, so under Level 4 was another thin zone of the same kind (Level 5). Aside from Spanish and aboriginal pottery, only a limestone discoidal stone and a fragment of cinder-like metal are worthy of note. Level 6 was of brown clay, 6 to 7 inches thick, which rested on the virgin red clay (Level 7). Both of these strata were sterile.

After the borrow pit was cleaned out, it was seen to be basin-shaped with a well-like depression in the center. This hole had vertical walls on three sides, but on the fourth side, nearest the building in Section D, there was a 2-foot "step" into two parallel basin areas. The rim between these three areas was peaked and from 6 to 10 inches thick. From the well and these trough-like areas, the ground sloped up to the general ground surface level. A *tinaja*, complete except for the rim, and with its mouth facing in the direction of the well, was found in the highest of these troughs.

Boyd, in viewing the troughs with the *tinaja* in place, saw a close analogy to the watering places of the Indian villages of Central America. He postulated that the upper trough, which was 5 by 2 feet with a maximum depth of 15 inches, was used for drinking water with the *tinaja* functioning as a filtering system. The neck of the vessel, which had been broken away, gave an enlarged opening through which water could have been dipped more easily. The next trough would have caught the overflow from the drinking trough and could have been used for the watering of cattle. In turn, the "well" would have caught the overflow from the "cattle trough" and could have been used for washing purposes.

About 7 feet to the west of the "well" escarpment was the stump of an oak tree. This stump, sitting where it had grown, atop the red clay and 4 feet 3 inches beneath the surface of the ground, is mute testimony that the pit was open for some little time after it was originally excavated to provide clay for the building of the mission. This fact, when considered alongside the possible use of the borrow pit as a well, suggests that the pit was largely open throughout the life of the mission and that the various strata which filled it were later accumulations. Possible exceptions to this statement are Levels 5 and 6, both thin, which may have accumulated during use of the well area.

It will be remembered that between the red clay of Level 7 and the humus of Level 1 were five alternating strata of brown clay and yellow sand. These strata possibly represent alternation of different agencies of deposition, with the brown clay being a water-laid deposit and the yellow sand either a water-laid or wind-blown deposit. As there are only five strata, the alternation obviously reflects a longer cycle than seasonal variation, and may possibly be the result of several clearings of the land with attendant soil disturbance of periods of drought in which the thin, wind-blown sand deposits drifted in. Level 1, with its quantity of artifacts of the mission period, including the axe haft belonging to the blade found in Section D, and its evidence of recent origin, as attested by part of a shotgun shell at a depth of 1 foot 6 inches, is probably largely the result of leveling and filling of the site surface in recent agricultural operations.

These comments on the process of filling of the borrow pit have a definite relationship to the interpretation of the cultural stratigraphy, for if the various levels do not represent growth during the life of the mission settlement, they lose their potentialities as indicators of cultural change during the mission period. Some change in techniques and cultural assemblage would be expected in a site which was occupied for possibly three-quarters of a century during a time of social unrest among the Indians, when some groups were migrating and when new technological advances were being introduced by the Spaniards. However, the nature of the strata in the borrow pit is such that they could hardly be expected to reflect these changes. In view of the relatively few sherds in the levels below the black humus, it is impossible to obtain a complete picture of the appearance and disappearance of pottery types if such did exist. Most of the types present at the site occur in most of the levels, and no clear-cut evidence was forthcoming from a level by level analysis. Appendix B contains a complete listing of materials found in Section E.

All three units of the excavations revealed both aboriginal and European cultural materials, which may be taken as characteristic of the late seventeenth century in the area. Differences in content of the units may be interpreted as the result of the random scattering of single or unique objects. There was an established tradition which kept its integrity throughout the time span of the mission.

The Leon=Jefferson Period

THE EXCAVATION OF THIS MISSION SITE revealed an archaeological complex previously only dimly suspected from surface finds on various sites. It is a complex consisting of both aboriginal and European materials representing the fusion of two diverse traditions and the consequent reorientation of the Indian culture in many of its aspects. This group of material obviously required designation by a name. The name chosen is Leon-Jefferson, a combination of the names of the counties from which it is known.[1]

The tentative time span given this new period is 1650-1725. The earlier date is approximately the time of the full functioning of the missions in the Apalachee territory. After 1704, when the Apalachee were almost totally destroyed by the British and Creek raids and the remnants migrated westward to the protection of French territory, records of the Apalachee are sketchy. It is certain that the area was nearly totally abandoned in 1716,[2] but a mission list compiled by Benavides in 1732 names some of the missions with the implication that they were still in existence.[3] Whether they were in actual operation or were merely in ruins is not known. In order to include any possible remnants of the group that might have carried on the Leon-Jefferson culture after 1704, the end date of the period is extended to 1725.

Pottery made up the bulk of the collection of cultural materials from the mission site, and was both aboriginal and European. The aboriginal types which can be considered as a definite part of the Leon-Jefferson complex are Jefferson Ware with its various complicated stamped types—Miller Plain, Aucilla Incised, Gritty Plain, Lamar-like Bold Incised, Alachua Cob-Marked, Pinellas Incised, Leon Check Stamped, Ocmulgee Fields Incised, and Mission Red Filmed—all of which are described in detail in Appendix A. The Spanish *tinaja* ware and the glazed Hispano-Mexican pottery form the non-aboriginal portion of the Leon-Jefferson pottery complex. Some of the aboriginal pottery of the Leon-Jefferson complex clearly shows European influence at work on the Indian culture. Miller Plain and Mission Red Filmed, characterized by plate forms and annular ring bases, are cases in point. Hardness, too, of much of the pottery surpassed the normal range in the Southeast, and may indicate improved techniques of firing learned from the Spaniards.

129

Aside from pottery, the aboriginal assemblage is almost negligible, the major items being a few projectile points and the limestone discoidals. Whether this situation reflects actual conditions in Leon-Jefferson times is not certain, and the excavation of a purely Indian site of the same period might alter the picture. It is reasonable, however, to assume that the true situation is the one presented at the mission site and that aboriginal items other than pottery had largely been discarded in favor of items obtained in trade from the Spaniards. In fact, there is some doubt that a purely aboriginal site of the time, that is, one without a mission, can be found in the region. Of the thirteen Spanish settlements, missions, and forts in the Tallahassee region in 1675, ten had a population of over 6,800 persons,[4] which must account for most of the Apalachee population.

The Leon-Jefferson Period presents a different type of European-Indian relationship from that which occurred in the region before the establishment of the missions when contact was limited to sporadic trade. With the establishment of the missions, trade would become more regular, and Indians living in or near missions would accept European artifacts through trade or gift, and then replace items with similar functions in their own culture. Later, as the contact became more intense, the Indian culture would change on material, social, and religious levels to the extent that it would be reoriented into quite a different pattern. It is quite evident, therefore, that the Leon-Jefferson complex must be viewed from an acculturational viewpoint and that a different kind of archaeological change occurred in this period than in earlier horizons where the various cultures were on more or less the same technological and sociological plane.

It is of some little interest, then, to attempt to determine what the aboriginal culture of the area was before the impact of the Spanish missions, in order to see how much it changed. The late prehistoric and early historic horizon in the area is known as Fort Walton,[5] and recent excavations in what is believed to be a site of the latter part of the time range of the Fort Walton Period near Tallahassee are pertinent to the present discussion. Griffin's excavations at the Lake Jackson site give us a large sample of Fort Walton Period pottery with which to compare that from the mission.[6] The first point which is immediately apparent is that stamping, the predominant decorative technique of the Leon-Jefferson aboriginal pottery, is virtually absent in Fort Walton times, and that when present in Fort Walton it differs from the types known in Leon-Jefferson. Incision, which is the predominant technique in Fort Walton times, is relatively rare in Leon-Jefferson, but the commonest type in late Fort Walton times, Pinellas Incised, the other apparently indigenous Leon-Jefferson incised type, is evidently a descendant of types of the Fort Walton Period. Certain elaborations of rim and lip treatment in the type Lake Jackson Plain of Fort Walton times also appear to be ancestral of some Leon-Jefferson specimens. Thus the relationship between the two, which should exist because they follow one another in time in the same region and are believed to be the products of the same Indians (the Apalachee), is suggested, but it is also apparent that the two periods differ greatly.

The technique of stamping could not have been derived from the Spaniards, and it was practically absent in Fort Walton times. It is necessary, therefore, to look elsewhere for its origin, which may have derived from the influence of other Indian cultures operating simultaneously with the European influence. The acculturational process was then complicated and multifaceted.

At the same time that Leon-Jefferson existed in the Apalachee region, a contact period culture, known as Ocmulgee Fields, existed in central Georgia.[7] In contrast to Leon-Jefferson, Ocmulgee Fields was in contact with the British, and the pattern of the relationship was distinctly different. Leon-Jefferson was based on the mission contact; Ocmulgee Fields on the trading-post pattern. That contact between the two occurred is attested to by the presence of sherds of the pottery type Ocmulgee Fields Incised in the Leon-Jefferson Period. The Ocmulgee Fields Period, however, cannot be regarded as the source for the complicated stamping in Leon-Jefferson, for that technique was not present.

In central Georgia, Ocmulgee Fields is preceded by Lamar, and in Lamar, complicated stamping is an important feature of the ceramic complex. In areas outside central Georgia, particularly toward the Georgia coast, Lamar is not replaced by Ocmulgee Fields, but continues with some changes as a Late Lamar.[8] It is perhaps to this general source that one must look for the origin of the complicated stamped pottery of Leon-Jefferson, because it is both temporally and geographically feasible.

Vessel shape is an important feature in the search for the origin of complicated stamping. In Fort Walton and Ocmulgee Fields the basic vessel shapes are bowls. The incised types of Leon-Jefferson also have this shape; thus technique and vessel form combine to suggest relationships. The complicated stamped vessels of Leon-Jefferson times, on the other hand, are relatively deep pots or jars, as are the Lamar vessels.

The St. Augustine Period of the Florida east coast, which is contemporaneous with Leon-Jefferson, shows a heavy Late Lamar influence, but differs in detail from Leon-Jefferson.[9] St. Augustine ceramics find many of their closest parallels in materials of a Late Lamar time span in coastal Georgia. King George Check Stamped of Georgia, which is very similar to San Marcos Stamped of Florida, is "on 'Lamar-like' pottery in association with Spanish pottery."[10] Granting that Late Lamar is the source of complicated stamping in both the Leon-Jefferson and St. Augustine periods in Florida, differences between these two contemporaneous Florida horizons may be due to regional differences within Late Lamar itself. Leon-Jefferson possibly received its influence from a Late Lamar centering in western Georgia and eastern Alabama, which differs somewhat from the Late Lamar of eastern Georgia.[11]

The most unusual of the pottery types in the Leon-Jefferson complex, Mission Red Filmed, is related to the historic pottery type of eastern Alabama and western Georgia known as Kasita Red Filmed, which is believed to have been manufactured by the Kasita and Hitchita Creek Indians.[12] Despite their similarities, the two types differ in many particulars. Vessel form in Kasita Red Filmed is predominantly the flattened shallow globular vessel with flaring rim, with some cazuelas, and rare plates and cups. Mission Red Filmed, on the other hand, has the plate as its principal form. Mission Red Filmed is harder, contains more tempering material, and has a black core, whereas Kasita Red Filmed has a buff to light brown or gray core.

The tentative identification of the mission as San Francisco de Oconee is of considerable significance in interpreting the aboriginal ceramic relationships, for it is known that various tribal groups, including one group of the Oconee, inhabited the region in mission times. If the excavated site was occupied by the Oconee whose homeland was in Georgia, many of the perplexing ceramic problems might have a simple and reasonable answer.

The summary of possible ceramic relationships has indicated that the aboriginal pottery of the Leon-Jefferson Period is related to four or five pottery traditions which may, or may not, have been related to one another. At any rate, Leon-Jefferson is the final stage of a functioning culture which had its roots far back in the prehistoric culture of Florida and Georgia.

Summary

THIS EXCAVATION has revealed a Spanish mission site at which aboriginal and European cultures coexisted and blended. Available evidence indicates that the mission was founded between 1633, when the missions were started in the St. Augustine-San Luis chain, and 1655, when they were known to have been in full operation. In 1704 many of the missions were destroyed by James Moore's raid. Historical records were used in establishing the end dates and for finding information on the approximate location of the missions. Through the use of the Spanish artifacts and the inscribed sherds, the time span of the mission was more closely delimited. The best evidence of a terminal date comes from sherds inscribed with the name of Father Criado who, according to Father Geiger, was at San Luis in February, 1704, and who was killed during the English invasion.

The work of Louis Caywood has demonstrated that some of the glazed earthenware came from Mexico. It is now evident that trade between Mexico and Florida occurred possibly as early as 1633, and became quite strong by 1700. It is of interest, also, to note that the majolica-like ware was introduced into Mexico almost as soon as the technique was introduced into Spain from Italy. Dating of the Spanish sites in Florida will aid in correlating the various other Spanish sites of the United States and Mexico with one another, since the historic period in Florida is almost as long as that of Mexico.

The crucifix corpus which was found is, in its configuration and technique of modeling, of a type in vogue during the seventeenth century in Spain. A crucifix is likely to be kept over a long period of time, which reduces its value as a dating device; but in the present instance the specimen seems to fit into the total picture.

Archaeologically, it has been possible to correlate the Ocmulgee Fields Period of Georgia with the Leon-Jefferson Period. There are also stylistic similarities between Leon-Jefferson and some Late Lamar sites peripheral to the Macon area, which have historic materials. Similarities have been noted in various pottery types from historic sites, undocumented as yet, in the Tampa and Manatee areas of Florida. It now appears that during this late time similar elements were found throughout the Southeast, but with regional variations which as yet have not been linked together. At present our best tie is with the St. Augustine Period, which was in existence before the digging of the moat at the Castillo de San Marcos in 1686, and which continued until about 1750.

The excavated mission was one of a chain that had a tremendous influence on the aboriginal culture. Through the missionary work of the Franciscan Fathers there was a partial, if not a total, replacement of aboriginal ceremonial and mental attitudes that undoubtedly were reflected in the social and material culture of the Indians. The economy was changed by the importation of various European materials which would speed up and make for more intensive agricultural activities. The mission period occurred at a time of general unrest among the Indians of the eastern United States, and the missionizing of the Apalachee group, which took place at a time when it would be the most acceptable to the group, was pushed forward by the intensive activities of the Franciscans.

It is to be hoped that in the future more work relevant to the various aspects of historic archaeology will be undertaken, for the writer believes that in working out the historical aboriginal sequence and its interrelationships to Spanish culture in Florida it will be possible to obtain a better idea of the dynamics of these changing cultures. The relatively long span of Florida's history should make it possible to correlate historic Florida cultures with protohistoric and prehistoric cultures in other areas and to obtain a better knowledge of the time periods and cultural changes in areas peripheral to Florida.

Notes

The Site and the Excavations

1. Js-2 is the symbol given this site by the Archaeological Survey of the Florida Park Service, under whose auspices the excavation was conducted. It is also known as the Scott Miller site (Willey, 1949, p. 301).

2. Most of the information on the Apalachee is drawn from Swanton (1922 and 1946).

3. Swanton, 1946, p. 90.

4. Boyd, 1939.

5. *Tinaja* is the word used in this report for the large earthenware vessels made and used by the Spaniards for olive oil, water, and wine storage.

6. A full listing of all surface material, as well as that from previous collections, will be found in Appendix B.

7. The site is in Section 20, T 1 S, R 4 E.

8. Cooke, 1945, p. 10.

9. Kurz, 1944, p. 1.

10. Wenhold, 1936. See also Boyd, 1939.

11. The informants are Bishop Calderón (Wenhold, 1936) and Juan Fernández de Florencia (Boyd, 1948b). Both of these men wrote of the mission chain as it existed in 1675.

12. Material in Florida Park Service collections.

13. Boyd, 1939, p. 273.

14. Florencia's figures for the population of Apalachee in 1675 give a total of over 6,800 for the mission settlements (see table 1). This may be an exaggeration since Moore in 1704 estimated the population to be 1,300 free Indians plus 100 slaves (Swanton, 1922, p. 122). Bienville indicated about 2,000 at the time of Moore's raid, and after this every census shows a decrease. About 1718 there were, including those around Pensacola and on the Savannah River, 738 Apalachee.

15. The writer wishes to acknowledge his thanks to the various individuals who aided this project. Dr. Mark F. Boyd's constant counsel and advice has been mentioned. Mr. Lewis G. Scoggin, Mr. M. B. Greene, and Mr. John W. Griffin, all of the Florida Park Service, through their cooperation lightened the technical details that necessarily accompany an archaeological excavation. Mr. E. M. Murphy, Jr., aided greatly in the supervising of the excavations, surveying of the site, recording of the data, and organization of the laboratory work. The contributions of other individuals are acknowledged at appropriate points in the text.

The Buildings and Their Contents

1. All pottery types mentioned here are treated in detail in Appendix A.
2. Identification of all animal bones is by J. Clarence Simpson, to whom the author is indebted for the information.
3. An analysis by J. J. Taylor, State Chemist for Florida, showed the presence of copper and zinc, and a specific gravity of 8.39. In his report, Taylor says, "This crucifix is apparently an alloy of copper and zinc. The specific gravity of this metal corresponds to a brass of 67% copper and 33% zinc. Gold, silver, tin, and lead were tested for but were not detected."

    In discussing this object with Mrs. Beatrice Williams, head of the Art Department, Florida State University, it was agreed that the type of sculpturing and casting was definitely of the Spanish seventeenth-century period.
4. Dr. Boyd thinks that this interpretation is the most probable of the four suggested to him by Father Geiger, which include in addition *Padre Prelado*, *Padre Presbítero*, and *Padre Prebendaro*.
5. Geiger, 1940. See also Documents 22 and 42 earlier in the present volume.

The Leon-Jefferson Period

1. This name was suggested to the writer by Gordon R. Willey.
2. Boyd, 1949.
3. This list will be found in Boyd (1939, pp. 260-261).
4. Boyd, 1948b. See also table 1, this volume, and footnote 14, Chapter I, of the present paper.
5. See Willey (1949, pp. 452-470) for a summary of the Fort Walton Period.
6. Griffin [1950].
7. Kelly, 1938, pp. 51-58; Fairbanks, 1949, p. 72.
8. Fairbanks, 1949, p. 72.
9. Smith, 1948; Griffin, 1949, pp. 50-52.
10. Caldwell and McCann, 1941, p. 41. See also Caldwell, MS.
11. Wesley R. Hurt, personal communication.
12. Southeastern Archaeological Conference, 1940.

SECTION III.

Excavations
at the Site of San Luis

by

JOHN W. GRIFFIN

The Site of San Luis

AN LUIS is intrinsically the most important and the most interesting site of the mission period in northwest Florida, for it was the key to Spain's precarious hold on the Apalachee region. It was there that much of the drama occurred which is recorded in the documents translated by Dr. Mark F. Boyd in the first section of this volume. To the casual observer nothing remains above the ground to indicate the former presence of an extensive settlement, but excavation has revealed the location of portions of the community, and future work will bring more information to light. The excavations recorded in this paper were preliminary in nature, but it is felt that with the paucity of data on the archaeology of the mission period in Florida, the results were worth presenting alongside Hale G. Smith's more extensive work at the probable site of San Francisco de Oconee.

The exact date of the founding of the settlement of San Luis is at present unknown. Mission activity was extended to the Apalachee territory in 1633,[1] and San Luis must have been founded as a mission between that time and 1655 when its name appears on a mission list.[2] By 1675, and probably for some time previously, San Luis had become the most important post in the area, as the following quotation makes clear:

In the village of San Luis, headquarters of the deputy governor (which it has always been) there is a population of one thousand four hundred persons, between men, children and women, a little more or less.[3]

Writing in the same year, Calderón says:

. . . In the mission of San Luis, which is the principal one of the province, resides a military officer in a country house defended by pieces of ordnance and a garrison of infantry.[4]

The documents translated by Boyd trace the history of San Luis from 1693, when negotiations for the strengthening of defenses were underway, until the abandonment of the site in 1704. These documents, together with the remarks which precede them, render any detailed discussion at this point unnecessary. Of particular interest is the map of San Luis which accompanies this volume (Pl. I) and which gives a fairly detailed picture of the site at the time of its destruction.[5] It would seem that San Luis was never re-established; certainly it, as well as the entire area, was unoccupied in 1716,[6] and the early nineteenth-century descriptions would tend to confirm its abandonment throughout the remainder of the eighteenth century.

Early nineteenth-century references to the site are relatively numerous. Andrew Ellicott, who saw the site sometime between 1798 and 1800, said that "it is now totally abandoned and scarcely a vestige of the settlement now remains, except the ruins of a fort, one or two pieces of old artillery, almost in a state of decomposition."[7] In the following passage, John Lee Williams describes the site as it existed in the early years of American occupation:

Among the curiosities of the country we discovered an old Spanish Fort on a commanding hill about half way from Oclockney to Tallahassee. The south line of it measured 71 paces, the north 55, the east and west ends about 46. It had bastions near the angles, and in the spring about fifty feet down the ravine, east of the works, we discovered the breach of a six-pound field piece, and near it another piece of the same dimensions, from which the muzzle was broken.[8]

Elsewhere, Williams thus characterizes the structures within the palisade:

Fort St. Lewis was situate two miles west of Tallahassee. Its form was an irregular parallelogram; the eastern and longest side was 52 paces. Within the moat, two brick edifices had been erected; one sixty by forty, the other thirty by twenty feet. There were bastions at each corner. The outward defenses are extensive. A covered way led to a spring, in a deep ravine, under the north-east[9] wing of the fort. Here we discovered two broken cannon, one of them having only the muzzle broken off; this has been removed to Tallahassee, and again awakens the echoes of the distant hill on days of rejoicing. Many articles of old iron have been discovered about this old ruin. Before it, trees and grape vines grow, in the order in which they were planted: the rows are distinctly traced, although overrun with a more recent forest.[10]

Excavations at San Luis

An anonymous description of 1825 has the following comments:

At Fort St. Louis, about 2 miles west of Tallahassee, have been found remnants of iron cannon, spikes, hinges, locks, etc., which are evidently of Spanish manufacture, and which have not been much injured by the rust.

Within the principal fort, for the outworks seem to have been numerous and extensive, are the ruins of two brick edifices, one was about 60 feet by 40, the other was about 30 by 20. These are in total ruins, and nothing but a mound appears where the walls stood, composed wholly of broken bricks, which have been composed of a coarse sandy clay and burned in the modern fashion. Yet on the very walls of these buildings are oaks 18 inches in diameter. On the same hill, and in fact within the outworks of this fort, are to be seen grape arbors in parallel lines, which still maintain their pristine regularity.[11]

From the quotations given above, it is obvious that the site was well known to many of the early American residents of the region, and that a certain amount of material was collected from the ruins. Treasure seeking, according to a contemporary news account, seems to have played a part in further disturbance of the site of San Luis. The site was never really "lost," but the exact location of the fort on the hilltop disappeared during the century following the descriptions given above. Although the early excavations in search of treasure no doubt played a part in this leveling, the practice of agriculture at the site probably was a more potent factor. By 1948 it was no longer possible to trace the fort outlines on the ground. The ravine remained, however, and gave some clue to the location of the structure. Surface indications, in the form of pottery or other artifacts, were scarce. Gordon R. Willey visited the site in 1940, finding but a handful of specimens. Most of these were plain aboriginal sherds, but three bore complicated stamped designs. A few Spanish olive-jar sherds were also found by Willey. On the basis of this material and of five sherds in the United States National Museum—one a Lake Jackson or Lamar type rim, one a sherd of Aucilla Incised, and the remainder plain—Willey felt justified in assigning a post-Fort Walton, or Leon-Jefferson, affiliation to the site.[12] This conclusion is amply substantiated by the excavations reported in the present paper.

Our first visit to the site in 1948 disclosed a bare handful of plain aboriginal sherds on the surface, with absolutely no Spanish indications. Several days were spent in the company of Dr. Boyd going over the surface of the hill with a mine detector. On the last day allotted to the preliminary survey, the mine detector gave a very positive indication at the point which later became Square O. The digging of a test hole at this point disclosed a portion of cannon, several hand-wrought nails, fragments of a Mission Red Filmed plate, Spanish and aboriginal sherds, and animal bones (horse or cow). The soil was dark at this point, and it was later discovered that the initial test hole had penetrated the filled eastern moat of the fort.

The preliminary investigation was so encouraging that we returned to the site and spent three weeks in more extensive test excavation. The test pit in which the cannon fragment was found was relocated, and it served as a base point for the investigations. From it a line of stakes was run east and west, and 5-foot squares were laid out with our test pit in Square O.[13] From this point a trench was extended 20 feet east and 35 feet west. It soon became evident that the dark earth in our original test hole represented a pit, and that virgin red clay lay close to the surface both east and west of this pit. As the form of the pit became evident in cross section, it was seen to be about 8 feet wide on the surface and 4 feet wide at the bottom, with a depth of approximately 3 feet. We tentatively identified this pit as the eastern moat of the fort, and our digging of another square 15 feet to the south disclosed the same profile, indicating that the moat ran north and south at this point.

Test pitting was continued westward until an increase of burned clay debris and a possible posthole 75 feet west of Square O indicated the desirability of expanding the excavation. A rectangular area covering twelve 5-foot squares was opened at this point and revealed other postholes and larger pits which were considered as evidence of treasure hunting in earlier years. The pitting had been so great that no alignment of more than two or three postholes could be recovered. The postholes that were found were from 1 foot to 18 inches in diameter and were placed about 2.5 feet apart, on center. The distance from the eastern moat is about right for these to have been part of the interior blockhouse shown on the map (Pls. I and II), and it is probable that a strip excavation of a large area would reveal the outlines of this structure. Our time did not permit such an excavation.

Farther to the west, 180 feet west of Square O and 35 feet south of the line extending from that square, another test trench was dug

35 feet westward in an unsuccessful attempt to locate the west moat of the fort. This trench may have missed the moat at one or the other end, or it may, by sheer accident, have passed through the door, assuming that the moat did not continue in front of the door. At 180 feet west of Square O, and 80 feet to the south, another trench, 30 feet long, was dug. At 100 feet south of Square O this trench crossed a deep moat-like pit which is assumed to have been the south moat of the fort.

It is of interest to summarize the evidences of structure which were found, and to compare them with the contemporary map and descriptions and with the nineteenth-century descriptions. The legend on the map of 1705 accompanying this volume describes the palisade as being of upright posts four *varas* in height. Inside it a clay banquette rose to a height of seven *palmos*, thus providing a firing platform. Outside the palisade, or parapet, was the moat, which excavation disclosed to be at least 3 feet deep. Reference to the sketch map will show that it was regularly bastioned at the four corners. So far the excavations have located the moat along the south and east sides of the fort, but there is not, as yet, evidence of the palisade. Fragments of burned clay in the moat and in adjacent squares probably represent the clay banquette, which was no doubt baked at least in part by the fire which consumed the palisade.

The blockhouse within the fort is more troublesome. Though the map of 1705 shows one structure, Williams mentions the ruins of two, stating they were made of brick. The legend on the map gives the construction of the blockhouse as palm posts backed with clay bricks, strengthened within and without by a platform of planks. Williams and others believed that the bricks they found had been burned "in the modern manner," but it is possible that they were first sun-dried and then baked by the fire which destroyed the structure. There were no bricks in the excavation, but some rather large pieces of burned clay were found. Some of these pieces bore white plaster on one surface, and others showed definite imprints of wattles, indicating a type of construction at variance with either the Spanish or early American accounts, but in keeping with that found at San Francisco. As previously noted, post holes, which no doubt had belonged to the blockhouse, were encountered, and with future work in the area the problems of construction may be considerably clarified. The size of the central structure given in the Spanish account is about 85 by 58 feet, and it may be that Williams' two buildings were part of this one. Certainly a structure of this size, with a roof carrying eight artillery pieces, must have had considerable support in the form of bearing walls within it.

There is one more comment before leaving the matter of structure. The ravine ending in a spring is shown to extend from the region of the southeast bastion of the fort on the Spanish map, and it is located 100 feet south of Square O. Williams asserts that the spring was situated northeast of the fort. In this instance, the Spanish map seems to be the more accurate. Williams also states that the spring, in a deep ravine, was reached by a covered way. It should be noted that "covered way" does not necessarily mean "roofed passage." In fortification terminology the phrase refers to the area between the moat and the glacis, which is protected from the front by the glacis and "covered" (that is, defended) from the rear by the fortification. By extension, "covered way" could refer to the ravine itself at San Luis, which is covered from the fort.

Within the confines of San Luis, there were bones of horses, cows, and pigs in the fill of the moat, and although they probably were contemporaneous with the site, there is always the outside possibility that they (particularly the horse bones) represent latter-day burials. The few pieces of oyster shells may be taken as indications of food, and these must have come from some little distance. No charred vegetable products were present, but the nineteenth-century accounts speak of the overgrown rows of grapevines and trees, the latter presumably bearing either fruit or nuts. Dr. Boyd's translation discloses the additional use of at least fish and maize by the occupants.[14]

Artifacts from San Luis

A NUMBER OF ARTIFACTS, both ceramic and non-ceramic, came from the excavations at San Luis. These do not represent a complete inventory of the site, and they are not fully comparable to the material found by Smith at the Scott Miller site, because of the relatively complete excavation of the Scott Miller site and the frankly preliminary excavations at San Luis. Yet they do shed a certain amount of light on life at San Luis. Furthermore, through their resemblances to the material from the Scott Miller site, they strengthen the validity of the Leon-Jefferson Period as defined by Smith.

Modern debris, including that from the nineteenth century, did not occur in any quantity beneath the surface of the ground, and none was found below a depth of 6 inches. The actual surface of the ground was littered in many areas with tin cans, fence wire, and parts of automobiles and machinery. Little difficulty was experienced, however, in distinguishing most latter-day specimens from those dating from the time of the fort.

The most common non-ceramic artifacts found at San Luis were hand-wrought Spanish nails, of which there were 131. In their size, range, and shape these were identical to those found by Smith. It is of considerable interest to note that these nails were actually made on the site of San Luis, for Document 4 of the translations by Boyd in the first part of this volume gives the amounts paid to the black-smiths for doing the job. Glancing at this list, one will observe that the nails were the most expensive item in the construction of the fort.

One of the most interesting finds was a broken portion of the barrel of a cast-iron cannon. The piece is a longitudinal section about 12 inches long and 4.5 inches wide, with segments of both the bore and the outer surface present (Pl. VI, 9). A reinforce ring is present on the specimen, and the thickness of metal in front of this ring is 45 mm., while that behind is 52 mm. The bore of the gun, as calculated from the segment available for study, is about 7.2 cm., or slightly less than 3 inches.

The legend on the contemporary map of San Luis which accompanies this volume (Pls. I and II) lists the armament of the fort as consisting of two six-pounders, four four-pounders, and seven *pedreros.* The problem is to decide which type of gun is represented.[1] Since *pedreros* are usually small guns with thin walls, they may probably be discounted as a possibility.[2] The bore diameter of nearly 3 inches approximates that of three-pound guns of the eighteenth century, and is smaller than the 3.75-inch diameter of six-pounders of that century and earlier.[3] Remembering that artillery of the late seventeenth century was not highly standardized, it seems reasonable to consider the fragment to be a portion of one of the four-pounders mentioned in the armament of Fort San Luis.

More confusing than the cannon itself are fragments of hollow projectiles, eleven in number, which were found in our excavations. The fragments found range from 6 to 11 mm. in thickness and suggest either diameters approximating the cannon fragment found, or slightly larger diameters which might fit the six-pounders at the site. One specimen has a fuse nipple. Although explosive shells date as far back as the fourteenth century, their manufacture in a small size is a much later phenomenon. According to Albert C. Manucy, "Shells filled with explosive or incendiary mixtures were standard for mortars after 1550, but they did not come into general use for flat-trajectory weapons until early in the nineteenth century. . . ."[4] Manucy and Harold Peterson, both of the National Park Service, have examined these fragments and suggested that they are from grenades rather than from artillery projectiles.

Armament is further evidenced by the presence of a pistol barrel with its muzzle burst and incomplete. The surviving portion of the barrel is 12.5 cm. in length and 2.4 cm. in diameter. The bore was apparently about 14 mm. (or about .58 caliber), but oxidation makes this measurement somewhat uncertain. The butt end of the barrel is octagonal, but apparently the barrel rounds toward the muzzle. Although slightly heavier, and apparently larger, this barrel is basically similar to the one found by Smith (Pl. VI, 8).

Three lead balls were found at this site. The first of these, somewhat irregular, is about 13 mm. in diameter. The second, somewhat flattened and irregular, and with three sharp parallel cuts on one side, is about 15 mm. in diameter. The third, faceted on all sides as though whittled from a piece of lead, is nearly the same size. All these balls, but particularly the first one, are of a size approximating the bore of the pistol barrel. The inventory of accessories for firearms at San Luis includes five gunflints, all but one of which are of a gray-brown flint that does not appear to be native to the region.

The remaining specimen is about 30 mm. square and fashioned from silicified fossil coral.[5] The specimen is of the same size as the undoubted gunflints, but differs in being uniformly double convex in section. It does not resemble any aboriginal form, and may probably be interpreted as a gunflint made on the site of native material.

While the fragments of artillery weapons and firearms give evidence of the military nature of Fort San Luis, the religious aspect of the frontier mission-military post is exemplified by a large portion of a broken rosary which we found. The portion recovered consists of thirty-nine beads, mostly in strands on links of copper wire (Pl. V, 2). The beads, which are of glass, were apparently originally blue, but they are now so thoroughly oxidized and iridescent that color determination is difficult. The shape is that of an elongated barrel, about 13 mm. in length and 4.5 mm. in diameter, with the surface covered by spiraling longitudinal depressions and ridges. Each bead is on a separate piece of wire which is looped at both ends and usually connected to the loop of the next bead. However, some longer separations occur, with three links of chain separating beads. The longest strand has eight beads, a three-link separation, a bead link from which the bead has disappeared, a three-link separation, and six more beads.

A rosary is supposed to have five units of ten beads each, called decades, each unit separated from the next by a single bead, which usually differs from the majority in size, shape, or material.[6] Pendant from the loop of the decades are five beads, like those separating the decades, from which the crucifix is suspended. The modern rosary has, therefore, fifty-nine beads. Part of the recovered rosary consists of a chain-link triangle with bead attachments at each corner. This is undoubtedly the portion from which the beads of the decades loop, and from which the crucifix and its companion beads are suspended. Examination of item 2 on Plate V will disclose chain separations above the triangle on either side, a blank bead link, a three-link separation, and the beginning of a strand of beads. This linking and the separation bead is lacking on the modern rosary, and may mean that the one from San Luis originally had sixty-one beads. It is interesting to note that in all four cases of links set apart by chain, the bead link itself is empty. This would seem to indicate that these spaces were occupied by beads of another type than those of the main portion of the rosary.

One may speculate on why these portions of a rosary were in the filled moat of the fort. A rosary is very unlikely to be thrown away by a Catholic, although when badly broken it might be destroyed. Fire may have been the agent employed in an attempted destruction of a broken rosary at San Luis, and may account for the heavy oxidization of the glass beads, which are not, however, misshapen by heat. Of course, it is always possible that the rosary was merely lost. Other possibilities include the finding of the piece, and its discard, by non-Catholic Indians after the abandonment of the post, or the discard of the piece by a mission Indian who had drifted away from the Church. But it is really impossible to determine whether priest or soldier, Spaniard or Indian, owned the piece.

Hardware found at San Luis, in addition to the nails mentioned above, was similar to that of the Scott Miller site. Two hasped hinges, ornamented exactly like those from Scott Miller (Pl. VIII, 5-6), interestingly enough, still function.[7] Another double pin had an iron ring attached (Pl. VIII, 9). A keyhole plate from a lock was found in Square O. There were four strap-like sections of iron, and fourteen miscellaneous scraps of rusted iron.

The excavations yielded no iron tools, but of considerable interest was a scraper chipped from a heavy piece of green glass (Pl. VI, 6).[8] It was 57 mm. long, 36 mm. wide, and 11 mm. in thickness, with the greatest thickness lying near the nose of the artifact. This interesting example of the extension of aboriginal techniques to European materials was undoubtedly made from a portion of a heavy bottle. Three pieces of sandstone, whose concave surfaces gave indication of their use as grindstones, and a fragment of a chipped stone projectile point or knife complete the list of tools from the site.

Ornaments were of copper, brass, and glass. Two pieces of copper tube were found, one being about 60 mm. long, the other slightly longer (Pl. IX, 5). These had been fashioned from sheet copper, the edges of which met, but did not overlap, and were probably used as beads. A smaller tubular copper bead, 15 mm. in length, had overlapping edges. All three specimens were about 4 mm. in diameter. Another piece of copper, 26 mm. long and 10 mm. wide, with one side turned under for 3 mm., had been incised and perforated in the center (Pl. IX, 9). This piece is apparently aboriginal in execution. Another thin strip of copper, 4 mm. wide and about 30 mm. long, was found twisted in a loop. It probably was a crude finger ring. Several parallel-sided strips of copper apparently served as raw materials for articles of the type described above.

Another ornament was an embossed brass plate about 65 mm. in length, ornamented with a floral design and beaded along the edges (Pl. IX, 8). Wood fragments adhered to the rear of this piece, and it probably represents an inlaid ornament on a wooden chest or box.

Among the beads was one of "jet," 11 mm. in diameter, flattened on the back and faceted on the face. The bead was penetrated by two holes, passing through the bead from the sides, and set at right angles to one another. Eight other beads, not including those from the rosary discussed above, were made of glass. Three of these were seed beads, 3 to 5 mm. in diameter; two were opaque light blue; and the other was translucent amber. There was one translucent light-blue oblate-spheroid bead, 5.5 mm. in diameter, and a fragment of another light-blue, probably elongate-spheroid, bead. The longitudinal half of an opaque white bead, 12 mm. long, with groups of three spiraling blue lines was found (Pl. IX, 6). Two other beads of this same type were fused together. Except for the opaque white beads with blue spirals and the jet bead, all the beads are of types found in other historic sites in Florida.[9]

Domestic containers, other than pottery which will be described shortly, consisted solely of glass. Altogether ninety-two pieces of glass came from the excavation. Some of these no doubt date from the American period, but the vast majority of the fragments would appear to belong to the period of Spanish and Indian occupancy. Almost without exception the color of the glass is green, and many of the pieces have the iridescent patina associated with old glass. Thickness ranges from 3 to 13 mm., and the curvature of most of the specimens indicates that they came from bottles, some of which were apparently square, while others were of the squat round "wine bottle" variety found by Smith at the Higgs site.[10] One bottle neck in particular is identical to those from the Higgs site. Nothing more of a non-ceramic nature remains to be mentioned except some molten pieces of lead and brass and one tablet-shaped fragment of brass, which was 34 mm. long, 23 mm. wide, and 10 mm. in thickness.

The ceramics of the Leon-Jefferson Period, to which San Luis belongs, have been described in detail by Smith in the preceding paper, and will be discussed here only in general terms to note their occurrence at the site and the differences which exist between the type descriptions and the San Luis specimens.

Unglazed olive-jar, or *tinaja* sherds, represented by 918 examples, are the most numerous non-aboriginal ceramic specimens. Exterior surfaces range from white through buff to terra cotta. Several specimens are from large flat-bottomed vessels rather than the more common amphora-like shape. One large fragment of a vessel side has an incised design, scratched on after firing. Glazed olive-jar sherds are also found, but there are only thirteen of them. The glaze is green, and is applied only on the inner surface, except in two specimens (one of them a ring-shaped neck), which are glazed on both surfaces. One sherd has a touch of red glaze at one corner of its green-glazed surface.

TABLE 3

POTTERY DISTRIBUTION AT SAN LUIS

	O	OL3	Area A In	Area A Out	Area B	Area C	Total
Aboriginal Pottery:							
Jefferson Stamped and rims	52	74	15	19	9	4	173
Residual Complicated Stamped	106	60	41	25	26	1	259
Unique Complicated Stamped	18	0	0	2	1	0	21
San Marcos Stamped	41	0	0	0	2	0	43
Leon Check Stamped	10	0	0	1	0	1	12
Other check stamped	25	1	5	4	0	0	35
Mission Red Filmed	103	1	5	2	2	3	116
Miller Plain	274	19	47	62	35	15	452
Ocmulgee Fields Incised	48	1	6	4	6	0	65
Aucilla Incised	17	4	1	5	5	0	32
Other types and uniques	37	0	9	2	1	4	53
Residual Plain	398	63	113	103	204	57	938
Total Aboriginal Sherds	1,129	223	242	229	291	85	2,199
Non-Aboriginal Pottery:							
Unglazed olive jar	47	12	52	33	767	7	918
Glazed olive jar	1	1	3	0	8	0	13
Majolica	24	1	6	5	10	4	50
Other European	12	0	0	0	2	0	14
Mexican painted	2	0	0	0	0	0	2
Total Non-Aboriginal Sherds	86	14	61	38	787	11	997
Total Sherds	1,215	237	303	267	1,078	96	3,196
Hand-wrought nails	23	4	12	25	62	5	131

Fourteen sherds are grouped as "other European" in table 3. Six of these are on a reddish paste, about 6 mm. thick, and are brown glazed on both surfaces. Four sherds of earthenware are on a finer paste than the glazed *tinaja* sherds and have a blue-green glaze.[11] One sherd with a reddish paste, seemingly a flaring rim of a bowl, is glazed with a rather dull, light gray-green. The three remaining sherds in this grouping are too small for description.

Fifty sherds are classified as majolica, the term being equivalent to Smith's Hispano-Mexican. Nineteen of these are of the blue, black, and white polychrome which is known to have been made in Puebla, Mexico, and which has been found throughout the areas of Spanish influence in the United States (similar to Pl. X, 3, 6).[12] Five are decorated with blue conventionalized floral figures only (similar to Pl. X, 5). Four are small fragments of polychrome ware in which the designs are executed in yellow, green, and black. Fourteen have green conventionalized floral designs with parallel black lines at lip, shoulder, and base (similar to Pl. X, 4). All these types occur most frequently on shallow bowls or plates. Eight other sherds are classified as majolica in table 3, but are really quite a different thing, being more closely related to the Delft tradition. They are on a soft paste and have decorations in blue which are copied from Oriental vessels (Pl. X, 9). Two sherds from San Luis are of a type found in the nearly contemporaneous Higgs site near Vero Beach, but not found at the Scott Miller site. They are red and black painted Mexican colonial pieces, termed Mexican Ware, Type A, by Smith in the Higgs site report.[13]

Turning now to the aboriginal ceramics, which outnumbered the European two to one at San Luis, it is evident that most types are the same as those described by Smith from the Scott Miller site. Mission Red Filmed is represented by 116 sherds, of which almost half are from a single plate, painted solid red on both surfaces, which was found in Square O. Apart from a solid red rim sherd, apparently from a cup or small pitcher and with a portion of what appears to have been a loop handle, all sherds of this type are from plates. With the exception of the specimens mentioned above, which are solidly painted, all specimens are zoned. Representative sherds are shown in Plate XI, 1, 3, 4.

Miller Plain is represented by 452 sherds, if the writer correctly understands the criteria for determining the type. Most of these sherds seem to be from plates with annular ring bases, although some shallow bowls (in the aboriginal rather than the European sense) are also indicated.

The problem of Jefferson ware at San Luis involves a difference in classification procedure that must be noted. The writer followed Smith's classification of the complicated stamped Jefferson types and the Jefferson pinched and punctated rims, but separated the residual complicated stamped from these. In addition, the residual plain category may include some body sherds which are not of the Jefferson paste. Only seven handles were found. Table 4 compares the occurrence of various types of Jefferson ware at Scott Miller and San Luis.

TABLE 4

JEFFERSON WARE AT SCOTT MILLER AND SAN LUIS

Type	Scott Miller	San Luis
Stamping, Type A	198	12
B	15	8
C	7	62*
D	14	5
Rim, Type 1	41	6
2	22	4
3	1	8
4	12	1
5	132	67
Total	442	173

* *This large number is mostly accounted for by sherds from one vessel.*

Leon Check Stamped, as defined by Smith, is represented by twelve specimens, but there are also thirty-five sherds of another type of check-stamping at San Luis. These are treated with rectangular checks, 3 to 5 mm. in length, with the cross lands either thinner or the same size as the lineal lands. The paste is sand-tempered. These sherds have not been assigned a type name, but their occurrence should be noted.

A pottery type observed at San Luis, but absent from Scott Miller, is San Marcos Stamped.[14] All specimens were of the variety produced by a simple stamp placed over itself at right angles. The majority of the forty-three sherds noted came from a restorable small globular vessel with a high, slightly flaring rim, which had originally been fitted with a loop handle. The stamping on this vessel occurs only below the shoulder. The category of unique complicated stamped, consisting of twenty-one sherds, includes partially obliterated motifs which apparently do not qualify as any of the described varieties of

152

Jefferson ware. The motifs are curvilinear and bear some resemblance to Late Swift Creek Complicated Stamped.

Aucilla Incised is represented by only thirty-two sherds. Ocmulgee Fields Incised, on the other hand, appears more frequently here than at Scott Miller, being represented by sixty-five sherds (Pl. XII, 4). The final category in table 3, termed "other types and uniques," might be as well called miscellaneous. In addition to a number of fragments of Gritty Plain, making up about half of the total of fifty-three, there was one sherd each of Fort Walton Incised, Pinellas Incised, St. Johns Plain, and overall punctation. The remainder of the group were specimens with fragments of incision too small to classify as any type.

Table 3 gives the distribution of both aboriginal and European pottery in the excavations at San Luis. For purposes of analysis, the excavated squares were combined into three sections. Section A includes the squares in the eastern part of the excavation and is subdivided into four groupings. Two groupings, Squares O and OL3, are in the eastern moat of the fort. The third grouping consists of squares inside (that is, west of) the moat; the fourth, of squares outside (that is, east of) the moat. Section B includes the squares near the postulated center of the fort, the area of the postholes believed to be part of the blockhouse. Section C includes squares to the west part of the site, and the trench across the south moat of the fort.

It is of interest to note the dominance of aboriginal pottery in Sections A and C, near the edge of the fort, and the overwhelming preponderance of European ware in Section B, within the fort. One might expect less Indian pottery within the fort itself, and seemingly this expectation is fulfilled. From another point of view, these distributions are of interest, for they point out the dangers involved in assuming that a limited test adequately represents conditions at a site. Evidence from the digging of only Square O would have pointed to a very small quantity of European ceramics in relation to Indian pottery; and data from the digging of only the squares grouped as Section B would have suggested the opposite conclusion. This differential occurrence of materials is less likely to obtain on a small aboriginal site in which areas of use are relatively unspecialized than it is on a site such as San Luis, where there are not only two major groups of people, Spaniards and Indians, but also such very specialized areas of use as the fort, the mission, and houses. It is, however, a factor to be remembered in all analysis. The distribution of the hand-wrought nails, the most frequently occurring type of artifact other than pottery, is given at the base of the same table. It is of interest to note that their distribution coincides very well with that of the Spanish pottery.

There is a close similarity between the Scott Miller site and San Luis in the proportion of non-aboriginal sherds to the total. At Scott Miller 31.7 per cent of the sherds fell into this category, whereas at San Luis there were 31.2 per cent. There seems to be a rather constant proportion of roughly one-third of non-aboriginal pottery at these sites of the mission period. Whether this can justifiably be extended to surface collections as a possible indication of an actual mission settlement is not as yet proved. The writer, however, suspects that percentages which fall grossly below such a figure would not indicate an actual mission settlement. In other words, the mere presence of one or two non-aboriginal sherds in a rather large surface collection is not adequate evidence for identifying a site as a mission. Although this hypothesis remains to be tested in the field, it is a point to bear in mind.

Conclusions

THE TEST EXCAVATIONS at San Luis have provided a certain amount of data on a Spanish mission settlement, combined with a post of military and civil authority, abandoned in 1704. Since the construction of the fort, around which the work was concentrated, occurred in the late seventeenth century, the cultural complex recovered probably belongs predominantly to the years 1690-1704. Certainly, none of the material should be later than this time, although some may be slightly earlier. Appendix B to this volume contains a trait list for Smith's excavations at the Scott Miller site and for the excavations at San Luis. This list of materials, together with the documentary sources, provides new insight into actual living conditions in the Spanish missions of Apalachee of the late seventeenth century.

From the point of view of the aboriginal ceramics, the complex at the two sites is very similar. The presence of San Marcos Stamped, an east-coast Florida type, and the variations of proportion of certain other types may possibly be indicative of the different characters of the sites compared. The Scott Miller site, the subject of the preceding study by Smith, is probably San Francisco de Oconee. San Luis was predominantly Apalachee, but some evidence of all the Indian groups present in the region might be expected, as it was the seat of the deputy governor and the largest community in the area. Work on still other sites of the period in the area is needed to clarify fully the ceramic situation.

From the point of view of culture change, and the interinfluencing of cultures, the copying of European forms in some of the aboriginal ceramics is obvious. We may also cite again the scraper chipped from glass. Glass beads and copper ornaments provide tangible evidence of a more direct influence of Spaniard on Indian, namely, trade. Although it is, of course, impossible to state which metal artifacts were possessed by Indians and which by Spaniards, the documents show that trade had provided the Indians with many European articles. The documents, too, are the source for information on the influences on the social and religious life of the Indian.

Acculturation is rarely one-way; in fact, by definition it is two-way, thereby differing somewhat from the concept of assimilation. There is no direct archaeological evidence of Indian influence on Spanish life, unless the aboriginal features of the mission buildings represent such influence. The use of corn (maize) by the Europeans is perhaps the major technological borrowing from the Indian, but Smith has also suggested that aboriginal ceramics were used by the Spaniards. Other evidences of interinfluence are inherent in the archaeological materials and the translated documents, and still further evidence lies buried in the ground and in untranslated manuscripts. The period is a fertile one for the social scientist interested in the dynamics of culture change, and the present paper can do no more than suggest the problem.

Turning now to considerations of a different level, it seems desirable to review our present knowledge of the locations and identities of the various missions of Apalachee. San Luis is a known point, and its identity may be regarded as firmly established. The Scott Miller site is most probably San Francisco de Oconee, although as Smith has pointed out this should be taken as a tentative identification. Other locations from which Spanish materials have come are known for the region, and may be re-examined in the light of documentary references and archaeological findings.

Table 1 in Smith's study lists the missions from San Miguel de Asyle, the last in Timucua territory, to San Luis, as they existed in 1675.[1] Smith has indicated that San Lorenzo de Hibitachuco (Vitachuco) is possibly located located about 2 miles south of Lamont on the west side of the Aucilla River. If the Scott Miller site is really San Francisco de Oconee, then La Concepción de Ayubali lies between it and the previously mentioned site, but has not yet been located. San Juan de Aspalaga and San Joseph de Ocuya could very well be represented by the two sites west of the Scott Miller site which Smith has mentioned. The distance from San Joseph to San Pedro de Patali is 4 leagues, about 10.5 miles, which would place the latter somewhere in the neighborhood of Lake Lafayette, although the actual site has not been located.

In the immediate area of Tallahassee and San Luis, the picture becomes clouded by the number of the missions. Although only two are listed on the direct route to San Luis from San Pedro, three others—Candelaria, San Martín, and Santa Cruz—are also in the immediate neighborhood.[2] Little can be done about identifying these five sites at present, but it is of interest to note that materials found and recorded during Territorial days may indicate some locations. Two sites, respectively located one-half mile south and three miles east of Tallahassee, were noted by John Lee Williams, and have been summarized by Boyd.[3] South of San Luis, "on the road to the sea," was a mission of three small villages of non-Apalachee Indians. West of San Luis, and seemingly on the Apalachicola River, were three other missions whose locations are but vaguely given.[4] It is obvious that while a beginning has been made in the determination of the mission sites of Apalachee, much remains to be done before all of them may be located.

But the missions of Apalachee were not alone in Spanish Florida. From the territory of Apalachee to the city of St. Augustine there were nine missions in Timucua territory, none closer to the latter city than 16 leagues west of the St. Johns River. At present only one site along this chain may be tentatively identified.[5] This is Santa Catalina, very possibly located near the head of Itchetucknee Spring. The recorded measurements bring one near this point, and from the bed of the stream J. Clarence Simpson, John M. Goggin, and others have recovered quantities of Spanish material.[6] Near Rochelle, southeast of Gainesville, Goggin has found a site which produces Spanish pottery similar to that from Scott Miller and San Luis.[7] The aboriginal pottery, as one might expect since this is in Timucua territory, differs from that of the Leon-Jefferson Period, and Goggin has chosen the name Potano Period to designate such material in the area.[8] The remainder of the missions of Spanish Florida, particularly those north of St. Augustine into Georgia, constitute a separate problem, and will require effort as intensive as that expended on the St. Augustine-San Luis chain.

In one sense, the problem of the Spanish missions of Florida is related to the larger problem of Spanish missions in the hemisphere, and particularly to those in North America. When enough data are available from the various regions to which Spanish mission activity was extended, it will be possible to study the varying reactions and adjustments of divergent aboriginal populations to a similar impact. In this connection, however, one should not assume that the impact was identical in the different geographical areas involved. Matters of colonial policy, location in relation to international affairs, isolation, and environment, as well as the personalities of the individuals involved, will combine to complicate the problem. Some comparative data from California, Arizona, and New Mexico are now available, particularly from the latter two, and more will be forthcoming in the future.[9] Latin America, too, is an important source for data on

Spanish mission activity. It is not the purpose of the present paper, however, to bring these comparative data into focus.

So far as the Spanish missions of Apalachee are concerned, the translation of contemporary documents and the excavations at two sites have provided us with a solid foundation from which to view the period and its characteristics. The picture which emerges is not one of cloistered gardens, tolling bells, and peaceful idyllic communities. Rather it is one of crude structures and few tools, of poverty and discord, of war and martyrdom; but it is a picture of greater interest than one painted with the brush of romance, for it is related to reality.

Notes

The Site of San Luis

1. See Boyd, this volume, for a summary of mission effort in Apalachee.
2. Boyd, 1939, p. 261.
3. Juan Fernández de Florencia, translated by Boyd, 1948b, p. 184.
4. Bishop Calderón, translated by Wenhold, 1936, p. 9.
5. Document 40 of Boyd's translations in the present volume accompanies this map.
6. Boyd, 1949, p. 18.
7. Quoted in Shores, 1927, p. 112.
8. Quoted in Shores, 1927, p. 115, and in Boyd, 1939, p. 265.
9. As will be indicated shortly, this probably should read southeast rather than northeast.
10. Quoted in Shores, 1927, pp. 115-16, and in Boyd, 1939, pp. 265-66.
11. *Pensacola Gazette*, April 2, 1825. Quoted in Boyd, 1939, p. 267.
12. Willey, 1949, pp. 285-86.
13. Because of the preliminary nature of the work, and the rather scattered test excavations, no excavation plat is included with this paper. One was made, however, and will be available for coordination with future work.
14. See above, Document 6, for example.

Artifacts from San Luis

1. It will be remembered that fragmentary cannon were found on the site in the early nineteenth century. See p. 140 above.
2. Manucy, 1949, p. 37, notes, however, that *pedreros* were made in calibers up to fifty-pounders.
3. Albert C. Manucy, personal communication. I wish to acknowledge my gratitude to Mr. Manucy for his help in regard to artillery at San Luis.
4. Manucy, 1949, p. 65.
5. This silicified coral is a common artifact material in the Tampa Bay region.
6. Father Charles W. Spellman was kind enough to examine the rosary fragments and discuss the problem with the writer.
7. Many of the wrought-iron artifacts are in much better condition than those of steel. This is, of course, to be expected because of the known greater resistance of wrought-iron to corrosion.
8. This artifact has been discussed by Griffin, 1949b.
9. See, for example, Griffin and Smith, 1948, pp. 12-14, and Sleight, 1949, pp. 27-28.
10. Smith, 1949, Pl. 2.
11. The color is near Blue Spruce (Maerz and Paul, 1930, Pl. 30, H7). The green *tinaja* sherds are closer to Holly Green (*Ibid.*, Pl. 23, L1) and Mt. Vernon Green (*Ibid.*, Pl. 23, J8). The *tinaja* glaze is also more "pebbly."

12. It is of interest to note that among the royal cédulas in the Archivo General de la Nación in Mexico City are documents stating that taxes were levied against the cathedral church at Puebla for the support of the Florida missions in the late seventeenth and early eighteenth centuries. This information was kindly supplied by Father Charles W. Spellman, who found the records while doing research on the Florida missions.
13. Smith, 1949, pp. 12-13; Pl. 1.
14. Smith, 1948, pp. 314-15.

Conclusions

1. See figure 1 of the present volume, and the reproduction of a contemporary map in Boyd (1939, p. 254).
2. See Wenhold, 1936, and Boyd, 1948b, p. 185.
3. Boyd, 1939, pp. 267-69.
4. See Wenhold, 1936, p. 9; Boyd, 1948b, p. 186.
5. In addition to the possible site of San Miguel as suggested by Smith.
6. Personal communications.
7. Goggin, et al., 1949, pp. 10-11.
8. Goggin, 1949, fig. 3; Griffin, 1949, p. 50.
9. The bibliography for these areas is quite extensive. Special note should be made of the recent monograph on Awatovi in Arizona, which the writer considers to be the finest report yet issued on a Spanish mission site (Montgomery, Smith, and Brew, 1949).

APPENDIX

Leon-Jefferson Ceramic Types

by

HALE G. SMITH

and

Trait List of Two Spanish Sites of the Mission Period

by

JOHN W. GRIFFIN

and

HALE G. SMITH

Leon=Jefferson Ceramic Types

The ceramic descriptions contained in this Appendix apply to the presumed site of San Francisco de Oconee, reported in this volume. The analysis is based completely on sherds from this site. The maximum time span of the site is from 1633 to 1732, with a probable actual range of 1650-1704. Table 2 gives the total sherd count of the site on which the descriptions are based.

Non-Aboriginal Pottery

SPANISH TINAJA WARE

Some 2,427 sherds from Spanish *tinajas* accounted for the bulk of the non-aboriginal pottery at the site. These vessels, used for water, olive oil, and wine storage, were probably all wheel-made, and the vast majority are of an unglazed, grit-tempered, pink paste.

The necks and rims found indicate vessels with very short necks, if any, with a comparatively small, thickened, rim opening. Vessel shape is elongate, with maximum diameter high on the vessel, and with a rounded bottom. One such vessel found in the borrow pit (Pl. X, 10), complete except for the rim, measured 46.5 cm. in height with a maximum diameter of 29.5 cm. Glaze, when it is present, appears on the vessel interior and exterior, or on the interior only, but never only on the exterior. A color analysis of the glazed specimens, by Ripley P. Bullen, is presented in table 5. Three basic colors of glaze—red, green, and gray—are found, with variations particularly in the blue-green-gray series. Bullen suggests that the green

TABLE 5

GLAZED EARTHENWARE FROM SCOTT MILLER SITE

Outside white slip (?), inside red glaze	32
Outside white slip (?), inside green glaze	18
Outside white slip (?), inside purple glaze	6
Outside white slip (?), inside blue-green glaze	12
Outside white slip (?), inside blue-gray glaze	27
Outside green glaze, inside green glaze	8
Outside lines or dots of green glaze, inside green glaze	7
Outside blue-gray glaze, inside blue-gray glaze	8
Other sherds with suggestion of glaze on inside	39
Other sherds with suggestion of glaze on both sides	10
Total	167

glaze became purplish with refiring during the burning of the mission. He also believes the blue-green may be a variant of green, but that the blue-gray is distinctive and probably represents a "true," or intentional color. A *tinaja*-like ware, but with a white or gray glaze, which was sometimes decorated with blue lines, was found in Section D. The sherds suggest comparatively small vessels, such as flat-bottomed pitchers and jars.

HISPANO-MEXICAN POTTERY

In comparison to the *tinaja* fragments, sherds of other non-aboriginal wares were in a definite minority, but of extreme interest are 146 sherds of glazed earthenware designated herein as Hispano-Mexican.

From the eighth century until 1566, when "Moorish writing, dress, and style of decoration were prohibited"[1] in Spain, the pottery of the Iberian Peninsula was in the pure Oriental tradition. The latter part of the sixteenth century saw Italian influence in the form of conventionalized floral scrolls, birds, and other motifs on the Spanish ware which was being produced at Talavera de la Reyna (Reina), the center of Spanish earthenware production. In the seventeenth century the style became even more ornate, with careless pictorial copies of the Italian majolica in evidence.[2] As early as 1570, the tradition of Talavera had been introduced into colonial Mexico, particularly in Puebla, where a similar ware is being made to this day.[3] Louis R. Caywood believes that the sherds at the mission site came from this source, and dates one type of the blue ware (Pl. X, 3, 6) between 1600 and 1650. According to Caywood, "The pottery was made from two kinds of clay, white and red, combined in equal parts. The glaze is tin and lead."

On all the specimens, except one divergent sherd to be mentioned later, the initial glaze is creamy white, but the dominant color in the design applied over this glaze on the vessel interior permits division of the ware into three types. The first type is characterized by a predominance of green in the decoration. These sherds have one, two, or more black lines encircling the vessel which delimit the design area (Pl. X, 4), and which occur generally below the lip and at the junction of base and side in bowl forms. The green glaze was applied heavily with a wide brush, and the pattern executed is composed of highly conventionalized floral designs, geometric in appearance. The broad "leaf" designs are often supplemented with dots placed sporadically throughout the pattern. On one sherd, golden lines have replaced the black lines near the base of the vessel, and on another the green "leaves" are outlined with a smeared red glaze.

The second type, while predominantly yellow, is in reality polychrome. Bands of different shades of yellow, separated by white and black lines, encircle the vessel. Beneath these bands the decoration consists of conventional flower designs with black stems and a black circle terminating each stem (Pl. X, 2). The circles are filled with orange, yellow, and green in various shades, with an occasional circle left white. Occasionally the floral pattern is brushed on without the black lines, thus giving the effect of mass design rather than individual patterns. One sherd has an area outlined in thin black lines and filled with various shades of yellow over which short black lines and dots occur.

[1] Cox, 1944, p. 327. [2] *Ibid.*, pp. 328-332.

[3] All information in this paragraph is from Louis R. Caywood, National Park Service, who has been doing research on glazed earthenware from mission sites in Sonora, Arizona, New Mexico, Texas, and Louisiana. The dates are from Cervantes (1939).

Appendix

The third type, with predominantly blue decoration, can be further subdivided into two sub-types. The first sub-type consists of bowl forms with an exclusively blue-glazed decoration of conventionalized floral patterns (Pl. X, 5). The single or triple lines which delimit the design area are blue rather than black or golden. The second sub-type, in a flaring-rimmed deep-dish form, has a design which is basically a reduplicated geometric black line and dot pattern either surrounded by broad heavy blue lines or painted over with blue glaze. A double-based section of a bowl with a blue-glazed design was found on the surface. Vessels of this type, like gravy boats, are actually two vessels, one placed inside the other before the application of the glaze, which with the damp clay holds the two together.

Three basic forms seem to be represented in the collection of Hispano-Mexican pottery, all of them bowl or deep-dish forms. One restorable bowl is 16.3 cm. in diameter and 6.4 cm. in height, with an annular ring base 6.4 cm. in diameter. A second form, represented by sherds, is a shallow bowl or deep dish with a flaring rim ranging between 2.5 and 3.8 cm. in width. The diameter of this shape seems to fall around 23 cm., and the height is about 5 cm. Variation in height and diameter is apparent. Thickness is also variable, but averages around 8 mm. The third form is represented by only a single large section of a vessel, which is glazed with a heavy blue-white coat rather than the customary creamy white. The decoration is in blue and is a conventionalized floral pattern (Pl. X, 8). The form is a shallow bowl, about 20.8 cm. in diameter and 5.3 cm. high, with a flat handle-like projection. This piece, the writer believes, is not of Spanish origin, but rather came from some area in the Near East, possibly Turkey.

CHINESE PORCELAIN

Some Chinese porcelain fragments from a rectilinear vessel were found below undisturbed rubble on the floor of the larger room of Section D. Porcelain was not manufactured in Europe until 1700, but was imported from the Orient at and before that time.[4] The fragments at the mission came to Florida either by way of Spain or Mexico.[5]

Aboriginal Pottery

Some of the types listed below have previously been described by Willey,[6] but are redescribed here on the basis of an intensive analysis of the sherds from the mission site. Following the formal descriptions of these types, several types believed to be evidence of trade and certain unique specimens are mentioned.

Type name.—MILLER PLAIN

Definition as a type. This paper. A brief type description based on Smith (1948) is given by Willey (1949, p. 491). Based on 574 sherds.

Ware characteristics.

   Method of manufacture. Coil fractures present.

   Temper. Fine sand and grit in moderate to small amounts.

[4] Cox, 1944, p. 641.

[5] See Higgs (1942) and Smith (1949) for Chinese porcelain found at a site near Vero Beach, Florida.   [6] Willey, 1949.

Paste texture and color. The paste is well mixed, compact, and slightly contorted, with a black core.

Surface texture, color, and finish. The interior surface is finely scraped, while the exterior surface is rougher. The surfaces were smoothed with water after scraping and before firing. Both surfaces range in color between dark gray and black, and may be the same or different colors.

Hardness. 4.5 to 5.0.

Thickness. 4 to 8 mm.

Form.

Shallow bowl. Rims are usually incurved (17), but a few are straight (17) or flaring (14). The vessel wall is sometimes constricted at the point where curvature begins. Decoration, which occasionally occurs in the form of rim indentations, gives a lobed pattern. Lips may be flat or rounded, with the flat ones being either the same width as the body of the vessel, or overhanging the interior for approximately 1 mm. Bases are rounded, flat (2), or possess annular rings (1). There are no appendages.

Plate. Rims range from 2.3 to 6.1 cm. in width, and are either flat or have a concave-convex curvature to a maximum depth of 7 mm. The rim meets the concave base of the plate at an angle, and when the rim is also concave the juncture between it and the base is a peaked ridge (Pl. XI, 6). Lips are of several varieties. Flat lips (17) are placed at an angle of about 45 degrees to the plane of the inside surface of the rim. The exterior edge of the lip may be rounded into the rim exterior. Frequently the lip is peaked at its center by a double, flat bevel (8). In other cases the entire lip may be rounded (15). Bases were probably of the annular ring type (8). There are no appendages.

Small-mouthed water bottles. Three specimens. One has an opening 10.8 cm. in diameter with a collar estimated to be 6.3 cm. long. The rim is flaring and the lip is rounded.

Lugged shallow bowl. One specimen, presumably from a vessel with two opposing lugs.

Pitchers. Thirteen pitcher-handle sherds, both oval and round in cross section.

Geographic range of ware. Full range is unknown. Occurs on mission sites in Leon and Jefferson counties. Willey (1949, p. 491) notes its similarity in form to vessels of the Ocmulgee Fields Complex of Georgia. Similar forms are widely distributed in the Southeast and the Mississippi Valley.

Chronological position. Leon-Jefferson Period.

Ware name.—JEFFERSON WARE

Definition as a ware. This paper. A brief description based on Smith (1948) is given by Willey (1949, pp. 492-93). Six groups are differentiated within the ware, but have not been given the formal status of types; four types of complicated stamping, plain pottery with pinched and punctated rims, and plain body sherds. The following discussion is based on an examination of 3,873 sherds.

Ware characteristics.

Method of manufacture. Coil fractures present.

Appendix

Temper. Small to abundant amount of prepared grit and sand, with occasional use of coarse quartz sand or sherd tempering.

Paste texture and color. Paste is well mixed, fairly compact, moderately grained, with laminations along the vessel walls in some cases. A few sherds have a lumpy, coarse-grained, somewhat contorted paste. Core color runs from gray through buff and brown to black. Exterior color of one or both surfaces may extend halfway through the core. Surface and core color may be identical.

Surface texture, color, and finish. Interior surfaces were scraped smooth while the vessel was still wet. Surface texture ranges from rough through smooth to imperfectly polished. Exterior surfaces were scraped before decoration was applied, but in some cases, where the vessel was left plain, exteriors were not smoothed after being scraped. Surfaces range from black and dark brown to gray and buff. Black exteriors frequently have light gray interiors. Firing clouds appear on some exteriors. In a few cases the vessels were improperly air-dried and pre-firing cracks resulted. In two sherds of Type B Complicated Stamped, gas bubbles occur.

Hardness. Exterior, 3.5 to 5.0; interior, 4.0 to 4.5.

Thickness. 4 to 8 mm.

Geographic range. At present unknown.

Chronological position. Leon-Jefferson Period.

TYPE A COMPLICATED STAMPED (198 sherds)

Decoration.

Technique. Paddle impressed on soft unfired surface of vessel. After stamping, the exterior surface was lightly scraped, partially obliterating the design. The scraped lands have an imperfect polish.[7]

Design. A pattern of from three to five concentric rectilinear impressions, with some overlapping, but not to any great extent. In applications the designs range from clear to barely discernible. Lands range from 1.5 to 3 mm. in width. The center diamond may be open or closed, and occasionally a raised circle replaces the diamond. Illustrated on Plate XI, 7-8.

Distribution. Probably over most of vessel.

Form. Elongated globular vessel. Rims are flaring and folded. On the folded rim the stamping terminates at the juncture of the rim and body. At the base of the fold punctates made with a blunt instrument encircle the vessel; usually this is about 2.3 cm. below the lip. Lips are rounded. One lip was punctated on its outer half with a blunt instrument. The impression was from the lip downward, and the bottom of the punctations have an overhanging edge of about 1 mm. creating the effect of scallops around the vessel.

Relationships of type. In motif this type is similar to St. Andrews Complicated Stamped of the Weeden Island Period (Willey, 1949, p. 436). It has some elements in common with pottery of the St. Augustine Period of the Florida east coast (Smith, 1948).

[7]The terms *imperfectly polished* and *highly polished* follow the definitions of March (1934, Pl. 2).

TYPE B COMPLICATED STAMPED (15 sherds)

Decoration.

Technique. Paddle impressed on soft unfired surface of vessel, with some smoothing before application. Application is careless, with overlapping of stamping. Lands on some sherds are imperfectly polished.

Design. A pattern of concentric circles with raised dot centers. Lands measure 1 to 5.5 mm. in width, but lands on a single group of concentric circles are approximately the same width. The raised dot is in proportion to the circles. (See Plate XI, 9-10).

Distribution. Probably over most of vessel.

Form. Total vessel shape is unknown. Rim is flaring, with stamping ending 2 cm. below the rolled and flattened lip; rim is roughly smoothed from the top of the stamping to the lip, and a row of punctates made with a blunt instrument surrounds the vessel at this junction.

Relationships of type. Motif similar to degenerate complicated stamped of Weeden Island times in the Tampa Bay area (Willey, personal communication).

TYPE C COMPLICATED STAMPED (7 sherds)

Decoration.

Technique. As in Type A Complicated Stamped.

Design. A pattern of triangles and circles. Equilateral triangles are placed either base to base or side by side and are surrounded by circles or oval-sided elements. Overlapping occurs, but is not common. The design is bold, large, and open. Lands average 2.5 mm. in width. Inside dimension for triangles is 15 mm., and for circles 11 to 14 mm. Illustrated on Plate XI, 11.

Distribution. Probably over most of the vessel.

Form. Sherds indicate a large vessel with a flaring rim. Lip, base, and appendage data are lacking.

Relationships of type. Motif similar to degenerate complicated stamped of Weeden Island times in the Tampa Bay area (Willey, personal communication).

TYPE D COMPLICATED SHERDS (14 sherds)

Decoration.

Technique. As in Type A Complicated Stamped.

Design. Herringbone pattern with very little overlapping. Lands range from 2 to 5 mm. in width.

Distribution. Probably over most of vessel.

Form. Total vessel shape unknown. Rim is folded and flaring, with a row of punctates, executed by a sharp instrument or a blunt instrument, around the vessel at the base of the fold, which is from 1 to 3 cm. high. Lips are rounded and as thick as the rim.

Relationships of type. Motif is similar to Crooked River Complicated Stamped of the Weeden Island Period (Willey, 1949, pp. 435-36).

Appendix

Form. Collared ollas, shallow bowls, and water bottles are all found. Rims are straight to flaring, and may be thickened or folded. Lips may be rounded, flat, or annular ring (5). There is an occasional pitcher handle. The pinched and punctated rims have been divided into five types, which may be described as follows: *Type 1.* Flaring rim and rounded lip. Immediately below the lip a line of punctates made with a blunt instrument encircles the vessel. Punctates are mostly crudely executed, and pinching often occurs with them. The depressions are 4 to 10 mm. in diameter. (Pl. XI, 13). *Type 2.* Rim is straight and flaring. Blunt pointed punctates are found around the whole lip of the vessel. Diameter of punctates is from 8 to 12 mm., and size is such that a thickened rim is sometimes required. Outer surface of lip on specimens with large punctations sometimes has scalloped effect. In one specimen punctates had been outlined on exterior of vessel, leaving a ridge between the depressions and the vessel body. One specimen was treated with rectangular punctates, 5 by 6 mm. in size. One folded rim was punctated around the lip, and at the juncture of rim and body deeply scraped grooves encircled the vessel. (This type is illustrated on Plate XI, 12.) *Type 3.* Slightly flaring rim with a pinched decoration encircling vessel directly below the lip. The lip is rolled and rounded (Pl. XI, 14). *Type 4.* One specimen has a slightly flaring rim with crude punctates executed with a wedge-shaped stylus encircling the vessel. This specimen has a flat lip extending upward at a 45 degree angle from the vessel interior. Another specimen has a rounded lip and a straight rim, with rectilinear punctates, made with a split stick and/or reed and 2 by 5 mm. in size, encircling the vessel (Pl. XI, 15). Others are of the same general character. *Type 5.* Flaring rim which is thickened or folded. A row of generally large and deep punctates encircles the vessel at 1 to 2.5 cm. below the lip. In shape the punctates are oval, pointed oval, and semicircular, executed with a blunt instrument. Outlines are irregular because of application on wet paste, and generally the punctated areas has been smoothed over (Pl. XI, 16). Table 6 shows the distribution of the rim types in the various sections of the excavation.

TABLE 6

DISTRIBUTION OF JEFFERSON PINCHED AND PUNCTATED RIM TYPES

Type	Sec. A	Sec. D	Sec. E	Surface	Total
1	11	3	21	6	41
2		3	16	3	22
3			1		1
4		2	10		12
5	40	11	60	21	132
Total	51	19	108	30	208

Category.—RESIDUAL COMPLICATED STAMPED

Description. All the sherds having a Jefferson paste and partially obliterated complicated stamping in which the motif was not discernible were placed in this category.
This is not a pottery type.

Type name.—GRITTY PLAIN

Definition as a type. This paper. This type was represented by only a small
percentage of the sherds found, and may actually be nothing more than a paste
variant of Jefferson ware.
Ware characteristics.
  Temper. Prepared grit, sand, clay, and sherds.
  Paste texture and color. Twenty-two sherds have fine sand tempering with a very
    small amount of the other materials, and a gray or black core. The rest of
    this type have moderate to large amounts of tempering, including all materials
    mentioned, with sand used to a lesser extent. The paste is generally contorted
    and fairly compact, ranging in color from buff through gray and brown to black.
  Surface texture, color, and finish. The large particles of tempering material make
    the surfaces generally lumpy. Vessel walls were scraped and smoothed prior
    to firing, and tool marks are often evident on the exterior, which was not so
    finely smoothed as the interior. Surface color ranges from gray through buff
    and brown to black. Some temper actually extrudes onto the surface.
  Hardness. 3.5 to 4.0.
  Form. Unknown.

Type name.—LEON CHECK STAMPED

Definition as a type. Willey, 1949, p. 491-92. Willey's description is based in part
on Smith (1948) and in part on material from his own collections.
Ware characteristics.
  Method of manufacture. Coil fractures present.
  Temper. Prepared grit and sherds or burned clay.
  Paste texture and color. Well-mixed, coarse-grained, compacted paste which breaks
    irregularly. Temper visible in quantities on the interior surface. The core
    is black.
  Surface texture, color, and finish. Interior surfaces smoothed by scraping, and in
    some cases imperfectly polished. Exterior surface ranges from black to buff,
    with firing clouds present. Interior surface ranges from black to gray.
Decoration.
  Technique. Paddle impressed on the soft unfired exterior surface of the
    vessel. Surface scraped after application, which in some cases all but
    obliterated the stamping.
  Design. Check stamped (Pl. XI, 18-19). Interior dimensions of the checks
    range from 5 to 8 mm. Lands vary in thickness because of scraping. On
    some specimens the stamping is bold and distinct, but on the majority it
    is difficult to distinguish. Sometimes the vessel was initially stamped at
    an angle to the lip, and then re-stamped at a different angle, thus giving
    a superimposed check stamp.
  Distribution. Over the entire vessel.

Appendix

Form. Large globular vessels with outflaring rims thickened below the lip. On one specimen the fold extends 2 cm. below the lip, and a line of punctates 8 mm. in diameter encircles the vessel at the base of the fold. Lips are folded, rounded, or very thin.

Hardness. 4.0 to 5.0.

Thickness. 3 to 8 mm.

Geographic range. Centers in Leon and Jefferson counties.

Type name.—MISSION RED FILMED

Definition as a type. This paper. A brief description based on Smith (1948) is given by Willey (1949, p. 490).

Ware characteristics.

Method of manufacture. Coil fractures present.

Temper. Fine sand and finely crushed prepared grit in moderate amounts.

Paste texture and color. Paste is like that of Miller Plain, being well mixed, compact, and slightly contorted; some lamination occurs. The core is black.

Surface texture, color, and finish.

Plate form. Most sherds of the type are from plate-form vessels. Surfaces were finely scraped and smoothed before firing. Exterior surface is either white or black, with the white areas frequently being fire clouded. Interior surface is also white or black, with the former predominating, and painted red, with areas of the surface showing through to form part of the design. Surfaces have an imperfect polish.

Other vessels. Exteriors and/or interiors are red painted, and some sherds are highly burnished. Red color runs from a dark maroon, through a brilliant brick color, to a dull, flat, "fugitive red." Two sherds show evidence of two parallel lines of black paint atop the red surface.

Decoration.

Technique. The plates are red zoned between incised and broad trailed lines, or are merely painted in zones (Pl. XI, 1-4). Some of the original surface of the vessel was left unpainted. In the other forms the complete exteriors and/or interiors of the vessels were painted red.

Design. Designed areas appear only on the plate forms. Bands around the lip and triangular and circular motifs predominate. The red zones are set off by incised lines from 1 to 3 mm. in width. Rim sherds are occasionally decorated with incised loops, concentrically arranged in groups of three, pendant from the lip, and repeating around the plate. In some cases a dark fugitive-like red paint was applied after firing.

Distribution. Red zoning appears only on interior of plate forms.

Form. Plate forms appear close to those of Miller Plain, with annular ring bases definitely associated. One beaker form, with a bright-red exterior and a dark brownish-red interior, was found. One sherd appeared to be from a small elongated vessel with a flaring rim. Another sherd came from a vessel of a lobed jar of Middle Mississippi type (Pl. XI, 2). Still another sherd came from a small wide-mouthed vessel with a slightly flaring rim.

Hardness. 4.0 to 5.0.

Thickness. 5 to 9 mm.

Geographic range. Unknown at present, but at least as far west in Florida as the Chattahoochee River (Bullen).

Chronological position. Leon-Jefferson Period.

Relationship of type. Related to Kasita Red Filmed, which has a distribution "from western Georgia (Kasita) and eastern Alabama (Coweta) through central Georgia (Macon Plateau) to Oconee River. About the area of Kasita and Hitchita Creeks of late 17th and early 18th century. May extend farther west in Creek area." (*Newsletter*, Southeastern Archaeological Conference, Vol. 2, No. 2, 1940). Also similar to a red filmed ware found in the St. Augustine region from sites of a comparable time (Smith, 1948).

Type name.—AUCILLA INCISED

Definition as a type. This paper. A brief description based on Smith (1948) is given by Willey (1949, p. 491).

Ware characteristics.

Method of manufacture. Coil fractures present.

Temper. Sand and medium- to large-sized particles of grit in moderate amounts.

Paste texture and color. Paste is well mixed and compact, and the core ranges in color from dark gray to black, with the latter predominating.

Surface texture, color, and finish. Both surfaces are finely scraped and smoothed, and the surface texture ranges from smooth to imperfectly polished. Both surfaces are the same color, which ranges from black through gray to buff. Firing clouds appear occasionally. Some sherds from the site have color variations from refiring during the burning of the mission.

Decoration.

Technique. Wide to medium-wide, deep to shallow, incised lines and elongated oval and dot punctations.

Design. Seven motifs are distinguished. *1*. Loop design of five parallel lines (Pl. XII, 9). *2*. Two parallel wavy lines (Pl. XII, 13). *3*. Chevron design in two or three parallel lines, sometimes with punctations immediately below the lip, or below the motif (Pl. XII, 1). *4*. Three parallel deeply incised lines forming a slanting, interlocking, L motif, which occasionally forms a guilloche (Pl. XII, 2). *5*. Rectilinear designs combined to make variants of the designs listed above. Some rim sections punctated. *6*. Incised sherds showing sections of curvilinear loop designs. *7*. Rectilinear and curvilinear patterns which are filled, or have their backgrounds filled, with punctations (Pl. XII, 17). The distribution of these types in the various sections of the site is given in table 7.

Distribution. On shoulder of vessel.

Form. Shallow bowls and cazuelas. The majority of rims are incurving, but a few are straight. Lips are either flat or rounded. Lip lugs were found on two sherds.

Hardness. 4.0 to 5.0 plus.

Thickness. 3 to 9 mm.

Geographic range. At present known only from Leon and Jefferson counties.

Chronological position. Leon-Jefferson Period.

Appendix

Relationship of type. Probably a descendant of Point Washington Incised (Willey, 1949, p. 463) and Pinellas Incised (Willey, 1949, p. 482) of the Fort Walton Period. Also related to Ocmulgee Fields Incised.

TABLE 7

DISTRIBUTION OF AUCILLA INCISED DECORATIVE TYPES

Type	Sec. A	Sec. D	Sec. E	Surface	Total
1	1				1
2	1				1
3	2	1	4	1	8
4	5	1	26		32
5	23	3	31	6	63
6	2	1	10	2	15
7	2		4	1	7
Total	36	6	75	10	127

Type name.—PINELLAS INCISED

Definition as a type. Willey (1949, p. 482). This type was called Fort Walton Incised originally (Smith, 1948). See also Griffin (1950).

Ware characteristics.

Method of manufacture. Coil fractures present.

Temper. Sand and medium- to large-sized particles of grit in moderate amounts.

Paste texture and color. Paste is well mixed and compact; core is black.

Surface texture, color, and finish. Surface texture ranges from smooth to imperfectly polished. Some sherds have a lumpy texture even though they are smooth. Both surfaces generally black.

Decoration.

Technique. Incision.

Design. Three or four parallel lines encircle vessel below the lip (Pl. XII, 6). In some specimens these lines dip to form loops (Pl. XII, 8). May or may not have punctates encircling vessel immediately below lip, or below the parallel lines. One sherd has a small lip projection (Pl. XII, 7).

Distribution. On shoulder of vessel.

Form. Shallow bowl with an incurved rim which is sometimes thickened. Lips are flat.

Hardness. 4.0 to 5.0.

Thickness. 4 to 8 mm.

Geographic range. Northwest Florida, southeastern Alabama, and southern Georgia.

Chronological position. Fort Walton, Safety Harbor, and Leon-Jefferson Periods.

Relationship of type. The specimens found at this site are somewhat degenerate examples of the Pinellas Incised type. In motif they relate most directly to Pinellas Incised B and C, as defined by Griffin at the Lake Jackson site (Griffin, 1950).

In addition to the pottery types named and described above, there are other aboriginal sherds from the site which deserve mention. Eighteen sherds are considered

173

to be trade sherds actually brought to the site during its occupancy. Twelve of these are of the type Ocmulgee Fields Incised, which is predominantly a central Georgia type.[8] Two sherds are Lamar-like Bold Incised[9]; one of these is decorated with a deeply incised rectilinear pattern with an elongated oval punctate in the center of the interior diamond (Pl. XII, 10), and the other has a chevron motif executed in broad and deep incising (Pl. XII, 11). Four sherds of Alachua Cob-Marked, a type named by Goggin in the Gainesville region,[10] were found.

There is also a group of sherds which may be called special or unique. One of these is a rim sherd from a cazuela vessel with an incised motif similar to Ocmulgee Fields Incised (Pl. XII, 3). This sherd is very hard (5 plus) and is tempered with a small amount of fine sand. Three sherds with concentrically incised circles (Pl. XII, 14) are of the variety of Ocmulgee Fields Incised found by Hurt in southeastern Alabama.[11]

One sherd, with a rectilinear incised design and punctate filled background (Pl. XII, 16), is similar to specimens of Fort Walton Incised found by Griffin at the Lake Jackson site.[12] Two sherds from a shallow bowl have elongated oval punctates encircling the vessel in two rows, with every other punctate in the top row placed vertically; the others are horizontal (Pl. XII, 15).

Certain complicated stamped sherds shown differ in their design motif from other complicated stamped types at the mission, and are set apart for this reason. Some of them are limestone-tempered (Pl. XI, 17).

[8] A type description will be found in Willey (1949, p. 494).

[9] A type description will be found in Willey (1949, p. 493).

[10] Goggin, 1948, p. 3.

[11] Wesley R. Hurt, personal communication.   [12] Griffin [1950].

Trait List of Two Spanish Sites of the Mission Period

The trait list which appears below summarizes the archaeological materials found at the site of San Luis and the presumptive site of San Francisco de Oconee, both of which are described in the preceding sections of this volume. Detailed information on many of the traits listed will be found in the text and illustrations. The materials from San Francisco are presented in terms of the sections from which they came; the "surface" category includes previously excavated specimens. An "X" in the listing indicates the presence of a trait, with no quantitative evaluation.

Site location and construction details are not given in the trait list, but it is evident that both settlements occupied similar sites on high ground not adjacent to lakes or rivers, but on good agricultural land. The water supply seems to have come from springs and wells. Wattle and daub construction was used at both sites, but there are differences in construction related to factors of function, San Francisco being a mission, whereas San Luis was a fort. Neither site yields any evidence of the use of brick, stone, or other "permanent" structural materials.

TRAIT LIST

Trait	A	D	San Francisco E	Surface	Total	San Luis
Plant and Animal Remains:						
Domestic cow or oxen					x	x
Domestic pig					x	x
Domestic horse						x
Deer bones					x	x
Oyster shell					x	x
Corncob		1			1	
Peach pit		3			3	
Objects of Iron:						
Musket barrel			1		1	
Pistol barrel			1		1	1
Flintlock striker	1				1	
Cannon fragment						1
Grenade fragments (?)						11
Lance head				1	1	
Sword or dagger guard				1	1	
Chain mail (?)				1	1	
Spur rowel	1				1	
Anvil			1		1	
Hoe			2	1	3	
Axe blade		1			1	
Axe haft			1		1	
Chisel		1		1	2	
Nails	88	345	x	x	680	131
Ornate spring lock			1		1	

Trait	A	D	San Francisco E	Surface	Total	San Luis
Square spring lock			1	1	2	
Keyhole plate		1	1		2	1
Key				1	1	
Ornate wrought-iron hinge		1	1		2	2
Fragmentary hinge		2			2	
Double-L bracket		1			1	
Slide bolt				1	1	
Chest handle		1			1	
Single pin		1			1	
Double pin		1			1	
Rings on pins			2		2	1
Iron ring			1		1	
Miscellaneous iron		1			1	18
Objects of Copper, Brass, and Lead:						
Corpus from crucifix, brass	1				1	
Brass fragments	x	x	x	x	x	x
Embossed brass ornament						1
Censer fragment (?)			1		1	
Copper bead links and chain						strand
Tubular copper beads						3
Copper ring						1
Copper ornament						1
Copper fragments			1		1	x
Lead (?) finger ring			1		1	
Lead impressed with matting		x			x	
Lead fragments		x			x	x
Lead musket or pistol balls				1	1	3
Objects of Glass:						
Glass fragments	4	35	1	x	40+	92
Glass scraper						1
Seed beads						3
Light-blue bead, oblate						2
Blue bead, white lines	1				1	
White bead, blue spirals						3
Rosary beads						39
"Jet" bead						1
Objects of Stone:						
Gunflints	1	1	1		3	5
Marble (altar stone?)				1	1	
Small triangular point	1		1		2	
Large triangular point		1			1	
Large notched point		1			1	
Broken projectile point						1
Small chert scraper	1				1	
Pounders, granite and quartz		1	4		5	
Grindstones		1	x		1+	3
Limestone awl-sharpener			1		1	
Granite maul fragment	1				1	
Stone discs	1		x		1+	

Appendix

Trait	A	D	San Francisco E	Surface	Total	San Luis
Ceramics:						
Pottery discs			4		4	
Circular "jar lid"				1	1	
Hispano-Mexican (majolica)	22	23	88	13	146	50
Lusterware		2			2	
Tinaja (olive jar)	322	1,789	221	95	2,427	931
Chinese		2			2	
Nineteenth Century				151	151	x
Other European						14
Mexican Painted						2
Mission Red Filmed	29	6	33	7	75	116
Miller Plain	40	38	480	25	583	452
Aucilla Incised	36	6	80	10	132	32
Ocmulgee Fields Incised		6	6		12	65
Lamar-like Bold Incised		1	1		2	
Pinellas Incised			6		6	1
Leon Check Stamped	11	4	49	5	69	12
Other check stamped						35
San Marcos Stamped						43
Jefferson Stamped A	116	36	34	12	198	12
Jefferson Stamped B	4		11		15	8
Jefferson Stamped C			7		7	62
Jefferson Stamped D		1	13		14	5
Jefferson rims	51	19	104	30	204	86
Residual complicated stamped	398	54	312	129	893	259
Plain sherds	990	850	1,028	585	3,453	938
Gritty plain	29	24	93	56	203	26
Unique complicated stamped	2	3	10		15	21
Alachua Cob-Marked		2		1	3	
Fort Walton Incised						1
St. Johns Plain						1
Miscellaneous						24

Bibliography

Anonymous.
    1825. "Miscellany," *Pensacola Gazette*, February 26.

Anonymous.
    1843. "Old Fort San Luis," *Apalachicola Commercial Advertiser*, June 7.

Bolton, Herbert E.
    1925. *Arredondo's Historical Proof of Spain's Title to Georgia.* University of California Press. Berkeley, California.

Boyd, Mark F.
    1935. "The First American Road in Florida: Pensacola-St. Augustine Highway, 1824," *Florida Historical Quarterly*, Vol. XIV, Nos. 2-3, pp. 72-106, 138-192.

    1936. "The Fortifications at San Marcos, Apalachee," *Florida Historical Quarterly*, Vol. XV, No. 1, pp. 1-32.

    1937. "The Expedition of Marcos Delgado from Apalachee to the Upper Creek Country in 1686," *Florida Historical Quarterly*, Vol. XVI, No. 1, pp. 2-32.

    1938. "A Map of the Road from Pensacola to St. Augustine, 1778 (with nine plates)," *Florida Historical Quarterly*, Vol. XVII, No. 1, pp. 17-23.

    1939. "Spanish Mission Sites in Florida," *Florida Historical Quarterly*, Vol. XVII, No. 4, pp. 254-280.

    1948a. "The Siege of Saint Augustine by Governor Moore of South Carolina in 1702 as Reported to the King of Spain by Don Joseph de Zúñiga y Zerda, Governor of Florida," *Florida Historical Quarterly*, Vol. XXVI, No. 4, pp. 345-352.

    1948b. "Enumeration of Florida Spanish Missions in 1675," *Florida Historical Quarterly*, Vol. XXVII, No. 2, pp. 181-188.

    1949. "Diego Peña's Expedition to Apalachee and Apalachicola in 1716," *Florida Historical Quarterly*, Vol. XXVIII, No. 1, pp. 1-27.

Burch, Captain Daniel E.
    1824. Interview with Captain Daniel E. Burch, *Pensacola Gazette*, October 9.

Caldwell, Joseph, and Catherine McCann.
    1941. *Irene Mound Site, Chatham County, Georgia.* University of Georgia Press. Athens, Ga.

Caldwell, Joseph, and Frederick Hulse.
    MS. "Excavations at Fort King George, McIntosh County, Georgia," manuscript on file at the State Department of Natural Resources, Division of State Parks, Atlanta, Ga.

Carroll, B. R.
    1836. *Historical Collections of South Carolina.* 2 vols. Harper and Brothers. New York.

Cervantes, Enrique.
    1939. *Loza Blanca y Azulejo de Puebla.* 2 vols. Mexico City.

Cooke, C. Wythe.
    1945. "Geology of Florida," *Florida Geological Survey, Bulletin 29*. Talla-hassee, Fla.
Cox, Warren E.
    1944. *The Book of Pottery and Porcelain*. 2 Vols. Crown Publishers. New York.
Crane, Verner W.
    1928. *The Southern Frontier*. Duke University Press. Durham, N. C.
De Lacy, John Devx.
    1801. "Letter to Thomas Jefferson, Pensacola, December 18," in Library of Congress. Photostat in P. K. Yonge Library of Florida History, University of Florida, Gainesville, Fla.
Dunn, William E.
    1917. "Spanish and French Rivalry in the Gulf Region of the United States, 1678-1703," *University of Texas Bulletin No. 1705*. Austin, Tex.
Ford, James A.
    1936. "Analysis of Indian Village Site Collections from Louisiana and Mississippi," *Anthropological Study No. 2*, Department of Conservation, Louisiana Geological Survey. New Orleans, La.
Gatschet, Albert S.
    1880. "The Timucuan Language, Part III," *Proceedings, American Philosophical Society*, Vol. XVIII, No. 105, pp. 405-502. Philadelphia, Pa.
Geiger, Reverend Maynard.
    1937. "The Franciscan Conquest of Florida (1573-1618)," *Studies in Hispanic-American History*, Vol. I, Catholic University of America. Washington, D. C.
    1940. "Biographical Dictionary of the Franciscans in Spanish Florida and Cuba (1528-1841)," *Franciscan Studies*, Vol. XXI. St. Anthony Guild Press. Paterson, N. J.
Goggin, John M.
    1948. "Some Pottery Types from Central Florida," *Gainesville Anthropological Association, Bulletin No. 1*. Gainesville, Fla.
Goggin, John M.; Mary E. Godwin; Earl Hester; David Prange; and Robert Spangenberg.
    1949. "An Historic Indian Burial, Alachua County, Florida," *The Florida Anthropologist*, Vol. II, Nos. 1-2, pp. 10-25. Gainesville, Fla.
Griffin, John W.
    1949a. "The Historic Archaeology of Florida," *The Florida Indian and His Neighbors* (John W. Griffin, ed.). Winter Park, Fla.
    1949b. "An Authentic Glass Artifact," *American Antiquity*, Vol. XV, No. 1, pp. 56-57. Menasha, Wis.
    [1950]. "Test Excavations at the Lake Jackson Site," *American Antiquity* (in press).
Griffin, John W., and Hale G. Smith.
    1948. "The Goodnow Mound, Highlands County, Florida," *Contributions to the Archaeology of Florida, No. 1*. Florida Park Service. Tallahassee, Fla.

Bibliography

Haggard, J. Villasana.
    1941. *Handbook for Translators of Spanish Historical Documents.* Archives
        Collections, University of Texas. Semco Color Press. Oklahoma City,
        Okla.

Hamilton, Peter J.
    1897. *Colonial Mobile.* Houghton, Mifflin and Co. Boston and New York.

Hawkins, Benjamin.
    1848. "A Sketch of the Creek Country in the Years 1798 and 1799," *Collections of the Georgia Historical Society,* Vol. III, Part I, pp. 1-88.

Higgs, Charles D.
    1942. "Spanish Contacts with the Ais (Indian River) Country," *Florida Historical Quarterly,* Vol. XXI, No. 1, pp. 25-39.

Kelly, A. R.
    1938. "A Preliminary Report on Archaeological Explorations at Macon, Georgia," *Bureau of American Ethnology, Bulletin 119,* pp. 1-68. Washington, D. C.

Kurz, Herman.
    1945. "Secondary Forest Succession in the Tallahassee Red Hills," *Proceedings of the Florida Academy of Sciences,* Vol. 7, Nos. 2-3, pp. 1-42.

Leonard, Irving A.
    1936. "The Spanish Re-exploration of the Gulf Coast in 1686," *Mississippi Valley Historical Review,* Vol. XXII, No. 4, pp. 547-557.
    1939. *Spanish Approach to Pensacola, 1689-1693.* Quivira Society, Vol. IX. Albuquerque, N. M.

Maerz, A., and M. Rea Paul.
    1930. *A Dictionary of Color.* McGraw-Hill Book Co. New York.

Manucy, Albert C.
    1949. "Artillery Through the Ages," *National Park Service Interpretive Series, History No. 3.* Washington, D. C.

March, Benjamin.
    1934. "Standards of Pottery Description," *Occasional Contributions from the Museum of Anthropology of the University of Michigan, No. 3.* Ann Arbor, Mich.

Montgomery, Ross Gordon; Watson Smith; and John Otis Brew.
    1949. "Franciscan Awatovi," *Papers of the Peabody Museum of American Archaeology and Enthnology,* Vol. XXXVI. Cambridge, Mass.

Moore, Clarence B.
    1901. "Certain Aboriginal Remains of the Northwest Florida Coast," *Journal of the Academy of Natural Sciences of Philadelphia,* second series, Vol. XI, Part 4. Philadelphia, Pa.

Pittman, Lieutenant Philip.
    1934. "Apalache During British Occupation," *Florida Historical Quarterly,* Vol. XII, No. 3, pp. 114-122.

Shores, Venila Lovina.
    1927. "The Ruins of Fort San Luis near Tallahassee," *Florida Historical Quarterly,* Vol. VI, No. 2, pp. 111-116.

Sleight, Frederick W.
  1949. "Notes Concerning an Historic Site of Central Florida," *The Florida Anthropologist*, Vol. II, Nos. 1-2, pp. 26-30. Gainesville, Fla.
Smith, Buckingham.
  1860. Without title page. (Three documents in seven sheets in the Spanish, and two in the early tongues of Florida-Apalachian and Timucuan.)
  1866. *Narrative of the Career of Hernando De Soto in the Conquest of Florida as Told by a Knight of Elvas and in a Relation by Luys Hernández de Biedma.* Bradford Club. New York.
Smith, Hale G.
  1948. "Two Historical Archaeological Periods in Florida," *American Antiquity*, Vol. XIII, No. 4, pp. 313-319. Menasha, Wis.
  1949. "Two Archaeological Sites in Brevard County, Florida," *Publication No. 1, Florida Anthropological Society*. Gainesville, Fla.
Southeastern Archaeological Conference.
  1939. *Newsletter*, Vol. I, No. 2. Lexington, Ky.
  1940. *Newsletter*, Vol. II, No. 2. Lexington, Ky.
Swanton, John R.
  1922. "Early History of the Creek Indians and Their Neighbors," *Bureau of American Ethnology, Bulletin 73*. Washington, D. C.
  1946. "The Indians of the Southeastern United States," *Bureau of American Ethnology, Bulletin 137*. Washington, D. C.
Wenhold, Lucy L.
  1936. "A 17th Century Letter of Gabriel Diaz Vara Calderón, Bishop of Cuba, Describing the Indians and Indian Missions of Florida," *Smithsonian Miscellaneous Collections*, Vol. 95, No. 16. Washington, D. C.
Williams, John Lee.
  1823. "Letter to R. K. Call dated November 1," *in* Caroline Brevard (1924) *A History of Florida*, 2 Vols., Publication No. 4, Florida State Historical Society. DeLand, Fla. (Vol. I, p. 263.)
  1827. *View of West Florida*. H. S. Tanner and the Author. Philadelphia, Pa.
  1908. "Journal of John Lee Williams," *Florida Historical Quarterly*, Vol. I, Nos. 1-2, pp. 18-29, 37-44.
Young, Captain Hugh.
  1934. "A Topographical Memoir on East and West Florida with Itineraries of General Jackson's Army, 1818," *Florida Historical Quarterly*, Vol. XIII, No. 1, pp. 88-104.

Index

Index

IBERVILLE, Pierre le Moyne d', 9.
Innocent XII, Pope, 33.
Irishman, deserts to Spaniards, 16, 50.
Itchetucknee Spring, 157.
Ivitachuco, *see* San Lorenzo de Hibita-
chuco.

JERGUETA, a cloth, 47-48, 100n.
Jesup, Thomas S., 3.
Jordán, Juan, 9.
Jororo (Jorroro), province of, 68, 87,
90.

KALUSA (Calusa) Indians, 99n.
Kasita (Kasihta) Indians, 8, 172.
Kelly, A. R., 136n.
Kinchafoone River, 99n.
Kolomi Indians, 8.
Kurz, Herman, 135n.

LACHUA cattle ranch, 68.
La Concepción de Ayubali, mission, 11,
12, 13, 14, 15, 16, 19, 26, 48, 49,
65, 66, 74, 75, 77, 78, 79, 80, 81,
92, 100n, 111, 112, 156.
Lake Jackson site, 130, 172, 173.
Lake Lafayette, 156.
Lamar Period, 131.
Lamont, site near, 111.
Lance head, 109, 175.
Landeche, Antonio de, 67, 85.
La Purificación de Tama, mission, 12,
14, 25.
La Salle, Réné Robert Cavalier, Sieur de,
9.
León, Fray Francisco de, 89.
Leon-Jefferson Period, 107, 129, 141,
145, 149, 157, 163-174 *passim*.
Leonard, Irving A., 5, 97n.
Leturiendo, Ignacio de, 74, 77, 82.
Louis XIV, of France, 10.

MACKEN, Robert, 104n.
Mackie, Captain, 93.
Maize (corn), 21, 23, 46, 47, 107, 124,
144, 156, 175.

Manucy, Albert C., 146, 159n.
March, Benjamin, 167n.
Marcial, Antonio, 85.
Marmolejo, Pedro, 70, 76, 78, 81.
Martínez, Francisco, 42, 43.
Massacre Island, 64.
Matheos, Antonio, 8.
Mayaca, province of, 35, 68, 90.
Mendoza, Father Manuel de, 16, 56, 74,
76, 77, 78, 79, 81, 87.
Menéndez, Thomas Marqués, 21, 23.
Mexía, Diego Dias, 57.
Mexía, Juan Ruíz de, 15, 16, 17, 47,
49, 64, 79, 80, 82.
Miccosukee, lake, 109.
Milk, 25.
Miller, Scott, 108, 112.
Miranda, Father Angel de, 15, 49, 64,
75, 79.
Miranda, Father Manuel de, 80.
Mobile, bay and town, 9, 14, 39, 40,
43, 71, 72, 84, 86, 102n, 108.
Mobile Indians, 43.
Molina, Joseph, 85.
Montes, Francisco de, 39.
Moore, James, 5, 11, 12, 13, 15, 16,
91-95, 100n, 102n, 108, 112, 135n.
Morales, Sebastian de, 53.
Moscoso, Sebastian de, 83.
Muscogean, terms of rank in, 98n.
Muscogee Indians, 3.

NAILS, 21, 23, 108, 115, 120, 124,
125, 142, 145, 150, 175.
Narváez, Pánfilo de, 107.
Navarette, Pedro Fernández, 33.
Nieto de Carvajal, Bernardo, 57.
Nieto, Fernando, 41.
Nuestra Señora de la Candelaria de la
Tama, *see* Candelaria.
Nuestra Señora de la Leche, 72.

OCHESE Creek, 9.
Ochlockonee (Ockolockony) River, 3,
11, 62, 107, 140.
Ocmulgee Fields Period, 131, 133, 166.
Ocmulgee River, 9, 91.

Index

Tisimea, province of, 68.
Tocuime, province of, 68.
Torres, Juan Joseph de, 17, 55, 62.
Torres y Ayala, Laureano de, 20, 22, 23, 25, 27, 98n.
Torture by Indians, 53, 75, 76, 77, 78, 79, 80, 81.
Toulouse, Count of, 64.
Tristan, Francisco, 69, 71, 72, 73.
Tuckabatchee Indian, 99n.
Tuskegee (Tasquique) Indians, 8, 26.

Urisas, Fray Manuel de, 89.

Vasquez, Fray Domingo, 89.
Vilas, Pedro de, 83.
Villalva, Diego Pablo de, 82.
Villalva, Father Juan de, 16, 80.

Wacissa River, 109.
Wakulla River, 1, 101-102n.
Wakulla Spring, 101n.

War of the Grand Alliance, 10.
War of the Spanish Succession, 10.
Waukeenah, town of, 109.
Weeden Island Period, 167, 168.
Wenhold, Lucy L., 97n, 135n, 159n, 160n.
Wheat, 48.
Willey, Gordon R., 109, 135n, 136n, 141, 165-174 passim.
William II, of England, 10.
Williams, Beatrice, 136n.
Williams, John Lee, 2, 97n, 103n, 140, 143, 144, 157.
Woodward, Henry, 8.

Yamassee Indians, 3, 99n.
Young, Hugh, 99n.

Zuñiga y Zerda, Joseph de la, 5, 13, 14, 18, 29, 30-32, 33, 35, 36, 38, 44, 45, 46, 48, 55, 56, 64, 66, 68, 69, 87, 99n, 100n.

189

PLATES

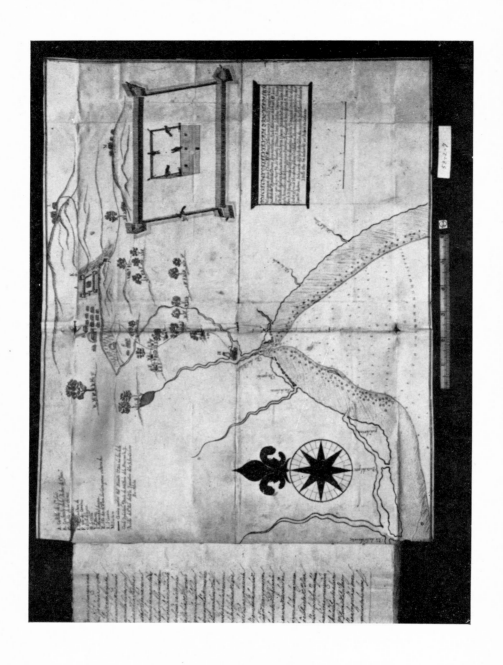

PLATE I

Map of San Luis Region

This map of Apalachee Bay and the region of San Luis, accompanying Document 40, was made during the reconnaissance of Admiral Landeche in August, 1705. For a translation of the legend in cartouche, see Plate II. Legend in upper left: *A*, Fort of San Luis; *B*, Convent of the Fathers of Saint Francis; *C*, village of the Chinos; *D*, the lakes; *E*, large lake; *F*, the two roads; *G*, well of water; *H*, the watch tower; *I*, San Marcos; *J*, spring of water; *K*, site where the bells were buried; *L*, Escambé; *M*, Bacuqua. The line shows the route followed by the Admiral Don Antonio Landeche with the infantry and artillery-men of the presidio of Santa María de Galve (Pensacola) and crews of the merchant vessels.

With reference to *E*, large lake, see note 77, page 101. Be it noted that this map shows the present-day Wakulla River arising from a lake. If the hypothesis presented in the before-mentioned note is correct, the lake must be the present-day Lake Munson.

PLATE II

The Blockhouse of San Luis

The reproduction is approximately the original size of the enlarged sketch of the blockhouse given in Plate I. (See Document 40.) The legend in the cartouche below this sketch is translated as follows:

DESCRIPTION OF THE BAY AND RIVER OF APALACHEE and of the road which goes from San Luis to San Marcos, together with that of the fort and blockhouse, their dimensions according to the Castilian yard [vara]. The longer side, which is the east-west, 84 yards, and the lesser, which is north-south, 48. The bastions [and] the traverse [travesa] 4 yards, the curtains 5 [sic] yards and 1/4, the outside height of each post [of the stockade] above ground level [is] 4 yards; within 7 palms [palmos] rises the banquette terreplein of clay, its width 3 palms. The blockhouse has a depth of 31 yards [and] a front of 21 yards, [and is] faced with palm posts and backed with clay bricks [masiado con adobes de baro] and above strengthened within and without by a platform of planks. On top are maintained four cannons of 4 [pounds] and four pedreros. In the gate of the fort another cannon of six [pounds] and another in the southeast bastion, and in the other three bastions, one pedrero in each one.

The Castilian yard is equivalent to 32.9 inches. In Brevard's "History of Florida" (Vol. I, page 265) is reproduced a letter of J. L. Williams to R. K. Call, dated November 1, 1823, wherein are given the following dimensions for the fort in paces:

Williams		At 39 inches to a pace, equals	Map legend	At 32.9 inches to a vara, equals
South side	71 paces	230 feet	} 84 varas	231 feet
North side	55 paces	178 feet		
East-west ends	46 paces	149 feet	48 varas	132 feet

The east-west dimensions are in close agreement and the north-south disagree by 17 feet. Williams' description is of a trapezoid, the Spanish description that of a parallelogram.

136

Los offiçiales de la R.l hazienda y caxa de esta provinçia, de la S.ta
villa de Cuyaua Don Thomas Menendez marques en hdad.s que
su Mag.d y Joachin de Florençia que sirve el officio de Thesorero y
tenedor de Bastimentos Cuyohentia Florençia del Proveedor
ocupado de orden de su Mag.d en las cobranças de lo situado de los
de Presidio. Certificamos que por la quenta y razon que se a tenido con
Industria se a tenido y tiene formada delos S.tos que en la provinçia
de Apalache se an hecho, en la fabrica de vna casa fuerte, de
Madera que se hizo para el Arossamiento y defensa, de la ynfan-
teria que alli assiste, de Guarnizon en la qual, los Indios de dha
provinçia travaxaron, siendo ellos la madera y manos como
que se hizieron Jun Mag.d mando, por la R.l Cedula se hiziera y de lo
se los a dicho pagado con la comida y alguna herramientas y clavasen
que se gasto en la dha fabrica todo de quenta de su Mag.d y lo que se
esto se a gastado, y en que tiempo es en esta manera

~ Primeramente comida por dos certificaçiones
del Cap.n Jazinto Roque Perez thenience
de dha provinçia y consta que corrio con
dha obra, que desde diez de octubre de mill
seiscientos y noventa y cinco que se enca-
rgo hasta su conclusion, y acabaron en la
comida de los Indios, Maestros offiçiales
y peones que en dha casa travaxaron
trescientas y cinquenta y seis medidas de
maiz para su comida que a dos reales
montan ochenta y ocho pesos y dos reales

~ Por seis quintales de fierro nuevo a diez
pesos quintal, por quintales y medio de

0.88 L 2

PLATE III

Page of a Typical Document

This is the first page of Document 4 of the present series, which is a certification of the construction costs of the blockhouse at San Luis.

PLATE IV

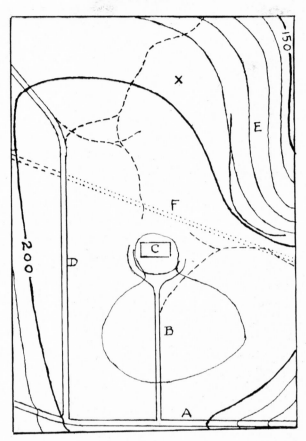

Aerial View of Hilltop Plateau at Fort San Luis Site
(North to top)

Contours at 10-foot intervals adapted from U.S.G.S. Tallahassee quadrangle sheet. *A*, paved county road, a relocated portion of Burch's road; *B*, driveway to Messer residence; *C*, residence of Mr. James Messer; *D*, private road; *E*, ravine with seepage springs at bottom; *F*, original tangent of Pensacola-St. Augustine road, laid out in 1823 by Captain Burch, and forming a chord to *A* off the sketch; *X*, site where numerous Spanish artifacts have been found, tentatively regarded as the site of the blockhouse. The tangent of road *D* is approximately 940 feet in length.

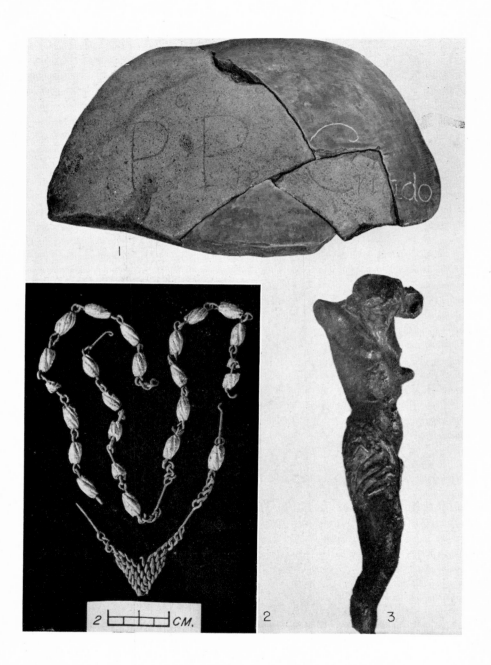

PLATE V

Religious Objects

(Scale variable)

1. Sherds of a Spanish olive-jar, incised with letters believed to be the name of Father Domingo Criado. Darker section, with a portion of the *C* and *a*, and the letters *do*, is hypothetical. Total length, 18 cm. San Francisco.
2. Fragmentary rosary, found in the moat of San Luis. Scale on photograph.
3. Corpus from crucifix, somewhat misshapen by fire. Height, 11 cm. San Francisco.

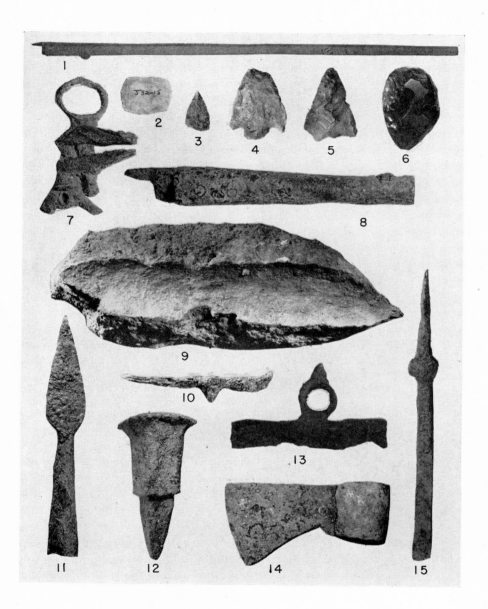

PLATE VI

Weapons and Tools

(Scale variable)

1. Musket barrel, octagonal, 114 cm. long. San Francisco.
2. Gunflint, 2.8 cm. long. San Francisco.
3. Small triangular projectile point, 3.1 cm. long. San Francisco.
4. Notched projectile point, 5.5 cm. long. San Francisco.
5. Broken projectile point, 5.5 cm. long. San Francisco.
6. Scraper chipped from glass, 5.7 cm. long. San Luis.
7. Flintlock, 7.6 cm. high. San Francisco.
8. Pistol barrel, 15.7 cm. long. San Francisco.
9. Fragment of iron cannon, 31 cm. long. San Luis.
10. Iron sword or dagger guard, 12.4 cm. long. San Francisco.
11. Iron lance head, 20 cm. long. San Francisco.
12. Iron anvil of unusual type, 29.5 cm. high. San Francisco.
13. Fragmentary iron hoe, 20 cm. broad. San Francisco.
14. Iron axe, 22.2 cm. long. San Francisco.
15. Iron chisel, 21.5 cm. long. San Francisco.

PLATE VII

Wattle and Daub Technique

An artist's reconstruction of the wattle and daub technique used in the Spanish missions of the Apalachee region. Upright poles have horizontal wattles lashed in place, and this framework is covered with clay (daub).

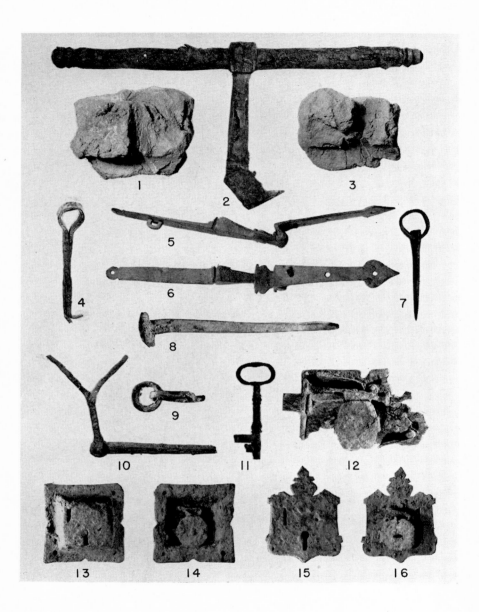

PLATE VIII

Construction and Hardware

(Scale variable)

1. Burned daub with wattle impressions. 10 by 8 cm. San Francisco.
2. Slide bolt, 29.2 cm. long. San Francisco.
3. Burned daub with wattle impressions. Scale as in item 1. San Francisco.
4. Pin, 12 cm. long. San Francisco.
5. Hinged hasp, side view. 37 cm. long. San Francisco.
6. Another view of the specimen illustrated in item 5.
7. Pin with ring; pin is 12.5 cm. long. San Francisco.
8. Large nail, representative of nails from both San Francisco and San Luis.
9. Ring on pin; ring is 2.7 cm. in diameter. San Luis.
10. Double pin, horizontal portion 11.2 cm. long. San Francisco.
11. Key, 13.4 cm. long. San Francisco.
12. Large lock, inside view. 18 cm. long. San Francisco.
13. Lock, front view. 9 cm. high. San Francisco.
14. Lock, rear view of the one in item 13.
15. Lock, front view. 11 cm. high. San Francisco.
16. Lock, rear view of the one in item 15.

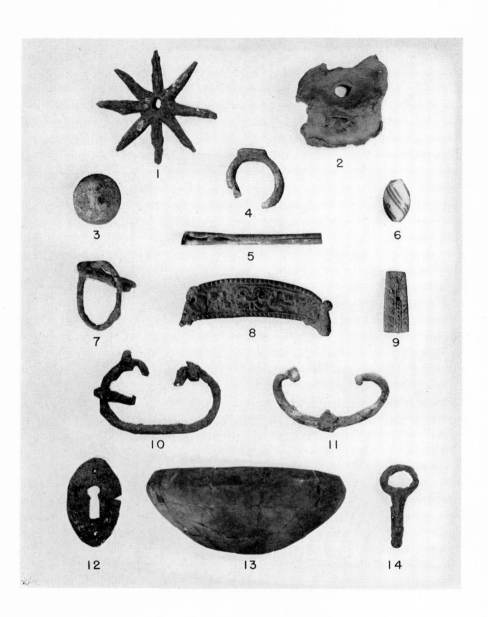

PLATE IX

Ornaments and Miscellaneous Objects

(Scale variable)

1. Spur rowel, 8.5 cm. diameter. San Francisco.
2. Brass, possibly part of a censer. 8.5 cm. maximum breadth. San Francisco.
3. Pottery disc, 3.5 cm. diameter. San Francisco.
4. Ring of lead, 2.5 cm. wide. San Francisco.
5. Rolled copper "bead," 6 cm. long. San Luis.
6. Blue and white glass bead, 1.2 cm. high. San Luis.
7. Ring on pin, 5 cm. maximum diameter. San Francisco.
8. Ornamental brass inlay, 6.5 cm. long. San Luis.
9. Copper ornament, 2.6 cm. long. San Luis.
10. Iron chest handle, 8.75 cm. wide. San Francisco.
11. Iron chest handle, 10.25 cm. wide. San Francisco.
12. Small keyhole plate, 2.5 cm. high. San Francisco.
13. Reconstructed Miller Plain vessel, 27.5 cm. diameter. San Francisco.
14. Small key, 6.5 cm. long. San Francisco.

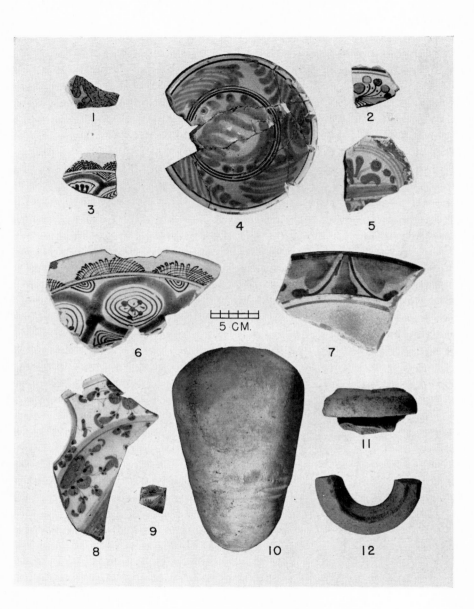

5 CM.

PLATE X

Non-Aboriginal Pottery

(Scale on photograph, except for item 10)

1. Polychrome, yellow, orange, green, and black on white. San Francisco.
2. Polychrome, yellow, green, blue, and black on white. San Francisco.
3. Polychrome, blue and black on white. San Francisco.
4. Reconstructed green and black on white bowl. San Francisco.
5. Blue on white, heavily painted. San Francisco.
6. Polychrome, blue and black on white. San Francisco.
7. Green and black on white. San Francisco.
8. Blue on white, soft paste, Oriental ware. San Francisco.
9. "Delft-like," blue on white. San Luis.
10. *Tinaja*, with neck missing. Found in Section E, San Francisco. Height, 46.5 cm.
11. Side view of *tinaja* neck. San Francisco.
12. Top view of *tinaja* neck (incomplete). San Francisco.

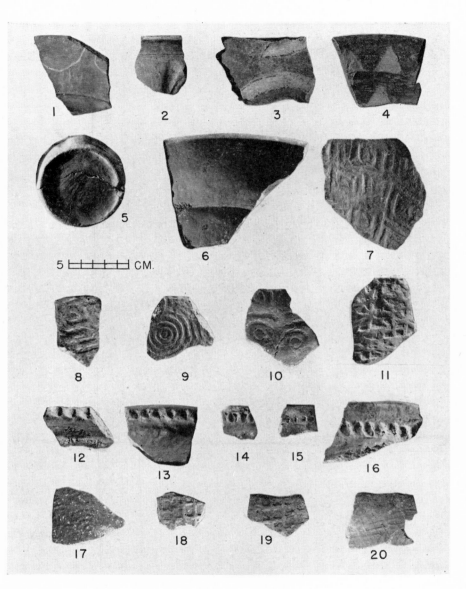

1

2

3

4

5

6

7

5 ⊢┼┼┼┼┤ CM.

8

9

10

11

12

13

14

15

16

17

18

19

20

PLATE XI

Aboriginal Pottery

(Scale on photograph)

1. Mission Red Filmed, plate rim. San Luis.
2. Mission Red Filmed, unique Caddo-like form. San Francisco.
3. Mission Red Filmed, base of plate, ring base on reverse. San Luis.
4. Mission Red Filmed, plate rim. San Luis.
5. Miller Plain, annular ring base. San Francisco.
6. Miller Plain, plate rim. San Francisco.
7. Jefferson ware, Complicated Stamped Type A. San Francisco.
8. Jefferson ware, Complicated Stamped Type A. San Francisco.
9. Jefferson ware, Complicated Stamped Type C. San Francisco.
10. Jefferson ware, Complicated Stamped Type C. San Francisco.
11. Jefferson ware, Complicated Stamped Type D. San Francisco.
12. Jefferson ware, rim type 2. San Francisco.
13. Jefferson ware, rim type 1. San Francisco.
14. Jefferson ware, rim type 3. San Francisco.
15. Jefferson ware, rim type 4. San Francisco.
16. Jefferson ware, rim type 5. San Francisco.
17. Unique complicated stamped with limestone tempering. San Francisco.
18. Leon Check Stamped. San Francisco.
19. Leon Check Stamped. San Francisco.
20. Unique check stamped. San Luis.

5 ⊞⊞⊞⊞ CM.

PLATE XII

Aboriginal Pottery

(Scale on photograph)

1. Aucilla Incised, type 3. San Francisco.
2. Aucilla Incised, type 4. San Francisco.
3. Ocmulgee Fields Incised. San Francisco.
4. Ocmulgee Fields Incised. San Luis.
5. Ocmulgee Fields Incised. San Francisco.
6. Pinellas Incised. San Francisco.
7. Pinellas Incised. San Francisco.
8. Pinellas Incised. San Francisco.
9. Aucilla Incised, type 1. San Francisco.
10. Lamar-like Bold Incised. San Francisco.
11. Lamar-like Bold Incised. San Francisco.
12. Unique incised. San Francisco.
13. Aucilla Incised, type 2. San Francisco.
14. Ocmulgee Fields Incised. San Francisco.
15. Unique punctated. San Francisco.
16. Fort Walton Incised, type 7. San Francisco.
17. Aucilla Incised, type 7. San Francisco.
18. Unique incised. San Francisco.